Pioneering Spirituality

Pioneering Spirituality

Edited by
Jonny Baker and Cathy Ross

CANTERBURY
PRESS
Norwich

© The Contributors 2015

First published in 2015 by the Canterbury Press Norwich
Editorial office
3rd Floor, Invicta House,
108–114 Golden Lane,
London EC1Y 0TG

Canterbury Press is an imprint of Hymns Ancient & Modern Ltd
(a registered charity)
13A Hellesdon Park Road, Norwich,
Norfolk, NR6 5DR, UK

www.canterburypress.co.uk

British Library Cataloguing in Publication data

A catalogue record for this book is available
from the British Library

978 1 84825 651 4

Typeset by Regent Typesetting
Printed and bound in Great Britain by
CPI Group (UK) Ltd, Croydon

Contents

Contributor Biographies

Jonny Baker is the director for mission education for the Church Mission Society. He founded and leads the CMS Pioneer Mission Leadership Training, which began in 2010. He is a member of Grace, an alternative worship community in London.

Stephen Bevans is a priest in the Roman Catholic missionary Society of the Divine Word (SVD) and Louis J. Luzbetak, SVD Professor of Mission and Culture (Emeritus) at Catholic Theological Union, Chicago. He has published widely on mission ministry and ecclesiology.

Andy Freeman is a lay pioneer working as part of the team at CMS, teaching ethics and pastoral care and enabling a Pioneer Hub in the South of England. Prior to this Andy spent nine years working with 24-7 Prayer, pioneering Boiler Room Communities around the world. He is part of the growing New Monastic movement in the UK and currently lives in Winchester.

Kim Hartshorne is a curate in the Church of England and leads a small missional community in a small market town that she and several women founded six years ago. They serve a marginalized group who would not be likely to attend traditional church. Before becoming involved in the missional community she worked as a community activist and before that had a career as an engineer in the aerospace industry.

James Henley is an ordained pioneer minister in the Church in Wales. He leads The Lab Newport, a community of missional young people in Newport, South Wales, whose members live in community on several housing estates across the city.

Tina Hodgett is Pioneer Team Vicar in Portishead. Known as the Team Pilgrim, she has a broad portfolio in community engagement, exploring new forms of mission, and accompanying others on their spiritual journey. Prior to ordination Tina worked in secondary education.

Beth Honey is an ordained Anglican pioneer minister and alongside her husband, Ben, leads Derwent Oak, a resident-led community in the Derwent ward of Derby city. The group's vision to build relationship and partnership is one that inspires bonfires, parties, prayer and shared endeavour, from a pool room set-up to street art projects.

Harvey Kwiyani is an African mission scholar and practitioner who has, for 15 years, served in missions in several countries in Europe and North America, working mostly among locals as a theological educator, missional coach and church planter.

Gavin Mart is a Methodist Pioneer based in North Wales where he founded Engedi Arts community, a gathering of artists and creatives from along the North Wales coast, based out of an abandoned high street hotel. He has curated several mixed media arts exhibitions over the last 15 years, most notably the ADVENTurous series inviting artists to unearth the biblical narrative of Advent.

Michael Mitton is a freelance writer, speaker and spiritual director. He is also the Fresh Expressions Officer for the Derby Diocese, and the Priest-in-charge of St Paul's Derby. He is the author of a number of books including *Restoring the Woven Cord* (BRF, 2010) and *Dreaming of Home* (BRF, 2012).

Kate Pearson is the Anglican Chaplain at the multi-faith chaplaincy of Warwick University. Before that she was a pioneer curate in an outer estate in Birmingham. Prior to ordination Kate worked for Anthony Collins Solicitors in Birmingham as a consultant and project manager in their Community Regeneration team.

Cathy Ross co-ordinates the MA for the CMS Pioneer Mission Leadership Training. She is also Tutor in Contextual Theology at Ripon College Cuddesdon and Lecturer in Mission at Regent's Park College, Oxford. She has worked in East Africa as a mission partner with NZCMS.

Johnny Sertin is married to Lisa and they have three boys. He is a member and activist in the Earlsfield Friary. His passions are road trips, North America, family adventures, making fire, guerrilla farming, homegrown food, coffee, film, rugby, second-hand shops, listening to the dawn chorus and collecting books he never reads.

Berdine van den Toren-Lekkerkerker has a Masters in Christian Studies from Regent College, Vancouver, and is currently studying for a PhD in Missiology. She worked in theological education in the Central African Republic, as Mission Education Advisor for CMS-UK and currently as a CMS mission partner.

Dr Benno van den Toren studied theology in Utrecht, Oxford and Kampen. He taught Systematic theology at the Bangui Evangelical School of Theology, Wycliffe Hall, Oxford, and currently in Groningen, the Netherlands. He has published widely on mission and theology.

John Wheatley is a youth worker on the Bournville Estate in Weston-super-Mare, where he lives with his wife, Cathy, as a part of a small missional community. John works for Frontier Youth Trust, resourcing and supporting StreetSpace, a networked community of missional youth workers.

Ann-Marie Wilson is a psychologist with over 30 years' experience in aid work in 14 countries and corporate HR, having studied business and cross-cultural studies. She founded and runs an anti-FGM charity, 28 Too Many (www.28toomany.org), focused on research, advocacy, networks and capacity development.

Foreword

BY PHILIP MOUNSTEPHEN

This book stands in a long and fine tradition. It's perhaps unusual to introduce a work whose topic is 'pioneering' in those terms. We sometimes think of pioneers as the shock troops of the emerging Church, the prophetic unveilers of an incoming reality – and rightly so. However, while pioneers are always concerned with the 'new', pioneering itself – and therefore a spirituality of pioneering – is nothing new *per se*. There will, of course, be much in this book to stimulate fresh reflection, and indeed the formation of new pioneering spiritualities, but the concept itself is not new.

Thus, while we might not have used the term before, a pioneering spirituality has always lain behind the Church's great movements in mission. It was a truly pioneering spirit that 1,400 years ago led Celtic monks, the *peregrinati* (the 'wanderers'), to range far and wide in taking the gospel across much of Europe, and beyond. It was pioneering spirituality that led Saddhu Sundar Singh, 'the apostle of the bleeding feet', to range far and wide across India and Tibet. The day after his heart was 'strangely warmed' in 1738, in Aldersgate Street, John Wesley found himself at St Paul's Cathedral where, as he wrote, 'I could taste the good word of God in the anthem which began, "My song shall be always of the loving-kindness of the Lord: with my mouth will I ever be showing forth thy truth from one generation to another."' Those words, from Psalm 89, became the very core of Wesley's own pioneering spirituality.

Within CMS, we find the same heritage. S. C. Carpenter, Dean of Exeter, writing way back in 1933, said of us, 'CMS was at times limited; at times injudicious, but always full of life: a guild with its own peculiar vocation within the Church' (Carpenter, 1933). It was a spirituality of vocation, a sense of being called by God himself, which led CMS to take risks, sometimes indeed to be injudicious, in the cause of mission, with remarkable results in shaping God's global Church. More specifically, Max Warren saw mission as our participation in history of that which God had initiated in Christ, and John V. Taylor awoke us to the essentially missionary nature of the work and ministry of the Holy Spirit. CMS from the very first has been infused with a deep pioneering spirit – and spirituality.

These lessons from history surely demonstrate that there can, in fact, be no true pioneering without a pioneering spirituality to underlie it and to provide its primary motivation. Without it, natural human inertia and self-preservation take over and we settle for the known and the comfortable. It is only a true pioneering spirituality that will ever drive us out to where God actually calls his whole Church to be, on the margins, in the unknown place of greatest need.

But if it is true that there can be no true pioneering without a pioneering spirituality, then it is surely also true that there is no true Christian spirituality that is not itself missional and pioneering. We tend unhelpfully to polarize what should rather be held together. Too often we caricature 'spirituality' as introspective, personal and static, while 'mission' and 'pioneering' are necessarily extrovert, relational and dynamic. And yet, as the chapters of this book so helpfully demonstrate, that is surely a false dichotomy. Spirituality is, of course, outgoing and relational; mission is certainly a matter for the reflective heart.

If we want the clearest possible demonstration of that then we have only to look at Jesus. At the heart of his spirituality was a determination to follow the Father's will, and to play his own unique role in the unfolding of the *missio Dei*. Jesus' spirituality was above all else a pioneering spirituality, a spirituality of mission: he certainly had no separate, individual, private spirituality that was divorced from his steadfast determination to play his part in the fulfilment of the Father's will. From manger to cross, his was only ever a pioneering spirituality. And Jesus the Son demonstrates to us that any true spirituality has to be infused with the pioneering Spirit of the Father. If it is not, we may doubt whether it deserves being called a spirituality at all.

The pioneer course at CMS has been a wonderful way of reminding ourselves that we stand in this great tradition that is rooted in no less a place than the mission of Jesus. May the chapters in this book, many of which flow out from the thinking and practice stimulated by that course, give us the courage – and the spirit – to walk in the same path, and to chart out a new future ourselves within this great tradition.

The Revd Canon Philip Mounstephen
Executive Leader of CMS

Reference

Carpenter, S. C., 1933, *Church and People 1789–1889*, London: SPCK.

I

In Their House

JONNY BAKER AND CATHY ROSS

Introduction

This is a book about pioneering spirituality. In what follows you will read many fascinating stories from people who are working out their spirituality in a variety of spaces and places where they are pioneering in mission. You will read of those trying to connect Bible stories with disenfranchised youth, a community reconnecting with the Eucharist, young mothers connecting with God through their babies, spirituality rediscovered through the arts, through pilgrimage, through the depth of community and hospitality in an African context, through identification with a thirteenth-century mystic, through the fight to eradicate female genital mutilation (FGM) and much more. What they have in common is that they are all searching for a spirituality that fuels the practice of mission, that sustains a life of faith in Christ where the priority is to be with those beyond the borders of the Church as we know it, to share Christ and join in with God's mission, with creation's healing. This is a spirituality of the road; a mission spirituality (Bosch, 2001). This is also a spirituality that looks for treasure in the other's place and space.

Several common themes have emerged: the importance of story, place, people, posture, and soulful treasure.

Story

There has been a rediscovery of the importance of story and story-telling in the world of theology. Liberation theology alerted us to the importance of experience and context while narrative theology encourages us to read the Scriptures as story rather than just a set of doctrinal propositions and principles. We are encouraged to reflect on theology as biography and how our own story and context have shaped our understanding of and relationship with God. Clearly, the Bible is a collection of stories, some of which resonate with our own life experiences and some of which are alien and other. The Bible hides nothing of the reality of humanity in the stories we read of prostitutes abused, sisters and daughters handed over to be raped, incipient ethnic cleansing; stories of loss and betrayal as well as stories of a new community, women affirmed in leadership and Jesus' ultimate sacrifice for us all. These are stories that have shaped history, places and people. And as we read them and ponder over them, as followers of Jesus today, we believe that these stories have the power to shape us and interact with our own stories. This is what forms our spirituality.

Let me (Cathy) give you an example. Recently I returned from a three-week visit to the Democratic Republic of Congo where we had been CMS mission partners 25 years ago. The story of Congo is not a noble one as the Belgians conducted a politics of greed and plunder to rob the country of its rubber. Terror and savagery were the order of the day as hands were cut off those men who did not bring in their required daily allocation of rubber. As King Leopold of Belgium's rubber policies spread, 'it branded people with memories that remained raw for the rest of their lives' (Hochschild, 2006, p. 165). One British missionary was asked poignantly and repeatedly, 'Has the Saviour you tell us of any power to save us from the rubber trouble?' (Hochschild, 2006, p. 172). This is part of the tragic story that has shaped Congo's past. Ugandan theologian Emmanuel Katongole believes that this same story of ambition, greed and plunder continues today, only with different actors. However, he maintains that there could be a very different story. This was a story of power and terror that wantonly sacrificed many African lives but as Christians we know a story of 'self-sacrificing love that involves a different notion of power and thus gives rise to new patterns of life, engendering new forms of community, economics and politics' (Katongole, 2011, p. 20). This requires a different story, a story that affirms the value and dignity of each human person and can shape new practices, polity and ways of living together in community.

This is where spirituality comes in. Our spirituality informs and shapes our life stories and fuels our engagement in mission. Katongole challenges Congo, and indeed all of Africa, to live out a different story informed by a very different set of values and practices which reflect the sacredness of human life and dignity. And how is that possible? As his response, Katongole narrates the stories of those who live a different way, the stories of those people who model the way of Jesus in their daily lives, who live out their spirituality by living a different story. He tells us of a Sudanese bishop who set up a peace village to fight tribalism in a small way; he tells us of Angelina Atyam, whose daughter was kidnapped by the Lord's Resistance Army, which led her on a journey not only of forgiveness but also of advocacy; and he tells us of Maggie Barankitse, who brought together orphaned and abused children of different ethnicities in her Maison Shalom (House of Peace) in Burundi.

In this book we read how the stories of these pioneers' lives have shaped their spirituality and involvement in mission. As we read these stories we begin to see the red thread of God's Holy Spirit at work, which may also inspire us to find that red thread in our lives. Katongole discovered that it is the stories that we carry that make a difference. If we carry assumptions of brutality, greed and chaos then that will carry over into our lifestyle, and the way we look at and organize the world. But if we can live out a different script – a story of love and sacrifice, one of justice and compassion, of beauty and belief fuelled by a spirituality that is nurtured by the bountiful love of God – then a very different story and way of being in the world can emerge. This is what we hope you will find in the chapters that follow.

It is interesting and perhaps not surprising that pioneers look to stories of other pioneers in mission. In this book, for example, Andy Freeman is inspired by St Francis, Kate Pearson by Angela of Foligno, Beth Honey by the early Irish Christians. These have all brought great changes and renewal in the world through their inspirational lives of mission and discipleship. Steve Bevans identifies these sorts of stories in his chapter as a key part of living out a mission spirituality. Those stories are also run through with that same red thread and it becomes something of a line that weaves down through the ages; the story we now find ourselves in.

Alastair McIntosh's book *Soil and Soul* (2004) tells the story of how the island of Eigg off the west coast of Scotland is freed from a landowner through setting up a community trust which campaigns to regain the island and free it from the domination of the laird. I (Jonny) am sure McIntosh would not use the word 'pioneer' for what he does but he clearly is, as the person who sees and then builds the change. It is a modern-day tale of David and Goliath. He draws on liberation theology and Walter Wink's trilogy of the powers with a threefold process of naming, unmasking and engaging the powers to describe the spirituality of the process. A big part of the battle is helping the islanders believe that this is even thinkable, possible or dreamable. One of their secret weapons is poetry. The bards are the storytellers who keep alive a counter-narrative to that of the wider dominant consumer private ownership narrative in an artful, soulful and powerful telling that helps people begin to believe in another way, another world. He suggests that prayer is one of the indispensable means by which we engage the powers and uncouple from our own participation in that domination system (McIntosh, 2004, p. 120). This may all sound rather political and dramatic, and it is. But its significance is that a pioneering spirituality is not about a story that is reduced to a set of privatized practices, something domesticated and co-opted unwittingly in service of the gods of the age. It is a spirituality shaped by a story that enables deep transformation in the world, and in our own hearts and minds. Ann-Marie Wilson's chapter, for example, explores how an active spirituality can support the eradication of FGM from the world.

At CMS one of the modules we explore with pioneers is on mission spirituality, and this, of course, opens up Christian spiritual practices. But its starting point is to help discern the spirituality in the wider culture that already demands our allegiance, the wider story or worldview of the culture, one predicated on the logic of consumption with its associated set of practices and rituals. There is no neutrality, as liberation theology so powerfully reminded us. A Christian spirituality requires an unlearning and a freeing from addiction to this wider spirituality of consumption and a conversion to the service of a different God out of a different story, a different way of living. Johnny Sertin explores how being and doing together can form a mission spirituality in this way. This is actually a tough side to spirituality, a sort of soulwork. Teresa of Avila (1987) uses the metaphor of preparing a garden to describe prayer which she says in the early stages is hard work. It is hard to do this alone and requires a community and practices to call us continually to follow in the way of Christ, to come home to ourselves and support us on that journey.

Place

There is a growing attentiveness towards and an appreciation of the importance of place. Social geographers remind us how knowledge and discernment are situated in particular places and communities. Of course, places are not just physical landscapes; they also embody and hold memories that contribute to a spiritual and emotional landscape of a place. As a New Zealander (Cathy), I hear of thousands of young people making an annual pilgrimage to Gallipoli in Turkey on ANZAC Day (Australian and NZ Army Corps) where tens of thousands of soldiers lost their lives in an ultimately fruitless campaign. The place has power to draw people there to evoke the memories and to share the pain. We saw a more recent example of this when the Germanwings flight plunged into the French Alps and families wanted to visit the crash site to be near their loved ones who had died.

For the Māori people of Aotearoa/NZ place is very important. At any formal introduction, they will tell you their mountain, their river, their village, and they will tell you all this before their name, such is the importance of place. For Māori, land is sacred, land is family and land can speak. Land ownership in Māori culture is very different from European understandings of it. Sadly, early settlers and missionaries were not attentive to this and the consequences have meant that some Māori have been deprived of their ancestral lands and marginalized from what they consider to be their homelands, their place. If the early settlers and missionaries had been able to listen to the culture and context, to the importance of place, and begin to appreciate differences in worldview, history may have played out very differently; the marginalization of one culture by another may have been avoided, or at least its harmful effects diminished. If we do not listen to the stories of the other, if we are not attentive to the importance of place, then their voices are not heard and invisibility and marginalization can result.

So place is important for our being in the world. German philosopher Martin Heidegger writes about dwelling as a way of existence. For him, it is much more than just living in a house; rather it is a way of being in the world. To be is to be in a place. 'Only by knowing our surroundings, being aware of topography and the past, can we live what Heidegger deems an "authentic" existence' (Marsden, 2014, p. 20). To be human we have to live in a place and 'to live is to live locally and know first of all the place one is in' (Marsden, 2014, p. 24). A theological expression of this is the Incarnation. Jesus fully immersed himself in our world, in our place and neighbourhood, and lived among us. This points to practices and virtues such as commitment to a place, radical hospitality, deep relationships, intentional engagement in the local community. This calls for a loyalty to and a delight in the local. It also requires a kind of expectancy to discern the presence of God already in that place. Kenyan theologian John Mbiti reminded us that the missionaries did not introduce God to Africa, 'rather, it was God who brought them to Africa, as carriers of the news about Jesus. African religion had already done the groundwork of making people receptive to the gospel of Jesus Christ' (Mbiti, 1986, p. 12). So we also need to remember that God's presence is already in a place as we seek to encounter this living God.

As you read the chapters that follow we hope you will note the attentiveness to place, the celebration of the local and the need to be fully immersed in the community in which we live and serve. John Wheatley and James Henley are examples of this in their living among young people and seeking to develop an active spirituality. That is a spirituality of place.

People

Spirituality is, of course, about people – the people we encounter on the way. The Emmaus road is perhaps the archetypal example of this. 'We discern in this familiar story the way a stranger becomes a friend, a guest becomes a host, one who listens becomes one who proclaims' (Bevans and Ross, 2015, p. xii). This encounter begins with sharing a journey and a story and ends with sharing a meal. So many of our human encounters mirror this – sharing of stories, friendship and food together. Telling stories and being heard are part of what it means to be human. Around the meal table – wherever that may be – stories can be told, many voices can be heard, memories can be created and nurtured. The youngest can be heard and listened to, the voiceless can be given a voice.

Jean Vanier claims that as we eat together we become friends – no longer guest nor stranger, no longer on the margins nor at the centre. Indeed, these categories begin to break down, as we were all strangers until God welcomed us into his household by grace to be his friends – the supreme act of God's hospitality. Friendship is a powerful force for good; friendship moves us towards wholeness and takes us beyond categories of marginalization. Jesus offered his disciples friendship rather than servanthood (John 15.15) and this is what the Eucharist, Jesus' sacrificial meal, offers us – an invitation to friendship, community and family. Kim Hartshorne's chapter explores how the Eucharist has become central in the Upper Room community in Cirencester.

Eating together is also a great leveller. Eating is something that we all must do, so it has a profoundly egalitarian dimension. Jean

Vanier, of l'Arche community, confessed that when he started to share meals with men of serious mental disabilities, 'Sitting down at the same table meant becoming friends with them, creating a family. It was a way of life absolutely opposed to the values of a competitive, hierarchical society in which the weak are pushed aside' (Pohl, 1999, p. 74). When we eat together, as we let down our guard and share stories, we begin to create relationship and this is at the heart of our spirituality – our relationship with God and neighbour. In a unique moment in the book of Ephesians, we see Jews and Gentiles coming together. The test of their coming together was the meal table; the institution that once symbolized ethnic and cultural division now became a symbol of Christian living. There is no more marginalization or schism between Jew and Gentile and it is symbolized by that most basic of human activities – eating and drinking together. Eating together is a mark of our spirituality and truly locates us in the *missio Dei*.

This kind of approach is a spiritual discipline. We need this encounter with the other person to open us up, to challenge and change us. Quaker scholar and educationalist Parker Palmer reminds us, in his intriguing book *The Company of Strangers: Christians and the Renewal of America's Public Life* (1986), of the importance of the stranger. Our spiritual pilgrimage is a quest, a venture into the unknown, away from safety and security into strange places, for if we remain where we are, we have no need of faith. The visitors to Abraham and Sarah, the stranger on the Emmaus road, brought new truths to their lives. According to Palmer we need the stranger. In his view 'the stranger is not simply one who needs us. We need the stranger. We need the stranger if we are to know Christ and serve God, in truth and in love' (Palmer, 1986, p. 131). So the stranger, the other, becomes a person of promise. The stranger may be unsettling, may challenge or provoke us, may provide a wider perspective. Remember the injunction from the book of Hebrews: 'Keep on loving each other as brothers and sisters. Do not forget to entertain strangers, for by so doing some people have entertained angels without knowing it' (Heb. 13.2). Strangers may transform us and challenge us. 'Hospitality to the stranger gives us a chance to see our own lives afresh, through different eyes' (Koenig, 1985, p. 6). As John Taylor reminds us in his book *The Go-Between God: The Holy Spirit and the Christian Mission*, 'If one is closed up against being hurt, or blind towards one's fellow-men [sic], one is inevitably shut off from God also. One cannot choose to be open in one direction and closed in another' (Taylor, 1972, p. 19).

When the Church Mission Society was exploring becoming an acknowledged community of the Church of England, there was a series of gatherings to discuss what was at the heart of her mission spirituality. Two of the themes that emerged were border crossing and hospitality. In Jesus' sending out of the disciples in pairs in chapter 10 of Luke's Gospel he instructs them to take nothing with them, to remain where they find welcome and to eat what is set before them (Luke 10.1–20). So the hospitality is not something that is provided as host but received as a guest 'in their house' as a border is crossed. Harvey Kwiyani's chapter reminds us of the importance of hospitality as the African pastors in Nottingham offer hospitality in what is for them a new and strange context.

This relates well to the earlier discussion of place – being at home in a place in pioneering often requires a leaving of home in order to find home in a new community and place. That wandering requires risk, trust and courage and it is far from certain what the outcome might be. As Michael Mitton suggests in his chapter, that is likely to be in shadowy or marginal places. Barbara Brown Taylor suggests that getting lost is a spiritual practice that we don't do enough of (Taylor, 2009, p. 69). To eat what is set before you suggests that the building blocks for life, for faith, for worship, for spirituality, are the things of the local culture, not the cultural baggage which the pioneer has been instructed by Jesus to leave behind. Tina Hodgett's chapter on her exploration of spirituality with new mums and babies is another great example of this friendship, which takes place in their house 'freestyle'.

As you read the stories of the pioneers' encounters with people in their communities, you will see how their lives have been transformed by this mysterious encounter that God enables between us: God's Spirit and the other. Our ego is broken open by encountering the Thou in the other, and through the Thou of other people we can meet the transcendent Thou, God. In a sense, this is the magic of mission and a challenge to our spirituality. When we cross a border, when we truly encounter the other, we are transformed and changed. We learn new things about ourselves and about the gospel.

Posture

Spirituality is about posture – it is about learning, listening, creativity, imagination, attentiveness, curiosity, hope.

> Mission is also done with a posture of curiosity, creativity, imagination – being curious about the world and the context, rejoicing in 'strange' ways of being and doing, imagining that another world is possible (to pick up the Occupy slogan) or indeed already here! (Bevans and Ross, 2015, p. xvii)

I believe this attitude fuels our spirituality – a posture of humility and curiosity that drives us to find out about the world, why things are the way they are, and what is our place in all of this. We have so much more to learn. Things are not always as they seem; life is more complex, more beautiful, more aweful than we sometimes acknowledge.

One of the most helpful insights we have found in the last few years regarding posture and spirituality is that in the process of inculturation there is a dynamic of insider and outsider at work, and two different postures are called for (Bevans and Schroeder, 2011, pp. 88–100). The outsider needs to learn to practise letting go – keeping quiet, leaving behind their practices and way of doing things, their language and culture, even their way of framing the gospel – all for the sake of the gospel. It is not that there is anything wrong with those things in and of themselves but they should not be imposed upon a new culture or context. By way of contrast, the insider, or local, should be encouraged to speak out, to risk, to experiment; to use their language, culture and arts in the forming of spiritual expression. This means that something genuinely local, of the place and culture – something indigenous – can emerge.

'God in all things' is something of a catchphrase in Ignatian spirituality (Martin, 2010, p. 5). Roman Catholic spirituality at its best opens up a view of all of life and creation as a sign and mediator of God's presence, as a gift. A contemplative posture of attention, of awareness of noticing, is to have eyes open where they have been blind. There is something wonderful and healing in all of this. For too long in western culture a hidden assumption has been that God is more present in particular church cultural expressions than anywhere else. At its worst 'the world', or the wider culture, has even been something to be afraid of, to be avoided. A pioneering spirituality in contrast finds God in all things, in the culture; through discernment and once eyes are opened God seems to be everywhere. We loved the story Johnny Sertin writes about of how the Masai are amazed to find that there are only seven sacraments in the Roman Catholic Church, when they assumed there would be at least 7,000! Harvey Kwiyani in his chapter similarly writes of the gift of holistic spirituality in African cultures.

Berdine and Benno van den Toren's insightful chapter explores a posture of spirituality in crossing cultures. When we adopt a posture of learning and humility; then we can allow God to come through the wounds. This is about being vulnerable, open, and willing to be wounded. Life will bring its pain, its dilemmas, its challenges. Our pioneering will not always be successful. The way of the cross is one of hiddenness, vulnerability, smallness and giving up one's life. If this all sounds rather grim, it is also about beauty, creativity, human dignity and flourishing. We experience the power of resurrection as well as sharing in the fellowship of Christ's suffering (Phil. 3.10). As one friend put it rather pithily, all is 'glory and grime, glory and grime'.

Soulful treasure

There is a storehouse full of spiritual treasures in the Christian tradition. Jesus tells a very short story where he likens the kingdom of God to someone who goes to this storehouse and takes out something old and something new (Matt. 13.52). It has been fascinating and wonderful to see the kinds of treasure that pioneers have been drawn to over the last few years. There seems to have been a particular resonance with contemplative spirituality and practices such as silence, the examen, retreat, spiritual direction, *lectio divina*, for example. When these get remixed with something new they seem to come alive in surprising and simple ways. *Lectio divina* used with the Jesus Deck at a 'mind body spirit' fair becomes a way of reading the Gospel with spiritual seekers. Communion round the meal table in a home reframes the Eucharist; stations of the cross etched in tattoos on the flesh of members of a Christian community tells the old story in a new way. Gavin Mart's chapter on unearthing spirituality through the arts is a reminder of how simple it can be to share this treasure.

Most often this something new is treasure that is already in the place: the culture, the language, the world in which the pioneer is seeking to be present – over the border they have crossed. While acknowledging that there is treasure from the tradition it can lack authenticity, resonance or even something as basic as connection without this remix. It can end up sounding as if it comes from or belongs in another world and therefore remain disconnected. There is something beautifully simple about using the stuff of a local culture as the building blocks for spirituality and worship. Jesus did this all the time in his use of stories about seeds, yeast, salt and light to mix the heart of the tradition with something new. At the last supper he took something old, the Passover meal, and something new – bread and wine shared in remembrance of him – to institute an incredible ritual that has been passed down the centuries and remixed in wonderful ways ever since. The pioneer is akin to a treasure seeker. The posture outlined above is so important in order to have eyes to see and ears to hear where this treasure might be in ordinary things. This is particularly powerful when it is combined with the insider speaking out, as outlined above. In other words, that treasure is something that is made or articulated or voiced from insiders to the culture with whom the outsider can then risk adding or introducing the gift of something old with it. Neither merely the old nor just the new have the same authenticity or depth. The spirituality of the kingdom is somehow found in the two together.

A group of pioneers, including three contributors to this book, travelled on pilgrimage to Ireland to visit sites of early Irish Christianity and reflect on their stories. Beth Honey shares some reflections in her chapter. One of the themes that came through is that those communities were places not only of wonderful mission and education but of soulful and artistic expression of spirituality. We felt both challenged and inspired by this. It is our hope that pioneers will enable a flourishing of artistic and soulful expressions of spirituality through the communities they help grow and nurture and through their own expression – through spoken word, music, song, photography, film-making, animation, liturgies, prayers, poetry, ritual, art installations, new practices, old practices reframed. This is worship that is created, made from local soil and cultures, homemade rather than from liturgical committees in church structures (though it might draw on those for some treasure!). We have encouraged the contributors to the book to include one or two pieces as part of their chapters, which we hope gives a flavour of this soulful expression.

In their house

One of the joys that we have found together with the pioneers who have trained at CMS over the last few years is that there is no solution you can pull off a shelf to tell you what to do in mission in a given context. Yes, there are examples that are inspiring, there are theoretical pieces that are profoundly helpful, and there is great wisdom to be learned from other mistakes and successes. But at heart it is a risk, an adventure of imagination, a creative response together with God's Spirit to leave home and cross a border to join in with God's mission: to make a way where there is no way. That can't possibly be boxed or packaged up – thank God! As we have read back through the stories, types of practice and communities in this book and pulled out some threads, we conclude that the same joy we have found around pioneering mission is true in the area of pioneering spirituality. There is no one, right way or approach to pioneering spirituality, there is simply great freedom in Christ. Those pioneering spirituality are using what helps and avoiding what hinders, exploring that freedom to open up whatever draws us into friendship with Christ and transforms the world. These stories offer a fresh perspective on what it means to live out a pioneering spirituality. We have been reminded that this spirituality is not focused around our own ways of doing things but takes place in the culture, place and communities we are among, 'in their house'. We hope it will spark your own sense of adventure, creativity, improvisation, imagination and pioneering spirituality.

References

Bevans, S. and Schroeder, R. P., 2011, *Prophetic Dialogue: Reflections on Christian Mission Today*, Maryknoll, NY: Orbis.

Bevans, S. and Ross C., 2015, *Mission on the Road to Emmaus: Constants, Context and Prophetic Dialogue*, London: SCM Press.

Bosch, D., 2001, *A Spirituality of the Road*, Eugene, OR: Wipf & Stock.

Hochschild, A., 2006, *King Leopold's Ghost: A Story of Greed, Terror and Heroism in Colonial Africa*, London: Pan Macmillan.

Katongole, E., 2011, *The Sacrifice of Africa: A Political Theology for Africa*, Grand Rapids: Eerdmans.

Koenig, J., 1985, *New Testament Hospitality: Partnership with Strangers as Promise and Mission*, Philadelphia: Fortress Press.

Marsden, P., 2014, *Rising Ground: A Search for the Spirit of Place*, London: Granta.

Martin, J., 2010, *The Jesuit Guide to Almost Everything*, New York: HarperCollins.

Mbiti, J., 1986, *Bible and Theology in African Christianity*, Nairobi: Oxford University Press.

McIntosh, A., 2004, *Soil and Soul*, London: Aurum Press.

Palmer, P., 1986, *The Company of Strangers: Christians and the Renewal of America's Public Life*, New York: Crossroad.

Pohl, C., 1999, *Making Room: Recovering Hospitality as a Christian Tradition*, Grand Rapids, MI: Eerdmans.

Taylor, B. B., 2009, *An Altar In The World*, Norwich: Canterbury Press.

Taylor, J. V., 1972, *The Go-Between God: The Holy Spirit and the Christian Mission*, London: SCM Press.

Teresa of Avila, 1987, *The Life of Saint Teresa of Avila by Herself*, trans. J. Cohen, Harmondsworth: Penguin Classics.

Wink, W., 1984, *Naming the Powers*, Philadelphia: Fortress Press.

Wink, W., 1986, *Unmasking the Powers*, Philadelphia: Fortress Press.

Wink, W., 1992, *Engaging the Powers*, Philadelphia: Fortress Press.

2

Dancing with the Missionary God: Towards a Mission Spirituality

STEPHEN BEVANS

Introduction: the notion of spirituality

This chapter presents the elements of a 'mission spirituality'. As I begin, however, I must acknowledge that to define 'spirituality' today is a bit of a risky business. There are, in fact, many definitions of spirituality, and while they all have a lot in common, they differ among themselves – sometimes very much. I'm sure not everyone will agree with the definition or description of spirituality with which I work here. Nevertheless, one has to start somewhere.

As I understand spirituality, I would conceive of it as a kind of 'framework' or 'set' of values, symbols, doctrines, attitudes and practices, which persons or a community attempt to make their own in order to be able to cope with a particular situation, to grow in the love of God and self-transcendence, and/or to accomplish a particular task in life or in the world. A spirituality, in other words, is like a reservoir from which a person or a community can draw to motivate action, to keep on track, to bolster commitment, or to avoid discouragement when times get rough. It is a way, in still other words, of tapping into the infinite, life-giving, refreshing and empowering presence of God's Spirit, so that people's lives, or the life of a community, can be lived in grace, gratitude and growth.

On the one hand, everyone has a spirituality – Christian or not, believer or not, pious or not. A spirituality – implicit or explicit, cultivated or neglected – is simply the way individuals cope with life. This is true at least as one regards human existence from a religious perspective. Spiritualities are very personal, and everyone develops one in some form or another. On the other hand, while allowing for individual differences, preferences and need, there are some spiritualities that are *systems* – particular, tried-and-true or freshly innovative ways of thinking, praying, imagining and acting that are developed to help women and men in particular circumstances find the stability they need, the challenge they require, and the growth that they seek. Thus, for example, we can speak about Anglican spirituality, lay spirituality, the spirituality of my own Roman Catholic religious congregation of the Society of the Divine Word, American or UK spirituality, presbyteral spirituality.

Mission spirituality

In order to develop a spirituality of this latter type, this chapter will attempt to sketch a framework of *mission* spirituality. This is a spirituality for women and men who want to grow and thrive in their identity as people consciously participating in the mission of the triune God, particularly insofar as such participation involves moving beyond their own zones of security in terms of culture, social status, language and location. Expressing this kind of spirituality in an image, mission spirituality could be described as a way of 'dancing with our missionary God'. It is the basis, I believe, of a pioneer spirituality.

Having said this, I do not believe that there is a particular, 'one-size-fits-all' mission spirituality. Mission spirituality, like mission itself, is always and everywhere a *contextual* spirituality. It will depend on *where* a person engages in mission (in affluent areas of North America or the UK, in poor Latin America or a housing estate in London, among youths frequenting clubs, at New Age fairs), *when* one engages in mission (as a newcomer in a situation learning the language, as someone beginning to withdraw from a ministry situation in retirement), one's experience (failure, struggle, identifying with the people in a particular culture), one's theological perspective (Rahnerian, Process, or focused on Roman Catholic papal and magisterial teaching, etc.). Because of this contextual reality, therefore, what I sketch here will be more of a template or checklist *towards* a particular spirituality of mission. Included are topics and questions that I believe every mission spirituality must address, but how they will be articulated will depend on a variety of contextual factors. One might say that I am presenting a number of *constants* of spirituality that will vary with every context. Readers may also recognize that there are issues and questions not addressed here. You are certainly free to add these to the template.

Our template will have six sections corresponding to six questions: (1) What Scripture passage anchors your mission spirituality? (2) Who are your heroes/heroines as you engage in mission? (3) What are the assets and liabilities of your own culture as you cross over to another culture or context? (4) What is your basic theological perspective as you minister in a missionary situation? (5) What is your experience as a missionary? And, (6) What practices might you engage in to deepen and develop your life in mission? The meaning of each of these questions is explained, followed by a number of possible ways in which they might be answered. Again, the point is not to offer a complete mission spirituality, but to engage readers in constructing or articulating their own.[1] You may want to pause after each section to ask how you might answer the question.

1 Scriptural foundations

Every spirituality needs to be rooted in Scripture, and mission spirituality is no exception. It is necessary to ask the question, therefore, what passage(s), books, or themes of Scripture are those that ground your missionary life?

Some passages may figure large at certain times during a life of missionary service. People may take strength and inspiration, for example, from some of the great vocation passages (such as Isa.

6.1–8; Jer. 1.4–10; Matt. 4.18–22 – the call of Peter and Andrew, James and John), or Jesus' invitation to Andrew and Peter to 'come and see' in John 1.35–39. Others may be buoyed up in difficulty by Jeremiah's sufferings (in chapter 38), by Jesus' Passion as a consequence of his own faithful missionary witness to the reign of God, or by Paul's being held under suspicion by fellow Christians (Acts 9.23–30) or those he had tried to evangelize (e.g. Acts 9.19b–25; 13.50–52).

There may also be passages that can provide basic guidance, inspiration and direction to the work of crossing a culture, struggling with a language, being accepted by a people, or bonding with people among whom one works. Paul's passionate statement that he had become a slave to all so that he could win more of them to Christ – indeed, that he had become 'all things to all people', so that he might 'by all means save some' (see 1 Cor. 9.19–23) – might serve as the anchor and beacon for missionaries in a very different culture from their own. One of my own inspiring passages is John 10.10: the reason for my ministry, the reason for witnessing to and proclaiming Christ, is to bring, like Jesus, abundant life to the world. One missionary in a course on missionary spirituality, my colleague Larry Nemer relates, chose as a foundational passage the story of the wedding at Cana in the second chapter of John's Gospel; the missionary, this person explained, is like water, but at the word of Jesus and in his hands he or she can be transformed into rich, joy-giving wine. The movement of the Acts of the Apostles has always struck me as a marvellous story of missionary spirituality. It is the Spirit, the primary agent of mission as Paul VI and John Paul II have characterized her (Apostolic Exhortation, 75; *Redemptoris Missio*, 30), that challenges, calls, pushes the Church beyond the boundaries of their understanding of the gospel to include all peoples and all cultures in the plan of salvation. It is precisely this move of the Spirit that calls the Jesus Community to be Church.

There is no 'normative' passage of Scripture for a mission spirituality. One reason for this, as I've said, is the changing context of people's missionary service. Another reason is that, as Christopher Wright has shown at great length, the *entire* body of

Scripture – Old and New Testaments, but especially the New – is the result of Israel's and the Church's reflection on the mission in which they have been called to engage (Wright, 2006). Readers might pause here and reflect on the scriptural foundations for their own missionary spirituality.

2 Missionary heroes/heroines

Particularly in the last decade or so, I have become more and more convinced of the importance of the example of the saints for my own spiritual life. Back in 1997 I was given an autographed copy of Robert Ellsberg's marvellous *All Saints*, in which he sketches the lives of 'saints' (canonized or otherwise, Christian or otherwise), one for every day (Ellsberg, 1997). For the next ten years these formed part of my daily reading. After a break of a few years, I have recently gone back to reading a short life of a saint each day; Ellsberg has provided these in a monthly booklet that contains the Scripture readings for the daily Eucharist.[2] There is something powerful about being in touch with that great 'cloud of witnesses' (Heb. 12.1) of our faith, and I have been greatly nourished in my faith and ministry by women and men like John Main, Cardinal Newman, Martin Luther King, Jr, Mary Mackillop, Mary Ward, Mahatma Gandhi and Pandita Ramabai.

A second element of a mission spirituality, I believe, is a rootedness in those women and men who have gone before us, set amazing examples, raised standards, and have helped us see our own humanness as we struggle and celebrate our participation in God's mission. Perhaps our heroes/heroines are the founders or past leaders of our own missionary congregation: Henry Venn, Max Warren or John V. Taylor, the great founder and leaders of CMS; Arnold Janssen, founder of the Society of the Divine Word. Perhaps the great missionaries of the past might offer us guidance and inspiration: Charles de Foucauld, for example, or Alopen of East Syria, John Carey of India, or Matteo Ricci, or Mary Magdalene the Apostle to the Apostles. Perhaps it could be missionaries who are also heroes and heroines from our own culture: an Oscar Romero from Latin America, an Alessandro Valignano from Italy, a Lorenzo Ruiz from the Philippines, a Samuel Ajayi Crowther from Nigeria. Or perhaps our models for mission are senior members of our congregation with whom we have worked. I think of a German SVD by the name of Fritz Scharpf from whom I learned so much as a young missionary in the Philippines, or my former teacher and then colleague Bernhard Raas from Switzerland.

Once again, it might be good to pause here and think about the great women and men who have influenced you in your life, who have lent you inspiration or perhaps a sympathetic, listening ear. These are the agents of the Spirit who shape our missionary spirituality, who help us dance with the missionary God.

3 Cultural assets and liabilities

We are all unique individuals, with individual strengths and weaknesses, and the development and cultivation of a mission spirituality is to bolster and harness those strengths and, if possible, blunt those weaknesses. But we are more than individuals. We are people of a particular time and generation. We are shaped by our families and by our social class and education. And we are formed and deformed by the culture in which we find our identity.

Culture is more than practices and cuisine. It is even more than values and attitudes. Culture shapes the way that we view – or, even better, *construct* – our world and our very selves. Westerners really do see themselves first as individuals and only subsequently related to others – even family. Latin Americans, Africans and Asians (if I can venture to say it) really do *not* see themselves first as individuals, but as vitally connected to family, community, or cultural group. What is the 'truth' here? Is the best form of organization of society hierarchical? Or is it democratic? There is no objective answer to this.

Culture is not something we can just take off or put on. While we can *acculturate* ourselves to various new circumstances, from the first moment of our lives we have been *enculturated* within our own culture by our family, our friends, our language, and the media that surround us. While some people are truly bi-cultural, and some people do manage to acculturate to a remarkable degree, most of us – the vast majority of us – never really move out of our original culture.

This is why knowing who we are as cultural beings – as citizens of the UK, as Italians, Germans, Polish, Americans, Chileans, Indians – is so important. Each of us brings a good amount of cultural baggage to mission, and we need to be aware of how that baggage can sustain us or how, as in the Latin for baggage, it is *impedimenta*: a real liability in our cross-cultural ministry. It is important to understand and believe that *every* culture is both good and bad in itself, and that every culture offers opportunities and impediments for growth in another culture or situation. No culture is all good. No culture is all bad.

As an American, for example, I bring a confidence to my ministry that is supported by a Yankee 'can do' attitude. I bring a sense of equality of all peoples that can help me build a strong sense of participation among the people where I work. I can easily work for a strong, well-educated laity. As a member of an affluent, powerful nation I have a confidence in myself and in my worldview, and a confidence in the capacities of others. But such confidence and surety can border on the arrogant. My sense of equality and participation might trample on people's sensitivities about distinct, important and even sacred roles in a particular society. My affluence can allow me to live in a way that actually separates me from the people among whom I minister. I speak with a frankness that my countrymen admire, but which often can be insulting to the men and women who are my hosts.

So part of my spirituality is to recognize who I am as a cultural being and make sure that my identity does not get in the way of God's work. I can never slough off that identity, but I can temper it quite a bit, and use its positive aspects for good. Working with my identity surely needs to find itself into my prayer life; it certainly points to ways that I can practise real 'self-denial' for the sake of my ministry. Once again, you might want to pause here to take your own 'cultural inventory'.

4 Theological perspectives

Every Christian is a theologian. We may not recognize that fact. We may deny that we think theologically – that we operate pastorally rather than theologically. But that very denial is already a kind of theology in itself. Our theology may be highly developed and articulated, or it may not, but when we understand that the basic dynamic of theologizing is simply part of faith, we see how inescapable it is. The mark of a good pastor, as spiritual writer Henri Nouwen suggests, is how conscious she or he is of that dynamic in her or his life (Nouwen, 1989).

Our theology shapes our world, and provides the framework for our spirituality. Depending on our understanding of God (judge, father, friend, Mystery), of Jesus (emphasis on his human nature, emphasis on his divine nature), of Mary (model disciple, the way to a basically angry God), the Church (missionary community, hierarchical community), we get energy for ministry, make time for prayer, feel challenged, intimidated or discouraged.

Cuban American church historian Justo L. González speaks about three basic types of theology that can shape the way we look at the world and do ministry (González, 1999). González speaks first of 'Type A' theology, which has its source in the North African Roman lawyer Tertullian in the third century, and emphasizes order and, to a certain extent, law. God is the lawgiver; human sin is disobedience; Jesus came to bring the new law and to mend the gap between humanity and God by his obedience unto death. 'Type B' theology goes back to Origen, the great scholar of Alexandria in Egypt. Steeped in Platonic philosophy, the focus of this type of theology is the mind's search for the truth, experimenting, even risking, using every rational and cultural means possible. In this type, God is the One, the contemplation of whom humanity failed to sustain and so needs to work its way back to; Jesus is the visible form of God, who helps us towards the goal of contemplation. 'Type C' theology has its model in the Syrian bishop and pastor Irenaeus, exile and missionary to the frontiers of the Roman Empire in Lyons in Gaul (today's France). This is a pastoral theology, rooted in experience. For Irenaeus, God is the great Shepherd, who fondly cares for his sheep. God did not make the world perfect, as Tertullian conceived of creation; nor did human souls exist before creation in rapt contemplation of the Godhead, only to be distracted and fall into bodiliness. Rather, humanity was created imperfect but eminently perfectible, and Jesus shows us the way to achieve our full identity as made in God's image and likeness. Each type certainly implies a distinct spirituality: Type A might emphasize a spirituality of strict discipline; Type B might conceive spirituality as a journey in dialogue with the world's many cultures; Type C might conceive spirituality in terms of a relationship that needs to be cultivated. My own sense is that Christians today still fall within one of these types, and this does indeed affect and form their spirituality – in this case, how they cope with cultural difference, with struggle and failure, with poverty or affluence.

As our theology becomes more and more conscious and explicit, it can become more and more consistent and self-critical. This is why the development of a mission spirituality is so closely connected with the articulation and critique of one's 'operative' or 'embedded' theology.[3] Is doctrine conceived more in the line of Type A, and so will breach no compromise as it is proclaimed cross-culturally? Is God a 'fellow sufferer who understands', as Alfred North Whitehead (1929, p. 532) once put it and which jibes with Irenaeus' image of a shepherd God? Is clarity on Jesus' divinity not all that important, as we struggle to understand the truth of revelation in other religions? What kind of God will understand our failures in mission? What kind of Church will encourage grassroots participation? These are theological positions we need to sort out to help us and guide us in our cross-cultural, missionary journey, as we continue to dance with the missionary God. Readers might want to pause to think of their own particular convictions in theology.

5 Mission experiences

Once again, a spirituality is never developed in the abstract. Spirituality is always rooted in concrete circumstances, and concrete experiences. If a missionary is struggling with learning a language, for example, his struggle will precipitate a certain kind of prayer (abandonment, for patience), a certain kind of asceticism (study, humility in seeming like a child, risking sounding awkward, being corrected), the importance of certain Scripture passages (e.g. Mark 10.13–16 about becoming a little child; John 3.3 about being born again), and the significance of certain missionaries from tradition (Cyril and Methodius and their important translation of the Bible, Matteo Ricci in China). If a missionary has been threatened with violence or death, or has experienced failure, or has after a long time been finally accepted by the people, all of these experiences will shape her spiritual life.

It will be important for missionaries to share their experiences so as to be able to be aware of and articulate them better. Such effort doesn't need to stop when a missionary returns home, or moves to another type of mission ministry. In fact, it is crucial that her or his experiences be told, and be appreciated. The search for such a support group and regular attendance at its meetings will be another way of cultivating a mission spirituality. Readers might want to recall the unique experiences in their own lives that shape their missionary spirituality.

6 Practices

Finally, although we have already spoken about them above, a mission spirituality is cultivated by commitment to certain basic practices. Contemporary theology has rediscovered the importance of frequently repeated actions – actions that create habits (Volf and Bass, 2002). As we commit ourselves to particular times and forms of prayer, to ascetical practices, to regular forms of behaviour, we are shaped by them in overt and quite subtle ways.

Any kind of spirituality involves the practice of regular prayer. That goes without saying. A mission spirituality, however, would make sure that the content of that prayer is one that reaches out to all the world. It might be one that uses the newspaper as a basic prayerbook. It is also a prayer that constantly calls to mind the people who are served, with all their cultural richness. It will be a prayer of kenosis or self-emptying. It will be a prayer that, where appropriate, will use the forms and content of the other faiths among whom missionaries work.

A mission spirituality will practise a simplicity of life, in solidarity with the poor of the world. This may be a real challenge to those of us from more affluent countries, but it is essential.

The spirituality that we are reflecting on here might practise two kinds of asceticism. One would be a kind of 'asceticism of risk'. By this I do not mean putting oneself in undue danger, courting violence or death for no good reason. This may be necessary, certainly (I think of missionaries like Dorothy Stang in Brazil), but this is not what I mean here; rather it is a practice of choosing to be stretched in everyday matters – in terms of language, perhaps, or in terms of pastoral assignments, the kind of things one reads. My experience is that often in cross-cultural situations we opt to spend time with our own cultural or language groups, in our own rectories and convents, eating familiar food. This 'asceticism of risk' would be an option to move beyond our comfort zones – perhaps not all the time, but certainly some of the time.

A second kind of ascetical practice would be in the area of learning to listen rather than to talk. This is hard work. So often missionaries occupy a position of power and prestige. From this position, they often talk too much, and too soon. A common saying in the Philippines where I worked as a missionary years ago was that the new missionary should not say anything for at least six months, perhaps up to a year. Then he might venture a humble opinion once in a while. But the main thing is to listen, to observe. To learn to really hear what is being said – so often 'between the lines' – to learn to really see what is going on in an unfamiliar context; this is a major exercise in self-denial. But it will pay large dividends in the future.

Finally, although I am sure there are other practices that missionaries could engage in, it is important to have a mentor or a spiritual director: someone to talk to. Larry Nemer lays down the qualities of such a person. The mentor/director should first be one who can listen with an understanding heart: 'someone who has time – someone who is willing to make [the missionary's] experience the priority of the moment'. Second, the person needs to have wisdom and experience, and so be able to advise the missionary on the 'right way' to do something or other in a particular culture. Third, the director/mentor should be someone who is 'serene, self-confident and not surprised by anything' (Nemer, unpublished). Our mission spirituality needs to be developed in dialogue, in real honesty and openness.

It might make sense at this point for readers to reflect whether there might be any other practices that would promote a spirituality that will sustain and inspire the hard but amazing work of mission.

Conclusion

What I have tried to do in these reflections is to lay out a template within which men and women in various stages of missionary service – preparation, newly arrived, veteran workers, those who have returned home or who are retired – can cultivate a spirituality that can sustain them, challenge them, console them, deepen them. Like spirituality in general, there is not one that works for everyone. And yet, any mission spirituality needs to be rooted in Scripture, in the Christian tradition, and in human experience. As one works to discover how Scripture can inspire, how tradition can challenge and anchor, and how human experience can continuously challenge, women and men in ministry will develop a mission spirituality suited for their particular situation, and conforming to the mind of Christ; therefore joining the dance as partners with our missionary God.

References

Ellsberg, R., 1997, *All Saints: Daily Reflections on Saints, Prophets, and Witnesses for Our Time*, New York: Crossroad.

González, J. L., 1999, *Christian Thought Revisited: Three Types of Theology*, Maryknoll, NY: Orbis.

Nemer, L., 'The Issues and Challenges of Cross-Cultural Mission in Promoting the Mission of the Church', unpublished presentation.

Nouwen, H., 1989, *In the Name of Jesus: Reflections on Christian Leadership in the Future*, New York: Crossroad.

Pope Paul VI, Apostolic Exhortation (EN), http://w2.vatican.va/content/paul-vi/en/apost_exhortations/documents/hf_p-vi_exh_19751208_evangelii-nuntiandi.html.

Pope John Paul II, *Redemptoris Missio* (RM), Encyclical Letter, http://w2.vatican.va/content/john-paul-ii/en/encyclicals/documents/hf_jp-ii_enc_07121990_redemptoris-missio.html.

Stone, H. W. and Duke, J. O., 1996, *How to Think Theologically*, Minneapolis: Fortress Press.

Volf, M. and Bass, D. C. (eds), 2002, *Practicing Theology: Beliefs and Practices in Christian Life*, Grand Rapids, MI: Eerdmans.

Whitehead, A. N., 1929, *Process and Reality: An Essay in Cosmology*, New York: Macmillan.

Wright, C. J. H., 2006, *The Mission of God: Unlocking the Bible's Grand Narrative*, Downers Grove, IL: InterVarsity Press.

Notes

1 I am highly indebted to my friend and mentor Larry Nemer, SVD for the development of this chapter. It was in conversation with him that the ideas in it have taken shape, even though, of course, I am responsible for its concrete development. Larry referred me to the groundbreaking work on mission spirituality: Michael C. Reilly, 1978, *Spirituality for Mission: Historical, Theological and Cultural Factors for a Present-Day Missionary Spirituality*, Maryknoll, NY: Orbis.

2 The service is entitled *Give Us This Day* and is available from the Liturgical Press at Collegeville, Minnesota.

3 The term 'operative' theology I owe to my former colleague Herbert Anderson. The term 'embedded' theology appears in Stone and Duke, 1996, pp. 13–16.

3

Preaching in Hades

MICHAEL MITTON

The harrowing of hell

> For Christ also suffered for sins once for all, the righteous for
> the unrighteous, in order to bring you to God. He was put to
> death in the flesh, but made alive in the spirit, in which also he
> went and made a proclamation to the spirits in prison. (1 Pet.
> 3.18–19)

This passage from 1 Peter is a strange passage, and one that has
teased and fascinated Bible scholars throughout the ages. Jesus, in
his resurrected life, somehow or other went and preached to the
spirits who were in prison. Among the varying understandings of
this passage has been the notion that Jesus visited the dark prison
of the underworld, traditionally understood to be the dwelling
place of the dead. For those of us brought up on the old words of
the Prayer Book Matins creed, we may recall reciting the Apostles' Creed, including the words, 'And I believe in Jesus Christ his
only son our Lord, who was conceived by the Holy Ghost, Born
of the Virgin Mary, Suffered under Pontius Pilate, Was crucified
dead and buried: *He descended into hell* ...' This has often been
referred to as the 'harrowing' (plundering) of hell, and there are
many medieval icons aiming to depict the scene.

The word Peter uses is *phulake*, the word for prison. The
imprisoned place of the dead was often called Hades. The Jews of
the first century had a very hazy understanding of life beyond the
grave. They saw it as a shadowy world where discarnate human

spirits roamed after death in a twilight world. It is very much like the underworld Aragorn has to visit in Tolkien's *Lord of the Rings*, before the great battle of Minas Tirith. Elrond gives him the sword of Anduril and tells him to take the Dimholt Road, the one everyone fears, because it leads to the haunted caverns where the Dead Men of Dunharrow live. In Peter Jackson's film version you see these green ghostly shapes being preached to by Aragorn, who eventually frees them. Well, this is something of the image that was in the minds of first-century Jews. This Hades place (or *Sheol* place, to give it its Hebrew name) was a fairly hopeless place. Isaiah could write about it, 'For Sheol cannot thank you, death cannot praise you; those who go down to the pit cannot hope for your faithfulness' (Isa. 38.18). It was a restless place of imprisonment, where the souls of the departed awaited the final judgement.

One understanding of 1 Peter 3.19 (and 4.6) is that Jesus visited this gloomy, restless prison, and many have explored the meaning of this idea. For me, whatever the true meaning of this passage, what I learn from it is that Jesus has a clear interest in visiting the shadowlands. He is interested in the places that look much more like death than life; he is interested in the places that are beyond the reach of human understanding; he is interested in the places that most of us would prefer to avoid. Not only is he interested in such places, but he actually has a message to preach in these places, a message that brings extraordinary resurrection hope. For me, the fact that Jesus chose to preach in Hades is one of the most hopeful aspects of the gospel.

So what is all this saying about pioneering and spirituality? I would argue that it is the pioneers who have an unusual enthusiasm and vocation for visiting Hades. By this I mean, the pioneer is one who, following the example of Jesus, is prepared to go to unevangelized places that others view as murky and dangerous. They have a particular fascination for forbidden territory and all that is out of bounds! The pioneer is not particularly interested in the acknowledged places of Christian life, such as inherited models of church. Their charism is to do with breaking new ground. And often that ground is ground about which the Church has been very suspicious. Examples of such ground have been the world of psychic fairs, tarot card readings, heavy metal, etc. It was not so long ago that charismatic evangelical teaching was to do with keeping clear of such places, because they would infect and corrupt you. Such Hades places were to be prayed against, not visited.

But now pioneers are boldly going into all kinds of worlds that have been judged in the past by some parts of the Church as being spiritually very dark and oppressive. And it is there they take the message of resurrection light, trusting that he who is in them is stronger than he that is in the world (1 John 4.6). And they also look out for signs of the presence of Jesus already there in that world, gladly preaching away, and quite at ease with the shadows.

Jesus was, of course, engaged in pioneering all the time. He kept on breaking out of the accepted forms of life, and entering the shadowy places where decent rabbis like him should not be seen dead. Thus he heads boldly into the home of the Canaanite woman, thinks nothing of being touched by the ritually unclean woman on his way to Jairus' home, and cheerfully invites himself into a tax-gatherer's home in Jericho. These are but a few of the many occasions where Jesus enters shadowy worlds that he was not supposed to enter, and there he preached good news. But there was a cost for him. This persistent engagement with forbidden worlds eventually cost him his life. And following his death on the cross he 'descends into hell', but there he is (if this understanding of 1 Peter 3.19 is correct) preaching the good news. And on Easter morning he rises from Hades, and you often see those icons where the resurrection is pictured as Jesus rising up from the tomb with lots of little people, freed from Hades, floating up beside him.

I would suggest therefore that pioneers are being faithful followers of Jesus, daring to accompany him to hitherto unblessed places and preaching good news. They take within them the presence and message of Christ, who was crucified and who also rose again.

But there is also another journey in all of this that gives integrity to our pioneering journey. Jesus did indeed visit the prisons of this world, and the prison of the underworld. But he was also willing to visit the prison of the inner world. We see this most clearly in the story of his temptations in the wilderness. To do all this pioneering and face the consequences of misunderstanding and judgement he had to do a significant piece of exploration first. To use language poetically rather than literally, he had to visit the Hades within himself.

The best insight we get into this is in Luke 4.1–13. This is a mysterious and extraordinary story of Jesus that comes straight after his baptism in the river Jordan. His public ministry gets under way as John drenches him in the Jordan, the dove flutters down from heaven, and the voice cries out that this is the beloved Son of God. All systems are set to go, but then are apparently stalled as Jesus is driven out to a wild wasteland for 40 days, just when you imagine he'll be enthused by the Spirit to get going on preaching, healing and delivering. But out he goes to that place of extremes of temperature, and starvation and wild beasts. And what happens to him there? Well, there is a great contest with Satan. It is a contest well understood by Egyptian monks and nuns, Celtic saints and many religious people over the centuries. It is an inner journey that has to battle with darkness. It is a spiritual battle in this desert journey, but such battlegrounds are often in the realms of our own vulnerabilities. And the fully human Jesus was no exception to this. Thus Satan probes into his soul at three tender points of his humanity:

- Jesus' human need for sustenance and all that gives him strength – 'turn these stones to bread …'
- Jesus' need for significance – 'all the kingdoms of the world can be yours …'
- Jesus' need for assurance of God's goodness – 'throw yourself down …'

There is something so deeply reassuring for us that Jesus had to face these temptations, and even more reassuring that he must have told them to his disciples who made sure they got written down in the Gospels. Jesus was led out into a wilderness by the Holy Spirit not for a charismatic glory party, but for something really very dark indeed. Jesus had to visit the 'Hades' within his own soul, the shadowy place where forces within his humanity could imprison him in all kinds of traps of fears, lusts, greeds – all those parts of our humanity that can be destructive. The Desert Fathers linked the wild beasts with what they called 'the passions'. So the story of Jesus in the wilderness with the wild beasts was understood by them as his battle with the passions within him that had the potential for great life, but also for great destructiveness. The wild beast is dangerous, precisely because it has the capacity to destroy. But in Jesus' case 'he was *with* the wild beasts', which suggests that he found a way of dwelling with them in such a way that they were no longer a threat. So Jesus patterns for us an extraordinary charismatic journey of the Spirit, whereby we allow him to visit the shadowy parts of ourselves in order that he may preach there some good news and send us on our way in the power of the Spirit.

Alongside Jesus in that wilderness with the wild beasts was also the presence of the angels who ministered to him (Mark 1.12). How they did this we don't know, but my guess is that at least one of those angels reminded Jesus of the word of the Father who announced from heaven, 'this is my beloved son'. Angels preach good news. They don't know how to do anything else. Angels can come in all forms of disguise, and they can often be found in wilderness places.

Jesus models for us a Spirit-led journey into wilderness places, where we have to visit the haunts of our shadow side and we will find there a real hotchpotch of fears, dreads, lusts, prides, needs, longings – we will often not know if they are right or wrong, light or dark, good or bad. But before we judge them, we must acknowledge them and accept that they are there and part of us. And then we have to find ways of letting Jesus preach good news to them, which he may well do through a ministering angel, and that angel may be in the guise of a friend, a book, a chance meeting, a television commercial – who knows what. We can't limit them!

The point is, though, that as Jesus was prepared to face his inner shadowy world, so it was precisely in that world that he was strengthened and renewed, and soon after his wilderness experience he heads into his home town of Nazareth in the power of the Spirit (Luke 4.16ff.) and goes into the 'inherited church', and there exposes the shadowy side in the minds and hearts of the people there. Moreover, he refuses to collude with their nationalist interpretations of Scripture, and he preaches a sermon on life-giving faith and chooses as examples the Gentile woman of Zarephath and the pagan captain Naaman. The orthodox Nazarenes despised women and Gentiles, so immediately Jesus is preaching into the Hades of their prejudices. Not all in Hades want to hear the good news. The familiarity of our prisons can give them a sense of safety. The Nazarenes, rather than welcoming their freedom through Jesus' message, seek to destroy him, but he walks through all those wild beasts, maybe because he is so at peace in himself.

The message in all this, therefore, is that if we are to be pioneers in this modern world, we will be following the example of Jesus, taking the good news of Jesus into the shadowy and imprisoned places. But like Jesus, we will meet many resistances, and we will be taken to the story of the cross again. Our way of thriving as pioneers in these shadowy places will be to allow the Spirit to drive us into the wilderness of our own hearts, that we may hear there the word of life and liberation. So just how do we do this? There are three things that have helped me.

1 The path of honest scrutiny

I've been in this church business a long time now and I have observed that if there is one thing more than anything else that contributes to poor leadership, it is lack of self-awareness. There are many leaders who are driven by impulses that they are not prepared to investigate. Many are desperately afraid of failure. Many have become 'workaholic', addicted to their work because they have lost their sense of self-worth. Many feel unloved by God but have not reached the point where they admit it. Some have lost their faith because so much about it has failed to work as they thought it would, but they have no one they can trust enough to discuss it with.

Pioneers will have to tread the path of honest scrutiny. Because of the hazardous nature of their work, they run the risk of being even more lonely, and therefore it is even more important to build in disciplines to acknowledge what is going on in the shadow-lands of the soul. Furthermore, if their missional call is to take them into uncharted seas, they must know how to navigate the waters of their own soul. The outer journey has to be resourced by the inner journey.

The only way we can possibly begin to acknowledge this stuff is by a deep sense of being beloved. It was the word of love from heaven that enabled Jesus to confidently face the wild beasts as well as to spot the angels who were there for him. A sense of being beloved does not come easily to many of us and we have to do a bit of work to find our way there. We need to be on the look-out for those signals from heaven that speak of God's tender and personal love for each of us. No amount of being told that God loves you will do it. You have to quest after it. In 2008 I took a three-month sabbatical and I was exploring the theme of homecoming (which eventually emerged as my book, *Dreaming of Home*, 2012). As it was my sabbatical, I gave up going to the church of which I was the priest-in-charge, and I decided not to go to church at all during my sabbatical apart from two occasions. The first was a visit to a Quaker meeting locally, and the other was to a church in California that I had been interested in visiting for some time. In both meetings I encountered the divine love: one in the silence of a Quaker meeting, the other in the high festival praise of a charismatic service.

The Quaker meeting was fascinating. I was completely new to this style of worship. I was taken there by a friend called Roger, who informed me that the moment the first person arrives in the room of a Quaker meeting, the service has begun. And so we arrived and sat in the Friends Meeting House in Bakewell on a warm sunny late September morning – about 30 of us including some remarkably well-behaved children. Stillness settled on the room, which gave me some thinking space, and it felt blessed thinking space. I looked out of the window at the beech tree that was swaying gracefully in the breeze, sprinkling its golden leaves onto the cars parked beneath it. And I felt sad, and it was the sadness of the loss of summer which I always feel, but other losses were also present in my soul, not least the recent loss of my brother who had died suddenly just three months before. My peaceful state was disturbed as the mix of feelings of loss and regret and dread of winter troubled their way into my silence.

Then an elderly lady stood up, with some difficulty, because she had recently broken her arm, which was supported in a sling. She had also been thinking about this autumn season and reminded us that soon the nights would grow long and it would be cold, and dark winter would be with us. I was far from comforted by this introduction! But she then went on to say how we need not be without hope. She told us about the Birkenhead poet A. S. J. Tessimond, who lived a very troubled life with a bipolar disorder. Tessimond had every kind of therapy, but none could rid him of his dark depressions, yet in his depression he wrote a poem called 'Day Dream' which speaks so eloquently of his conviction that there is a home, a place of safety and belonging, that will come one day.

And this elderly lady had learned the poem by heart, and in the quiet of that sacred chamber with the beech leaves fluttering behind her, she gripped the chair in front of her with her good arm, and recited the poem, which beautifully expresses a deep longing for a world where people will be at peace. It ends with the conviction that in such a world, people will smile even on a cold, rainy day in winter, the kind of day I usually find very bleak.[1]

She sat down and we were gifted with silence for a precious 20 minutes, and in that sacred space I offered my grief and fear and thought of dear old Arthur Tessimond and how he had reached out in his dark and found such precious words of hope. He became a preacher that day in my Hades and I felt hope as strong as I had ever known it. The wild beasts of despair and fear stopped their menacing prowling. Thank God for the poets. Thank God for silence. Thank God for the angels in the desert.

2 The presence of an *anamchara*

Many people nowadays have a spiritual director, accompanier, soul friend – call them what you will. They are people who are willing to give an hour or so as a friend to listen to you on your journey. I have visited my spiritual director now for 30 years. He is not a particularly disciplined listener. He interrupts me and we go off at tangents. But nonetheless I love sitting in his study with him as he gives me his full and prayerful attention, and I ramble on about my life, never quite knowing which way the path will turn in my ramble. Always, at some point in our conversation, he gives what the Bible calls 'a word in season'. It feels exactly right. It is a treasured insight – a piece of wisdom that is life-giving. It comes from someone who really does value me and values what I do, what I say and what I think. And he doesn't mind issuing the odd disturbing challenge as well. But it is safe because I know in that place I am beloved.

And I in turn offer spiritual direction to others – I feel enormously privileged to sit on my sofa at home and be entrusted with someone's journey. Always I feel the presence of God – I have a sense of knowing that this is what God wants to happen. Each person I see is involved in a very demanding ministry with many pressures, but here in the hour that has been set aside just for them, they are in a moment of precious withdrawal. They have come to a little island for a moment in time, and they become aware of their inner world.

Now, of course, anyone can do this on their own. But God has made us a community people, and somehow that *anamchara*, soul friend, can be for us a ministering angel who is able just to give us the support, energy and wisdom we need to face and subdue the wild beasts, and discover the right pathway forward. A good soul friend will not be fazed by the stories of the wild beasts, the passions; they will not be shocked by the temptations, the fears or lusts, the doubts, the worries about a puzzling God; they will be there come rain or shine, listening, holding, giving space.

Pioneers really do need spiritual accompaniers who understand the world they inhabit. We may need to do some work in training those who understand this journey. Pioneers can very easily feel misunderstood and they can feel very alone. It is easy for them to face debilitating doubts about their entrepreneurial ideas. They can feel the weight of the institution, and be very aware of the 'wild beasts' in the institution, while others who are more immersed in it fail to see. They can feel pressurized to produce results, raise finance, increase numbers, and in the eyes of some, save the Church from its relentless decline! A good spiritual director is able to journey with them and help them to find the message of Jesus. I don't know how many of those imprisoned spirits referred to in Peter's letter responded to the voice of Jesus preaching the good news. I like to think they all did. But my experience of life suggests that many of them were too preoccupied with the problems of Hades to hear the good news of heaven.

A good spiritual accompanier is able to help you detect the voice of Jesus amid all the inner and outer voices of despair. A spiritual writer who was very committed to this honest exploration was Thomas Merton, who died in 1968. One of his prayers has become particularly well known in recent years and can be found on many websites. It is sometimes called his 'Prayer of Abandonment'. It is a prayer that is an honest exploration of shadowy doubt, but that exploration opens him to a new experience of God's companionship:

My Lord God, I have no idea where I am going. I do not see the road ahead of me. I cannot know for certain where it will end. Nor do I really know myself, and the fact that I think that I am following your will does not mean that I am actually doing so. But I believe that the desire to please you does in fact please you. And I hope I have that desire in all that I am doing. I hope that I will never do anything apart from that desire. And I know that if I do this you will lead me by the right road though

I may know nothing about it. Therefore will I trust you always though I may seem to be lost and in the shadow of death. I will not fear, for you are ever with me, and you will never leave me to face my perils alone. (Merton, 1956, p. 81)

3 Patience with questions

As we pioneer into the shadowy places of our world and our own souls, we will meet with serious questions. The questions themselves can sometimes feel dark and burdensome. So what do we do with dark and burdensome questions? We either flee from them or seek to answer them as quickly as possible, and therefore not particularly effectively. But let's learn from the German poet Rainer Maria Rilke, who wrote:

> be patient toward all that is unsolved in your heart and try to love the questions themselves like locked rooms and like books written in a very foreign tongue ... The point is to live everything. Live the question now. Perhaps you will then gradually without noticing it, live some distant day into the answer. (Rilke, 1975)

We live in an age that wants quick and neat answers and finds it very difficult to stay with a question. Our Church is not immune to this – we want quickly accessible stories of success that answer the knotty problems of decline. We are facing a very simple major question: why are fewer people attending our churches? We must dwell for a long time in this question. We will miss something essential if we hurry to quick answers. One of the books I have found most helpful in recent years is Elaine A. Heath's *The Mystic Way of Evangelism* (2008). She is an American ordained Methodist minister and an assistant professor of theology. She opens her book with a basic thesis that the decline of the Church in the West is not something to fear or avoid. Nor are we to bolster ourselves up with encouraging stories. But we are to listen deeply. She speculates that we are being led into a corporate dark night of the soul, where there may be many more declines yet (Heath, 2008, p. 20). She reminds us of Brueggeman's words: 'In the end it is God, not the Babylonians who terminated the temple project' (1997, p. 109). We should not suppose that it is simply the march of secularism that is the cause of the decline of the Church. It may well be the reshaping of the Church by God. Heath writes that the dark night is

> a divinely initiated process of loss – so that the accretions of the world, the flesh and the devil may be recognized and released. It is a process of detachment from disordered affections, a process of purgation and de-selfing. Though the dark night is perilous, with no guarantee of a good outcome, it holds possibility of new beginnings. Out of the night the church could emerge into a dawn of freedom and fidelity. (Heath, 2008, p. 27)

She goes on:

> While the sun sets on Christendom in the West, the saints, mystics and martyrs beckon to the church as a great cloud of witnesses, calling us to transformation. The church will persevere through the night and emerge alive on the other side, not because of church programs, but because God's love has kept it. But to get there, we need the wisdom of the mystics, the holy ones of God. (Heath, 2008, p. 27)

If we become obsessional about church growth, we may well miss the prophetic word for our times. For me, one of the most significant prophetic words for our time is the Deutero-Isaiah verse:

> Do not remember the former things,
> or consider the things of old.
> I am about to do a new thing;
> now it springs forth, do you not perceive it?
> I will make a way in the wilderness
> and rivers in the desert. (Isa. 43.18–19)

The key word here is *perceive*. This is integral to Isaiah's call. He has to go to a people who are 'ever seeing, but never perceive' (Isa. 6.9). The exiles in their dark captivity in Babylon have to learn to see in new ways if they are to come to life. They cannot hanker after the good old days. The prophet helps them to catch a new vision. The mystic is the one who has learned to see in the dark, and in that respect they are very similar to the prophet. It is my conviction that the pioneers are likely to be the ones who are willing to spend time in the dark and not hurry into premature or superficial solutions. They are very well placed to become the seers. They are willing to enter into the unevangelized shadows both in the outer world and in the inner chambers of their own souls. And there they listen and see and wait for the revelation of the Lord.

Another metaphor we could use for this vantage point is that of the *edge*. Richard Rohr talks about living on the edge:

> To take your position on the spiritual edge of things is to learn how to move safely in and out, back and forth, across and return. It is a prophetic position, not a rebellious or antisocial one. When you live on the edge of anything with respect and honour, you are in a very auspicious position. You are free from its central seductions, but also free to hear its core message in very new and creative ways. (Rohr, 'From the edge of the inside')

This edge can be a shadowy and uncertain place without the securities of the centre. The pioneers must be allowed space to explore the edge. They must be given space to do this and not be put under pressure to produce impressive attendance figures. The centre must respect the edge, and the edge must respect the centre. Working together we may well find God's way on the mystical journey from the dark night to the place of illumination – of seeing the kind of Church God is desiring to build to serve our communities well in these times.

Let me end with the story of a Celtic saint who, I think, like many of his contemporaries was a pioneer. Fillan is one of those obscure saints about which very little is known. Originating from Ireland in the early eighth century, he went to Scotland and for some years lived the solitary life in a large cave in the fishing village of Pittenweem on the Fife coast. He became an abbot of a nearby monastery, but left there to move to Perthshire and is buried at Strathfillan not far from Crianlarich. Near here is a healing pool in the bend of the river, and it is a place that many came to who were battling with mental illnesses of different kinds. It is probably just my fanciful imagination, but I wonder if this might have been a particular ministry of Fillan – to minister to those who were suffering in their minds. And if that was the case, was he himself a sufferer who found that the risen Jesus visited him and preached his gospel of freedom into the dark corners of his mind? This is how I imagine him to be, and with this in mind I wrote these words shortly after I shared in a communion service last summer with some fellow pilgrims in his damp, dimly lit, yet holy cave in Pittenweem:

Curled in the corner of his dark, dark cave
Fillan sleeps a restless sleep
and dreams a dark night dream.
He pulls the goatskin coat over his sturdy shoulder.
A ray of moonshine leaks into his dank home
and strokes his furrowed forehead.
His breath rises as mist from his murmuring lips.

But in his dream
Fillan now journeys to his sparkling sunlit river,
to his sacred pool of healing.
He sees his troubled soul washed in the lucid waters
by the gentle hands of Christ
and his mind is once again made whole,
for these are waters that are graced with
peace for wounded minds.

Gracious Father,
when my mind is troubled and entangled
by the darkness of this broken world
lead me to your hallowed pools of healing
and immerse me in your peace.
Make me a messenger of this sacred stream
to the troubled souls I meet along my path.[2] (Michael Mitton)

References

Brueggemann, W., 1997, *Cadences of Home*, Louisville, KY: John Knox Press.

Heath, E. A., 2008, *The Mystic Way of Evangelism: A Contemplative Vision for Christian Outreach*, Grand Rapids, MI: Baker.

Merton, T., 1956, *Thoughts in Solitude*, Tunbridge Wells: Burns and Oates.

Mitton, M., 2012, *Dreaming of Home*, Abingdon: BRF.

Rilke, R. M., 1975, 'Letter 4, 16 July 1903', in *Rilke on Love and Other Difficulties: Translations and Considerations by John J. L. Mood*, 1975, New York: W. W. Norton and Company Inc.

Rohr, R., 'From the edge of the inside: the prophetic position', http://male-spirituality.net/article/edge-inside.

Note

1 The poem can be found in A. S. J. Tessimond, *Not Love Perhaps: Selected Poems*, London: Faber and Faber, 2008, p. 51.

2 Poem written by Michael Mitton in 2014.

4

Pioneers as Pilgrims

BETH HONEY

In April 2014 I joined with a group of pioneers on pilgrimage. We are all connected to the CMS pioneer community in one way or another, and are all involved in beginning and developing contextual Christian community. We were on pilgrimage in central and south-western Ireland in pursuit of early Christian sites. We were led by Michael Mitton and Russ Parker who were familiar with these sites and were trusted and wise guides, and who had plotted with Jonny Baker to gather us together. They all felt that there were some significant synergies between the mission and lives of the early Irish monastics and the pioneer gift and spirit.

We landed in Dublin, some of us strangers, some colleagues, some friends already. We travelled via Glendalough, the place of Kevin, via Kildare where Brigid claimed land with her cloak and lit a fire that burned for a thousand years, to the crossroads of Clonmacnoise where the River Shannon crossed the ancient highway or *esker* and where Ciarán died shortly after founding his community. From there we headed west and to the Aran Islands to spend two nights on Inis Mór, from where we headed to the Dingle peninsula to seek the place where Brendan put out in his boat to trust himself to God and the sea to find his place of holy encounter. At the end of this chapter there is a diary of our pilgrimage that may be helpful in getting a sense of the journey.

My inspiration behind joining this pilgrimage was the chance for reflection and inspiration for a new place and stage of life for my family and me. In May 2013 I moved to the city of Derby and since that time had been settling into a totally new context on a large housing estate very close to the city centre. We had begun to gather a community around us of those who have experienced church but are seeking its incarnation in that area and those who have not experienced church or much of faith at all. We had also found that our experience of any shared life on this estate was out and about, and a pilgrimage largely outside seemed to be appropriate for our context. If I am honest, I did not know much about the places that we were going to travel to, or even of the history of the individuals or communities we were looking for traces of. Yet I set out with some expectation to hear from God through the places that we visited.

I am also at a point in life where I am particularly considering the relationship between mission as exploring and mission as establishing home; mission as settling and setting out. While I set out on the pilgrimage with no particular itinerary of the spiritual gifts it may give me, I am aware of the power of journey and setting out: 'We are externally perplexed by how to move towards forgiveness or healing or truth, but we know how to walk from here to there, however arduous the journey' (Solnit, 2001, p. 50). This journey was to be varied and with some speed, but not too arduous. Pioneers often welcome adventure, and the sense that God will bring something new and surprising to our notice and experience. For this time in Ireland, we were not tourists, but expectant visitors.

Setting out

To be a pilgrim is to be in exile from home, to journey away from home and to come home and rediscover it. This kind of journey is one that identifies with an internal sense of exile and puts it in the forefront of experience to be able to understand and question it.[1] The pilgrim is therefore both away from home and seeking home in and through the journey, and this is where the family likeness between a pilgrim and a pioneer can begin to be seen. Early Irish Christian spirituality held together home and away; the settlement and community life alongside the journey, or the *peregrinatio* (Sheldrake, 1995, p. 58). This idea of pilgrimage was about casting out from the familiar, 'for the love of God', to find a place of his presence and blessing in unfamiliar places.

Exploration and rootedness appear as an attractive mix in a postmodern world seeking both new and familiar, which has brought a cultural and political re-emphasis on place and locality. 'Globalization, however, can also be characterized as a set of processes that have contributed to a reaffirmation of place-based identities, including that of Celticity' (Harvey et al., 2002, p. 8). Perhaps some of my questions about what the authenticity of this 'mining' reveals is to do with our moving a little beyond postmodernism: it is not enough to borrow images and find their use, but I sought an experience of their significance that could be woven into our stories. In this light, Celtic history and places have been mined for spirituality and image, to be used by and for emerging cultures: youth cultures, Christian spirituality across denomination and traditions, and, more recently, emerging Christian communities (Gibbs and Bolger, 2006, pp. 220–1). Such mining does not necessarily find the deepest seams, or indeed always explore complexity or compromise, but the contemporary connections of early Irish Christian community life are there to be experienced and learned from nonetheless.

Pioneering work often involves a sense of setting out, be it to a new place or context or to begin imagining worship or action in new ways, perhaps with new people and purpose. Pioneers themselves often share a sense of finding a home in this new place, yet feeling restless and somehow still in exile. There are also questions about the resilience needed to continue as a pioneer, both as individuals and within the communities that begin. How do we sustain ourselves? How do we sustain each other? How do we have deep roots and practices that will resource a community that will last? We do not assume that the communities we are in will be sustained by structures or even buildings, but how might they find their healthy life cycle? One of the features of sharing time with pioneers from the CMS community was the inspiration to be creative, especially with words. There was a lot of very good poetry shared, and spoken for the first time on this pilgrimage.

I wonder if the lasting history of much pioneering may be in a developing oral tradition, even if recorded in story and poetry.

We set out on this pilgrimage in this spirit of connections with the past and place, with a commitment to learn together, and to be held by the place we would journey through together. What gifts and challenges would we receive from each other and from these places in Ireland?

Home: a place to establish and a place to return to

The journey undertaken in this pilgrimage moved between some of the places that the early Irish monastic Christians called home: where they began to build and develop community or where they set off from. For this pilgrimage the process of the journey remained important, as cumulative experience and the quality of community among us as relative strangers at the outset gradually developed, and yet the sacred places visited proved to be the pinnacles of experience; often the points of destination are more important than the path taken in sacred pilgrimage (Park, 1994, p. 251).

The places were chosen by the early Irish monastics for their connections, such as the crossroads of Clonmacnoise, or an island that promised both remoteness for reflection and also good trade routes. It is possible to romanticize these settings in the relative comfort with which we experience them now, but they were landscapes to fear as well as to cherish and this was a deliberately harsh life (Sheldrake, 1995, p. 71). It is also worth reflecting on the dissonance with how we experience them today. During our pilgrimage, the site most influenced by tourism is the one closest to Dublin, Glendalough, but it was chosen for its remoteness (Ó'Ríordáin, 2001, Loc 783 of 1167). These places might well be treated as the basis for experience, as the early Irish monastics often did, but it must also be remembered that this experience cannot be called 'genuine' or 'authentic' in many ways. We had to find our own significance in the place as well.

Brendan, one of the key saints that inspired this pilgrimage as he is the saint most connected with adventuring into uncharted waters, an enduring theme in the call and spirituality of this particular group of pilgrims, sought to be a pilgrim on the sea. In doing so, he determined to seek God in the 'promised land', and to allow his boat to be directed by God through wind and wave.[2] Even Brendan returned home, however, and the prayer that is ascribed to him makes it clear that he holds home close even as he sets out:

> Shall I abandon, O King of Mysteries, the soft comforts of home?
> Shall I turn my back on my native land, and my face towards the sea?
> (Adam, 2000, p. 9)

Ireland was a place of relative cultural, if not physical, comfort for these early Christians as they felt they could grow communities of faith and make good connections with each other. To set out was to leave that relative comfort behind and establish new relationships and new places of worship in areas that were perhaps practically and geographically challenging, or simply lonely. There was not much threat of martyrdom for these early Christians and so they sought their martyrdom in other ways. Instead of death, exile from home, or indeed exile from human contact and comfort for a time of penance, were experiences they chose and often referred to as 'white' and 'green' martyrdom respectively. To leave home was a significant sacrifice for them, and I sensed during this pilgrimage that leaving home, while an adventure and a call and a joy for many pioneers, remains part of the cost of sustaining a pioneering spirit and gift. The white martyrs would seek to establish a home where they found themselves in exile, and sought to see God change first them and then their environment.[3] Many of us had become pilgrims to ask some of these deeper questions of ourselves.

Home: on *earth* as it is in heaven

This sense of home for the early Irish Christians is deeply connected to the land and the earth. One of the major reflections of the group in terms of daily worship was the influence of worshipping outside. We embraced the touching places of the standing stones, and discovered the waters of wells long associated with the early saints. Most of the Celtic 'churches' we prayed within were roofless too! This lends a different sense to seeking the presence of God. He is encompassing, uncontained, and there is a natural connection to the rhythms of weather and light that emerges. While this pilgrimage did not present so much of a physical challenge to us as pilgrims, there was a physical element to our experience of God and worship.

The early Irish monastics may not have experienced the remoteness of the landscape as relief, as many of our group did, but they did have to pay attention to the rocks and land they lived among. This is perhaps not unique to Christianity at that historical moment, and yet it became part of their spirituality. In a further nuance, Sheldrake notes that it is not nature itself that the Celts seek (compared perhaps to some modern Celtic understandings) but rather the God who can be found and known in and through that nature (Sheldrake, 1995, p. 73). Taking into account what has already been mentioned about the complications of the contemporary relative remoteness of landscape, this was particularly felt by the group on Inis Mór. Perhaps we had more time to encounter nature on this island, but the landscape certainly had an effect. Modern-day inhabitants on Inis Mór have to take the landscape into consideration on a daily basis, not least due to its rocky base. The many regular small enclosures bordered with dry stone walls are not for order; simply to use land at all, the rocks are cleared, and therefore form the walls.

This struck a note for me in connection with our Derby context. We have found in our cultural context that to cross thresholds into homes, or even public buildings, opens up a question of ownership and power, where the use of an outdoor space or indeed casual encounters as part of street life have led in an easier way to developing relationships of more equality. Outdoor space has been significant in forming relationships, therefore, and perhaps it is worth further exploring outdoor worship. This offers the scope for a more physical and less word-based experience of worship which may also be appropriate in what is largely a non-book culture. There is an echo here of the physical challenge of living day to day in urban communities like ours in Derby, which both shapes and is shaped by the environment as a result of being an 'outdoor' culture.

We had two Eucharists outdoors during the pilgrimage, and the connection between place and sacrament was enlivened and ener-gized by that experience. The elements had to be discovered along the way, and there was a sense of these coming 'from the earth' in a subtly different way from when the sacrament is conducted in an indoors context, where the natural symbolic link with daily life is the domestic table. The nature of home for the early Irish Chris-tians was as much about outdoors as about indoors, but remained deeply connected to a territory and a commitment to the created universe. This connection with God through what is created is sacramental, and again causes reflection on finding places of encounter outside as well as when gathered *in* for worship. This may have wider missiological implications when considered on a more paradigmatic level: that is, to encounter worship outside is about looking for the presence of God in the *world*. This has deep resonance for an understanding of seeking to see Christian community emerge out of a culture, rather than being placed over a culture. Viewing the earliest standing stone from Clonmacnoise brought this home to me, as it retained an early fertility symbol, even as it stood at the heart of this community.

Home: centred on God

Being outside in creation during this pilgrimage inspired not just awe but a sense of being held or comforted. What was striking, as we visited the places where these early communities gathered to worship, was the scale; they were built on a human or domestic scale. This is architecture not to glorify God and point to heaven, but to house the life of a community and root them to their place of communal life and the presence of God.

The churches or oratories we visited were almost universally small: the tomb of Ciarán, the oratory at the Seven Churches on Inis Mór, and another oratory on the same island in the place where Enda is remembered. They appear to be able to accommodate around a dozen people, and since our party was ten in all we mimicked that well and can attest to it. The 'minimum' for an early Christian site to be recognized as such is a standing cross or stone, a tomb, and an oratory (Jenkins, 2010). This would represent the centre of the community that would develop around that centre, as they built, or corbelled, stone *clochán* cells. These cells that made up these villages represent the usual domestic construction in early Irish history of the sixth to ninth centuries. They were simple 'beehive'-shaped structures, usually with one simple doorway with a single lintel stone above.

The experience of being inside such small places of worship and of solitary life and prayer, which were so normal and domestic, affected me considerably, on two levels. The first was a vocational level, as there is an echo here of what we are establishing in our new Christian community: community on a domestic scale, using what is familiar, but expecting the presence of God. This is already part of the culture of what we are developing in a less institutional model of church that is still a structured and intentional community. This can and will still be holy ground.

The second level was more personal. I entered this pilgrimage thinking that I wanted to seek the adventurous spirit of Brendan, but as we set out to follow his trail, we held Morning Prayer in a *clochán* on the Dingle peninsula. I had an overwhelming emotion that while I sought adventure, I did not wholly want to launch out; in fact I wanted to stay in the safe and comfortable place of security that appeared to be just the right scale for my hopes.

I reflected on this emotion with others and what it meant for me, but suffice to say here that the experience of being in that building in that place came together to help me begin integrating some of the adventure of Brendan with the community building of

Brigid, whose community at Kildare grew to quite a significance and was known as the church of the oak – or Kildare (Sheldrake, 1995, p. 19). The image of the oak tree has become important to our emerging community, in its stability, hospitality and its biblical context (see Isa. 61.1–4). What we know of these two saints is often difficult to rely on, but it was enough to be listening to stories of them in places associated with them to enable this connection and acceptance in me. Here was some of the gift of pilgrimage that I did not wholly expect.[4]

Home: making ecclesiastical connections

Early Irish monastic communities did not exist in isolation, and there are many similarities in how they were being built and developed; they had a family likeness rather than a blueprint or plan. There were ongoing connections with other monastic communities. Enda is a great example of this. He lived all his life on Inis Mór, training and then sending out other monastic leaders, and this is where Enda and Ciarán received the vision of a tree beside a stream bearing fruit, which they interpreted as a community once planted making connections from Clonmacnoise to Ireland and the rest of Europe. These connections were often about the spread of learning and culture, but they also represent a challenge to the notion that the rise of monastic community in early Irish Christianity was an indicator that the organizing influence of the Church was cast off in a sense of liberation to follow local forms of community and connections.

The question of contextual versus ecclesiastical was emotionally and spiritually potent on the pilgrimage. It was all too easy to compare free and open (even to the elements) early churches with those we found locked, perhaps for safety, or in one case at Clonmacnoise, to make the point (it seems ironically) that this was an active Church of Ireland concern, and not simply part of the heritage site.

Yet, in early Christian Ireland, it was not unusual to have abbatical and episcopal leadership side by side, and for these to be connected and overlapping with local clan and tribe authorities as well. This was not so different from the situation in England at that time, and it is therefore a mistake perhaps to consider the Irish situation as either in some way more *pure* or more vernacular. This mixed jigsaw of relationships of authority and jurisdiction was perhaps more tolerated, and even expected, in the seventh and eighth centuries, and does not perhaps necessarily suggest that the monastic model was triumphant. This was not a power struggle, but a situation that emerged, and may be quite familiar to how traditional church structures and new communities are gradually learning to live together, although we may be struggling a little more at our point in history with the sense of loss this invokes in many.

Some of the terms of this detailed historical conversation struck a clear chord, as the language sounds rather like the now well-known ecclesiological debate around pioneer ministry and Fresh Expressions of Church in the contemporary Anglican context: 'Could a primarily monastic church truly be church?' (Jenkins, 2010, p. 17). Jenkins goes on to recognize that there is complexity and diversity in the picture of pastoral care and jurisdiction, and terms this an 'ecclesial mixed economy' (2010, p. 18).

It was the former archbishop Rowan Williams who oversaw the ecclesiological developments that led to the exploration of a 'mixed economy' in the Anglican Church. In an interesting turn of events that gave me the sense that my pilgrimage, and discovery from it, was ongoing, I set about beginning this reflection as I also visited a poetry reading with Rowan Williams. I asked him how much his thinking had been inspired by this emerging web of ecclesiological organization in early Christian Ireland and his answer led me to another source of reflection.

Rowan Williams had been inspired by a book that hypothetically considers an Anglican bishop reorganizing his diocese along the lines of Celtic gifting (from the well-known early saints) and orders based on them. *Celtic Gifts: Orders of Ministry in the Celtic Church* by Robert Van de Weyer (1997) is one of an increasing number of books seeking Celtic inspiration for developing new communities,[5] although Van de Weyer appears to speak directly into the connections between the ecclesiastical structures and the possibilities of both lay and ordained following their gifting. It is not hard to see how this led Williams to develop and support the concept of lay and ordained pioneers set aside for innovative contextual church development, who are still part of more formal structures and can relate to them. Perhaps we can take some comfort in the situation of the early Irish Christians who lived with the mess of organization, sought connections with each other, and built up their communities.

Echoes from the earth: pioneers as pilgrims

Pioneers so often find themselves walking paths new to them, but with the sense that they are not the first ones to walk there, and that they do not do so alone. This pilgrimage cemented this in my mind as an essential element of the spirituality of the individual pioneer and the spirit of pioneering that can be treasured and nurtured. We walked together; we travelled together; we chatted and ate together; we drank together and prayed; we spent time alone, together. We heard stories long told and learned and told more of our own individual and collective story. We experienced that sense of pilgrimage where you enter a place to find out more about who you are and where you have been, to open up the horizon which you gaze at every day by allowing other horizons to pass you by.

Pioneers are pilgrims as they relate to place in a particular way. Some may be those who are new to a place and seeking out the story of that place and God even as they learn to tell their own story for that season. Some may be those who relate so strongly to one place or to one culture that they experience a sense of coming home – they will spend most of their lives in one place seeking God. The sense of making home on earth through the connection to the earth and to the places where worship and mission – the settling and the setting out kind – have occurred had the effect of building a sense of home among us, and, I believe, in each of us in some small but significant ways, as we committed to seeing and sensing God in those few days in a place familiar to some and new to many of us.

Afternote: Brendan and Brigid

Brendan the Navigator, associated with adventure and setting out to sea; Brigid, the mother of Ireland building her extended community at Kildare, inviting people in; but here he looks to earth and the land, and she to the horizon. What if they had met?

Well met

> Crossing a ploughed field she and Brendan exchanged spiritual thoughts. Brendan owned that he never stepped over seven furrows without turning his mind and heart to God, but Brigid confided to him that since the first day she set her mind on the Lord, the thought of him had never been out of her head. (Ó'Ríordáin, 2001, Loc 243 of 1167)

> A wonderful thought –
> Brendan, walking the furrowed field,
> Touching the earthy lines,
> Counting his prayers in perfect sevens,
> Looking to earth to follow his path.
> Brigid, her eyes to the horizon
> Noticing early the threats to her pasture
> Crossing to Brendan, as to the sea.
> The flow of God between them –
> His counting on Him,
> Her resting in the same.

A Diary

Day One

As we all landed and met new people we discussed what we already knew of Ireland and especially whether we had visited before now: seeking to put each other and the place in context of our stories.

Glendalough – most Celtic monks lived on islands, but Kevin was more of a recluse avoiding the crowds. As he attracted attention he retreated even further into the mountains. The irony being that this is the most populated holy site we will visit, and nearest to Dublin and connections now, and it is also a significant tourist attraction.

We shared Eucharist here – offering what remained to the earth and to those we would long to be sharing this journey with who are in our hearts. This was special, as I often sense those who are not yet worshipping as we worship.

There is a current Roman Catholic community here – although quite informal and offering prayer; we have not encountered them.

Interesting that we are seeking what is older and pre-medieval organization of the church – we are seeking the Irish Celts and there is a repetition of the notion that others have come in and laid on these foundations and built a different 'church' somehow.

We are seeking connections with these communities and individuals through our encounter with place and with each other, and with the connecting work that we are all seeking to do within our own contexts.

Day Two

Brigid – When we arrived the cathedral complex was locked, but the key was found in the heritage centre and we saw the round tower and the temple of fire. Brigid and the community she led, have some powerful messages. She dealt with power well, blessing what was there and building on it. The fire is said to have burned for 1,000 years and only women could keep it alight. Men and women worked together in her community, married and single, and she was also known as a motherly figure to the community as well as a symbol for that role domestically in Ireland. It was difficult for me not to wonder about the town of Kildare and the local community and how Brigid would live there now.

We travelled to Clonfert, Brendan's grave and cathedral. There was a contrast between the organization of the graveyard (church locked again!) and the freedom of a prayer tree that has been used haphazardly to express hope and pain.

Day Three

Clonmacnoise – Ciarán – the place he came to establish and where he died. There is more of a sense of tourism here – shop and visitor centre – but also a beautiful quiet roofless chapel where Ciarán is laid. Reflection here was on the church that is in use that was locked – locked to differentiate itself from the rest of the site, and the open glass altar established for the visit of John Paul II.

Settling into being on the move – and the flight to the secluded Aran islands lands us in the busiest hotel we have stayed in – a confirmation party is on! Feel a bit like Kevin – we came here to be apart!

Day Four

On Inis Mór: at the Seven Churches with Dara Molloy, a local Celtic priest, hosting a dispersed community of dreamers. He was a Roman Catholic priest, but was seeking liberation from the institution to rediscover his purpose and spirituality. He has lived on the island for many years and it felt like we were being taught history from someone who tries to live it as well as knows about it. We began at the bed of the Holy Spirit – a possible baptismal pool – and circled it and prayed for fruitfulness.

The Seven Churches may not be seven; it was simply a way of explaining that the church or community had reproduced. When there was an Abbot and 12 monks in their individual cells then it was time to begin again. So the title really means a church that has reached a certain point of maturity. As a group we found Dara fascinating and wondered together about his setting sail from the institution of the church. He didn't seem to have found himself anchored in the Trinity, however, and we pondered how we can rediscover roots while staying connected to God.

The monastic settlements and church building are on a domestic scale – built to fit their use by a small number of people; clocháns are the same. Sat in the clochán on Inis Mór: we learned about the difference between white and green martyrdom. Since Irish monks were not likely to be killed for their faith, they sought green martyrdom – the life of penance and seeking hardships, or white martyrdom – the life of being in exile from home, choosing to leave the plenty and resources of Ireland and family. They lived in the new community so that God would change them rather than they would change others. This seems a very important model for any incarnational mission to consider.

Day Five

Enda's place – he stayed in one place all his life – educating and resourcing those who went out. Prayed at this place for healing together, and the beauty of the coastal setting and the peace was powerful. The graveyard and labyrinth there provided a lovely place for some significant time of breathing in before we left the island.

Long day of travel to the Dingle – and beginning the trail of Brendan.

Day Six

The clocháns were not monastic inventions but the shape of the community of home in Ireland. We stopped at a café set up in a home too! I had a moment of connection in the clochán where we shared Morning Prayer today. I want to adventure like Brendan, but seek the security of home still.

Visited an oratory which is the oldest place of worship in the world – the atmosphere in there is solid. I can't explain it, other than years and years of prayer. It is indeed a place to hear God, but also hear the worship of God.

Enjoyed a relaxing evening in Dingle with local lager and local music.

Day Seven

Castlegregory – The sea was too wild for us to venture onto the island where the community was based Brendan left from. We sailed around the island – but we spotted dolphins who love the waves. We settled in a quiet bay for Eucharist again – noticing our increased connections over the week. I enjoyed running into the shallows in the bay – and they crept up on me and soaked me!

Day Eight

A significant time of sharing our collective memories of the pilgrimage, and then to the airport (in stages).

Further resources inspired by this pilgrimage

Sennach

by Michael Mitton[6]

Sennach founded a monastery on the island of Illauntannig, just north of Castlegregory on the Dingle peninsula, Ireland. Visitors to the island can still see the remains of the monastic community, including some beehive cells, a cross, church and burial ground. Access to the island is not easy!

Your hand that clutches the rim of your coracle
is the same that gently lifts its blessing
on your isle.
Such swells and currents don't disturb you
for you dream them in your salty sleep.
You feel the surges of God in these waters
divine heaves and sighs
signs of the yearnings of God;
glimpses of the grace of God
in the fin of a passing dolphin.
Is that why you set sail to this island
and built your tent from its rough earth?

I see you there, your blistered hand lifting dark stones
one upon the other
transforming these cold rocks into a vibrant home.
This your dysart, beckoning the surf of God
to break over the dry, dry land.

Oh Lord, when I settle too much on my mainland
take me back to these waters.
Let me feel again the movements of the great sea
the surgings of your restless heart.
Let me see the glittering surf
your life breaking through the waters
my soul at last in tune with yours.

13 April 2014, Dingle Peninsula

Song, Holy God

by Jonny Baker[7]

Holy God
Holy and strong
Holy and immortal
Holy One

All the world is holy
Shining with your grace
But in the blade of this moment
This is the touching place

Holy God ...

Ancient walls are leaking
Centuries of prayer
I can feel your presence
Like thickness in the air

Holy God ...

Listen to the Spirit
Quiet now my soul
In the gentle silence
Speak and I'll be whole

Holy God ...

All creation's sacred
And God is in all things
But you are now among us
Let me drink you in

Holy God ...

Sacred Imprint

by Andree Lee[8]

These waiting hills
empty now but for the shriek of chill winds
this bleakness of dung brown Wicklow rock
undulating heavy with the weight
of ancient memories
indented stone from faithful footfall
of hungered pilgrims questing for immanence
now lie silent yet restless
till pious pounding is renewed.

These dulcet streams by sun stricken gorse
honeyed trickle that once slaked parched souls
wearied from ceaseless journeying
still tenacious tumble, course unchanging
dead headed for the open sea
of homecoming dreams.

These once hallowed halls
embattled bastions of stone tombed saints
now echo plaintive with forgotten melodies
of yester year's sanctity
Ashen traces of burning hearts
long for remembrance
stir the inner clarion to once again
gather
wonder
and embrace by thin faith
another season of possibilities.

Written after visits to Glendalough, St Kevin's@Clonfert and St Brigid's@Cill Dara, 8 April 2014.

References

Adam, D., 2000, *A Desert in the Ocean*, London: SPCK.

Gibbs, E. and Bolger, R. K., 2006, *Emerging Churches*, London, SPCK.

Harvey, D. C., Jones, R., McInroy, N. and Milligan, C. (eds.), 2002, *Celtic Geographies: Old Culture, New Times*, London: Routledge.

Hunter, G. C. III, 2000, *The Celtic Way of Evangelism*, Nashville, TN: Abingdon.

Jenkins, D., 2010, 'Holy, Holier, Holiest': The Sacred Topography of the Early Medieval Irish Church, Turnhout, Belgium: Brepols Publisher n.v.

Jones, A., 2011, *Pilgrimage*, Abingdon: BRF.

Molloy, D., 2009, *The Globalisation of God: Celtic Christianity's Nemesis*, Aran Islands: Aisling Publications.

Mitton, M., 2010, *Restoring the Woven Cord*, Abingdon: BRF.

O'Carroll, B. and Felton, B., 2013, *The Story of Clonmacnoise and Saint Ciarán*, Shannonbridge: Ely House.

O'Meara, J. J. (trans.), 1991, *The Voyage of Saint Brendan*, Gerrards Cross: Colin Smythe Ltd.

Ó'Ríordáin, J. J., 2001, *Early Irish Saints: Celtic Spirituality*, Blackrock, Co Dublin: Columba Press, Kindle edition.

Park, C. E., 1994, *Sacred Worlds: An Introduction to Geography and Religion*, London: Routledge.

Reed, S., 2013, *Creating Community: Ancient Ways for Modern Churches*, Abingdon: BRF.

Sheldrake, P., 1995, *Living Between Worlds: Place and Journey in Celtic Spirituality*, London: DLT.

Solnit, R., 2001, *Wanderlust: A History of Walking*, London: Verso.

Van de Weyer, R., 1997, *Celtic Gifts: Orders of Ministry in the Celtic Church*, Norwich: Canterbury Press.

Notes

1 'Pilgrims move away from this sense of exile by renouncing what they once thought of as "home" and being willing to journey in search of God's presence in new places' (Jones, 2011, p. 70).

2 'Brothers, do not fear. God is our helper, sailor and helmsman and he guides us. Ship all the oars and the rudder. Just leave the sail spread and God will do as he wishes with his servants and their ship' (O'Meara, 1991, p. 10).

3 This was part of a conversation we had with Dara Molloy, a local priest, on Aran. See Diary, Day Four.

4 See the Afternote for a later reflection on reading about a possible meeting between these two saints, and a poem that emerged later too.

5 For example, Hunter, 2000, and Reed, 2013. There is not space here to discuss their use of Celtic models, but sufficient to say that having a clear model is not the only or perhaps most subtle way of hearing these echoes. There is something I found very significant in going to the places where these stories and models are traced from. The learning is perhaps more about commitment to place and to seeking God than to learning specific models. For further reading with a real sense of place and spirituality see Mitton, 2010.

6 Used with permission, see http://michaelmitton.wix.com/michaelmitton#!poetry/c1jwc.

7 Used with permission.

8 A participant on the pilgrimage. Used with permission.

5

Angela of Foligno as a Model for Pioneer Ministry

KATE PEARSON

A pioneer for women

I first 'met' Lella at a Quiet Day led by a Franciscan brother from the Society of St Francis. I, like many of my pioneering colleagues, had been drawn by the story of Francis of Assisi as a model for ministry and mission. Francis is wonderful; his vision for rebuilding the Church to which he was devoted is an inspiration for pioneers all over the world. He is, though, yet another man in the story of Christian leadership and mission; another pioneering male whose story I needed to learn to translate to work alongside my own story, as a woman. I am adept at translation, at finding myself in the gaps, as I would argue all evangelical women must learn to do if we are to flourish. Lella's story is different though. As a woman from the thirteenth century equally drawn by Francis' teaching and work, her life had a radically different outcome from Clare of Assisi's, who would have still been alive when Lella was born. Lella was extraordinarily active: a leader, a teacher, a mystic and spiritual guide. To find a story in church history that does not need translation for gender (although there is, of course, the need to translate over the passage of time) was an enormous encouragement to me and I hope will be to you, whatever your own gender.

Lella was in fact called Angela, taking the 'diminutive' name of Lella as an act of humility on her part as her fame grew. She is Lella to me, and she and her story have become increasingly important and familiar. Angela of Foligno (1248–1309) was a woman of her time in many ways. With more women than men in the population than ever before women therefore needed to find something else to do other than marry and have children, and the popularity of the mystical movement among women was on the rise. Angela's particular model of ministry and mission was, I believe, very distinctive from her mystical and Beguine peers and I set out in this chapter how she has inspired me and provides a great basis for discussion, debate and inspiration all of her own.

Talking about women

A roll of the eyes, a shortness in tone ... indications that the person I am speaking with is less than convinced that women *still* need 'special' treatment. Even in my aged and slow (but beloved) Church of England, women are now fully represented at every level of membership and leadership. Isn't it time we got over ourselves and stopped whinging? It probably won't surprise readers to hear that I think the answer is 'no'. Women have a track record of displaying a particular aptness for pioneering that could be a gift to the wider Church but is not yet being effectively recorded. My job in this chapter is not to point out the many discrepancies between the experiences of women and men around the world; you can find out the facts yourself, and there are a lot of them, if you look at the International Women's Day website. I also do not have the space for a sociological and biological debate on whether any differences between the genders are a product of our genetic make-up (our inherent gifts) or a product of our treatment within society over millennia as women have adapted to the opportunities and roles offered. Instead I am dealing with the facts as they present themselves: that while many complain of the feminizing of the Church, evangelism and mission remain very masculine functions (please note the use of masculine rather than male – I am certainly not asserting that every man is the same, nor would I assert the same for women). We are all aware, I'm

certain, of the critique of the word 'pioneer' which has masculine, and even imperialistic, connotations for many, as do some
of the strategies for church growth that are becoming increasingly popular. I know several pioneers, and not all women, who
adopt different strategies from those prevalent in the Church and
whose stories go untold; contextual missioners who are sharing
good news quietly and impressively but are unrecorded or celebrated. My purpose behind this chapter is not to draw yet another
line between 'what men are like' and 'what women are like' but
to offer as gift the story of one particular woman who I think
has much to offer our stories as pioneers, and to explore what
pioneering that is in touch with the feminine may look like. Not
because men can't do it – many already are – but because I believe
strongly that it is in the recognition of the full and extraordinary
diversity of God in creation and through our ministries that we
will enable those around us to seek wholeness through Christ. In
sharing our stories and experiences we make this more possible.

Meeting Angela

> In ... Blessed Angela of Foligno ... we have a mystic of the
> first rank whose revelations place her in the same class as St
> Catherine of Genoa and St Teresa. Known to her followers as
> the Mistress of Theologians ... (Underhill, 1949, p. 461)

Everything we know about Angela was dictated by her and
recorded by her scribe, a Franciscan brother, during the latter
part of her life (Foligno, 1993, p. 7), in a book of two parts: 'Memorial' and 'Instructions'. We know that she was married, with
children, but that not long after her conversion her entire family,
including her mother, died (McGinn, 1988, p. 143). This was a
grief that she bore for the rest of her life, and while even manag-
ing to rejoice in the freedom she had gained as a single woman
(Underhill, 1949, p. 216) we can only guess at her immense pain.
She does not give her grief much attention in her writings, but
we know that she carried her experiences of wife, daughter and

mother, along with the agony of experiencing their deaths, into her ministry (Gallyon, 2000, p. 3).

Angela was born just under 25 years after the death of St Francis of Assisi, and experienced a profound conversion to follow Christ most closely in 1285, when she was 37 years old (exactly my age at writing this chapter). She joined the Franciscan Third Order in 1291, professing her life vows, and embracing a life of poverty (McGinn, 1988, p. 143). Angela first stood out to me because of the parallels in our backgrounds in experiences of being a wife and mother and also the closeness in our age. She stood out to me, as distinct from other women under life vows, because of her uncloistered life; she spent her time with the Franciscan brothers in preference to the Poor Clares, and in a creative adaptation of the tertiary order, primarily an order of penitence (Bynum, 1984, p. 250), she took the life of a friar when this was not officially an option for women.

Angela brought her own, woman-shaped view of personal spirituality and mission, but she also had much in common with the First Order of Franciscans, adopting for all intents and purposes the life of a wandering friar. It seems likely that she was born into a wealthy family, and certainly knew much of 'worldly' and sensual pleasures, as evidenced in her writings. It is the absolution she received for her 'worldly sin' (about which the reader is tantalizingly left to guess) that released her into a vibrancy of relationship with God that made others blush and retreat. Certainly for me, it was a gradual releasing of the shame I carried as a young woman that took me from passive believer to determined (if inadequate) evangelist, but this took a long time. As I work alongside young women today in a church that ministers well to the arrogance of youth but less effectively to its more self-detrimental side, I recognize the devastating impact we can inadvertently have on the self-esteem of our younger congregations. I long for the power of Angela's absolution for people who need to see a glimpse of how extraordinary their God thinks they are, and a permission to get up and move on.

Angela's own conversion experience bears similarities to that of St Francis. She even has a 'naked conversion' where she takes off all her clothes and dedicates her life to Christ, an echo of Francis stripping himself of clothes when he walked away from his earthly wealth and family connections (Williams, 2003, p. 13); not a sight many of us would be prepared for in our churches! As well as the call to poverty, she bears the traditional mark of the Franciscan, which is a fascination with the Incarnation and a deeply personal experience which results in fervent prayer and positive action to serve the poor, teach communities and evangelize (Higgins, 2000, p. 165). There remains a dedication to a faith that is fully involved and alive in the culture around itself, rather than removed and distant, more focused on finding Christ in the here and now than distinguishing heaven from earth with tight boundaries. As pioneers I am sure we can say 'amen' to that.

Story: fraud or prophet?

Pioneers often find themselves on the edge, particularly of their local churches; we tread a line between being celebrated as innovators and prophets or rejected as troublemakers. This too was true for Lella. Early in her ministry she was even banned from the basilica at Assisi by the Franciscans themselves for the embarrassment she caused them (Foligno, 1993, p. 19). The episode finds Angela, overcome with emotion on seeing a picture of St Francis in the bosom of Christ, lying on the floor in raptures and shouting incoherently (Mooney, 2007, p. 58). Fortunately for Angela, one brother (who later became her confessor and scribe) wondered if maybe she could be a gift rather than a curse. He went to visit her and was impressed by her faith and practice. Dave Andrews argues that in order to enable transformation within the local church (or work within its structures) we each need a sponsor and two supporters (Andrews, n.d., p. 7). Angela had her sponsor in her Franciscan confessor. For pioneers who are yet to find the equivalent sponsor in their own settings, their ministry remains a lonely place, and being misunderstood is commonplace. Identifying the need for such a role and finding a person to act as sponsor may be a helpful first step in overcoming this isolation.

Personal practice: the examen

For me, the practice of the examen, the prayer of review, has become a crucial tool in my prayer life as I tread the line between tradition and experimentation. The intention is, at the end of each day, to invite the Holy Spirit in and to wind back the events of the day through my mind. I then invite God in as I explore the moments of consolation (glimpses of glory and goodness) and those of desolation (a sense of the absence of God through a lack of glimpses or a reaction in me or those around me). The prayer ends with a conversation with Jesus, and it has been in these moments that I have most often identified a relationship: an area of work or an idea that I would otherwise have missed but has the potential to be fruitful and hopeful. This practice reminds me that I am no fraud and gives me opportunities to give thanks and let go.

Reinterpreting the labels

The use of rhythms and rules of life are becoming more common among pioneers. They anchor us and provide a place of practice from which our ministries can grow. For Angela, the rule was transformative because of her interpretation of it. She entered into a rule of life that held her but also enabled her to step outside the confines of the roles of women at the time.

Despite the prevailing attitudes towards women and their apparent inexperience at leadership or spiritual knowledge in the twelfth and thirteenth centuries, women's involvement within religious life was energetic and active, with the new trends of penitential Christianity being particularly popular among women (Foligno, 1993, p. 36). This was a very recent trend in historical terms; women were presented with opportunities that had not been available for the previous generation. St Clare of Assisi, who was still alive at the time of Angela's birth, simply did not have the option of becoming a friar, much as she wished to follow Francis and his brothers in their way of life, and she led her religious sisters to a life of enclosure, albeit with the first rule of life written by a woman, and the 'privilege of poverty' which was granted just before Clare's death (Robson, 1997, p. 213), when Angela would have been a child. Angela grew up in a changing culture for women.

The key to Angela of Foligno's involvement in the women's movement of the time was her consistent reinterpretation of roles and opportunities. The Third Order of Franciscans was intended as a penitential movement, a sharing of the spirituality of the Franciscans in 'normal life' (Gallyon, 2000, p. 2). Yet Angela became a wandering friar, taking advantage of the opportunity that the Third Order provided to live under the Rule without having to be enclosed. This reinterpretation of a prescribed role, within the roles but outside of the intention, meant that Angela was part of a second generation of Franciscans (SSF, 2010, p. 4) who helped to create a viable method for the continuation of the spirit of Francis' teaching (Coakley, 1991, p. 454). Angela may have even benefited in her creative reinterpretation of role and expectation by the flexibility she had as a woman, kept at arm's length by many of the institutions of the Church (Bynum, 1984, p. 4).

Angela was in a sense a product of her time, but was also markedly different in that she deliberately stepped out of the (albeit new) boundaries of the roles of women mystics and communities. She was fully engaged in the culture of her time but was constantly reinterpreting that culture and institutions to enable her ministry to develop. This creativity may have been one of several factors that brought Angela a following, both men and women. These people committed to a women's movement that was entirely engaged with the Church of the time and was radically engaged with those in greatest need, while developing a life of penitence and contemplative prayer (Higgins, 2000, p. 144).

Story: it's the way we sing the song

The idea that a rule could be liberating at first seems perverse; how can binding oneself into a pattern possibly liberate? Yet more and more Christians on the fringes of inherited church are finding this becoming the sustainer of their faith practice, as well as being the bridge into experiencing effective community. For Angela, the rule was more than an anchor, it was an enabler to lead a lifestyle that was on the face of it entirely conventional and respectful to institutions but was radical in its reinterpretation. There is a brilliant song by Laura Marling, 'Alas I Cannot Swim'; in a live recording it starts out as a traditional folksong but half-way through with an increase in tempo and volume, it suddenly becomes a song of protest against the rules of convention and success. This is one of the songs that I play, very loudly, when I've disappointed another church leader with an off-the-wall comment, or walked away from an opportunity that might publicize but would constrain me. It is not just the words of the song that matter; it's the way we sing it. And it's the same for our rules, rhythms and patterns of prayer; rather than keeping us in check they can provide the pattern for protest and prophecy, against the individualization and unsympathetic measures of success, not only of society but of the Church. They can sustain us as we reinterpret the conventional rules around us through the radical love and compassion of Christ.

Personal practice: midday prayer

Frustrated with my inadequacy of saying Evening Prayer (which for me just did not fit with family life and the needs of my young daughter), I developed with my spiritual director an alternative form of prayer, at midday, which enabled me to connect to my environment. I adapted Church of England liturgy, which I memorized, and started and ended with some 'internal' singing of songs from Taizé and the Iona Community. I used this liturgy as I walked around the estate where I lived and ministered as I took a short break around midday, attempting to use a different route each time. The liturgy always included a form of recommitment to God; if my morning had been rubbish it meant I could start again, and if things were going OK it meant I could notice that and give thanks.

Creator of all,
you give us life,
you give us love,
you give us yourself.
Help me to give my life,
my love, myself to you.

As the rule keeps me, rather than I keep it, I aimed to do this most days but did not berate myself for those days I missed.

Sensual and alive

I've already told the story of Angela's rather erotic and outrageous display at the basilica in Assisi and there are other tales for the lover of medieval history to explore. Angela of Foligno was certainly not the first woman to have got in touch with her erotic nature through a deepening in her relationship with God, particularly through God incarnate, the Christ. This has been the case right from the start of the Church and Christians often sought out these women who express their love of God so outrageously. Mary Magdalene has been the subject of stories and myths surrounding her relationship with Jesus since the early Church; while mostly dismissed as fantasy, they arguably expose a gap in the Church's understanding of people able to demonstrate a profound love that baffles, that is more relational than rational, and taps into a great human need for intimacy and connection (Schaberg and Johnson-Debaufre, 2006, p. 33). Indeed, it seems that male friars often consulted women mystics, recognizing a connectedness with the divine from which they could benefit (Coakley, 1991, p. 455).

Feminist theology, documenting the development of faith in women and girls, cites the importance of understanding our faith in relationship with others (Slee, 2000, p. 6). Drawn to personal stories and connection, many women are adept at compromising in church worship and tradition in order to meet their need for community and connection (Brown and Gilligan, 1992, p. 2). Angela is a wonderful example of this interconnectedness.

She attended church and observed religious festivals throughout her life (Gallyon, 2000, p. 1), remaining fully connected to the community of believers, yet the moment of her conversion was significant, a milestone in her faith development that brought about a very personal response. Her experiences with the Holy Spirit enabled her to experience a love that far surpassed human or 'normal' expectations that the Church taught. Her actions may make us uncomfortable and this may not be the model of personal ministry that women aspire to, with its apparent overtones of mental health problems and public spectacle that would not help to enhance a reputation in the community; we must be careful in applying lessons in practice from 700 years ago to today. However, in its simplest form, Angela was a woman who refused to conform to those expectations of 'right and proper' behaviour around her, connecting deeply with a spirituality of emotion and expressiveness that appeared to draw people to her and enliven the Church. Could it be that pioneers themselves have created a new set of expectations for our behaviour and patterns from which we also need to be freed, allowing our spirit and God's to connect intimately?

Story: embracing our past

Like many pioneers, my background in church is chequered with multiple traditions and experiences as I've looked and longed for an 'authentic' expression of faith in Jesus. For some time, as I delved into the contemplative tradition (which still sustains me in many ways), I became a little embarrassed and uncomfortable at my charismatic past. I confess I have disparaged the 'Jesus is my boyfriend' culture as much as the next wannabe-alternative and I have degraded the faith I had as a teenager as immature and shallow. While I continue my journey into the rich stream of catholic tradition and prayer, I am also beginning to reconnect with my charismatic past. Lella and Francis are inspirations for me as I widen my understanding of where and how I might meet with God. Particularly formative was a meeting with a First Order

Franciscan sister, a real friar, who sat with me in silent prayer in the chapel in her community's house for a while, with the reserved sacrament (bread and wine reserved after a communion service to bring the presence of Christ into a sanctuary space) and its lit candle provoking a sense of reverential worship. Minutes afterwards she was, with huge enthusiasm and charismatic 'bounce', regaling stories of dancing down the aisle during a well-known national evangelical conference, wearing her brown habit, of course. Her enthusiasm for the Spirit at work in the hugest spectrum of Christian worship experience possible opened my eyes to an extraordinarily generous God who (to quote 'Lord of the Dance'!) 'will live in us if we live in him'. Francis was utterly evangelical; completely charismatic and totally catholic. As was Lella. And, if I ever get over myself enough, I will be as well.

Personal practice: the breath of children

Contemplative prayer requires practice. Being an undisciplined sort, I found I was very attracted to the theory, recognizing a natural connection between my charismatic past and catholic present, but struggled with the practice required to really benefit from silence. And then I noticed how calm I felt as I watched my baby daughter sleeping. So this became a practice of prayer. As I watched her breathe in I imagined her drawing the love of God into herself, and as she breathed out I watched her let go of all the doubts, confusion and stuff that holds her back. There is something about the breathing of a young child that seems calmer, more self-assured and more instinctively connected to the divine than anything else. This was the starting point for me to practise silence (my five-year-old daughter will be glad to know that I no longer sit on the floor of her bedroom watching her sleep) and to be able to focus on my own breathing (a common practice in silent prayer) without it becoming laboured. I taught this method of prayer to a group of mums that I met with weekly and it was transformative for several.

Authority not power

At a meeting with a group of pioneers recently I was challenged to recognize the difference that I carry as an ordained person, with a distinct role within the Church, compared with those 'without authority', or, as I understood it to mean in this context, with a person-given position of responsibility. It was a helpful challenge, and certainly in the Church I think there is probably a bigger difference in experience than I would like to admit. However, like everybody else, I am in pretty much the same position out in the wider community. The dog collar does not command the degree of respect and awe that it once did (for which I am grateful); these things need to be earned. Likewise, Angela had no position or official role; she was by nature of her gender entirely on the margins. Yet the very nature of who she was and how she went about her ministry lent her an authority that few could deny.

Angela was utterly committed to the experience of faith and journeying with Christ, knowing oneself and God so intimately that the heart is transformed and a community affected. This was a life that drew people to her; she had disciples and she was what one might now call a spiritual director to a number of Franciscan brothers – 'her sons'. There can be no doubt that Angela exhibited great leadership skill and style, not by her preaching or her great academic knowledge or theological insight, but by the truth of her experience of living in and among those who needed her. Her followers were able to benefit from Angela although she embraced a love that made her appear extremely eccentric and she devoted her life to a Church that would not recognize her leadership gifts. I suspect that Angela's experience might hit home for a number of men and women called to pioneer, whose gifts of leadership, innovation and mission are not recognized formally with a title, let alone any financial support.

You'll have gathered by now that Angela had a way around most things and within the debates of leadership she was clear that she was simply being 'motherly'. This is dangerous language for women who have long struggled against the stereotypes of motherhood (Bynum, 1988, p. 131) and against expectations of our biological functions, but bear with me if you are able (and skip this paragraph if you are not). Angela's role as a spiritual mother, she explained, was as someone who could enable others to access a feminine side of Christ previously obstructed from them, and to speak with an authority that was gained through experience rather than by right of position. It was an adaptation of language that gave authority without stepping out of convention. The catch with this approach to authority, though, is that one cannot simply decide to be a mother; either we literally give birth (which has been suggested to me by one bright spark as a way I could help to grow the Church ...) or we are graciously granted the role by those around us because of who we are and how we are. Motherhood always involves loss of some form, even when things are going well, as each stage is left behind and a child moves further away from its source (Miller-Mclemore, 2007, p. 65). The ability to recognize and embrace these losses – holding her disciples near but being ready to let them go to do more than her – provided a model of ministry for Angela that enabled her, while still having no power, title or money, to have a sense of authority that allowed her to teach and lead. I wish there was a short cut to being trusted with leadership and authority in a community. There is not.

Angela did not, it would seem, set out to found a community. Yet her role as spiritual mother and natural leader drew others, mainly men but also women (Gallyon, 2000, p. 4), and eventually she organized a community life for those around her. She was always quick to point to the influence of St Francis and the rule of life the Franciscans had adopted. Indeed, she was scathing of those who had stepped outside of the Church (Gallyon, 2000, p. 27), working instead to embed these principles and ways of life into mainstream Church and the life of a friar.

The natural evolution of her community remained deeply connected and rooted in her sense of authority, rather than leader, and in the distinction of her uncloistered life in comparison to other mainstream and notable women of the time. She drew to herself a community for all laity to be engaged in; a community of Christians who themselves led and formed communities. These were people with their own ministries and vocation who came together in community before progressing out into their particular and personal journeys once again. There was no overarching mission or purpose of Angela's communities; they were value and experience led, and members were free to come and go, staying for the time that they needed teaching. With all the marks of great leadership, Angela drew large numbers of friars and laity to herself (Petroff, 1991, p. 31). This does not dilute the great affinity and commitment this group would have felt to one another; they shared life vows, be they Third Order or First, kept their personal and community rules of life and went where the Spirit and opportunity led them.

Story: gracious accidents

Some of my best experiences as a pioneer in parish happened when I stopped planning and started to watch and wait for God at work so that I could join in. The estate where I worked as a pioneer curate, like many social housing estates on the edges of our cities, used to be a farm, and there are still physical features of that history around. Some of the roads are 'lined avenues' from the orchards, giving an elegance and green feel to the area, which can feel unusual in a social housing estate. There are many fruit trees still in existence, including cherry, plum and apple, and neighbours found these a nuisance as young people in the area used the fruit as missiles. Having listened to a neighbour about the plum tree on our road, I went out one Sunday with a stepladder, a number of buckets and a broom, and collected what good fruit remained and cleaned up the rest. I received a lesson in jam-making from a Franciscan sister who was supportive of the idea of 'turning bad news into good', from our reading of Deuteronomy 23.5. I made plum jam for the first time, distributing it among the houses neighbouring the tree, whose reactions ranged from surprise, congratulations for having the initiative, shock that I might consider the fruit edible, and even incredulity that I had 'stolen' the plums. Months later one of these neighbours, who had only opened the door a crack to me, stopped me in the street to give me a jar of his sister's marmalade. When I took his funeral a couple of years later (long after the consumption of my jam, I hasten to add), I was able to reflect on the development of my role along my road as a community enabler, quite aside from my formal role of church minister, which meant nothing to them until someone had died. While the ministry of parish priest is a powerful one, it is in the stories of community building and our minor prophetic acts, 'gracious accidents', that our authority as leaders is nurtured and our stories of a man who was raised from the dead and offers to do the same for us one day are heard. 'Gracious accidents' is a phrase I picked up from Joanne Cox Darling from the Methodist Church, in a discussion around the distinctiveness in practice that women pioneers are bringing; I'm so grateful to her, as it's a wonderful phrase to which I often return.

Personal practice: collecting stories for reflection

I mentioned to a group once that the problem with a ministry of 'gracious accidents' is that it becomes difficult to narrate, as the stories of which I become a part are simply not mine to share. Several times I went to set up a blog and then realized I would have nothing to write unless I was prepared to compromise pastoral integrity. I found I was becoming well fed from the stories of God at work around me and longed to find a way to share these to encourage others. Hindsight and the distance of time will enable some of that to unfold, and I must be patient. In the meantime, though, I am passionate about enabling others to capture and reflect on the stories around them. There is no need to reinvent the wheel either; Bishop Laurie Green's book *Let's Do Theology* simply explains and sets out a version of the pastoral spiral that can be used in small groups. One of my favourite memories of my time in pioneer curacy was working with this model alongside two older women who had moved to the estate as children from inner-city Birmingham, who told their stories and those of their neighbours. After an uncertain start, one hit upon the story of Naaman and the servant girl in 2 Kings. These women were, they realized, the servant girl who had been brought out of their homeland of back-to-back housing in the inner city into a strange new place where they held the traditions and practices of community and neighbourliness that they could offer as gift to those around. It was a wonderful moment, and for me it was the connection between our existing congregation and the new community forming in parallel that meant I knew there was a place for both to draw and learn from one another. And they have.

How to Lella

My own journey as a pioneer has recently entered a new stage where I've left parish (geographic) ministry and become Anglican Chaplain in a multi-faith chaplaincy at a large university. As well as being incredibly drawn to the particular university, its history and its culture, I have a theory (shared by many) that chaplaincy has been a space for pioneers for a long time. Without parish responsibilities I hope to be free to rest on the margins, to find myself in the gaps of busy academic life for staff and students. My theory is that the role of friar, and the model with which Angela of Foligno inspired me, is a good fit for the creative, diverse and fast-moving context of a university. I take with me the stories of my experiences in parish life and a commitment to those principles of Lella, which I have gleaned through study and prayer. I have a rule of life that encompasses my whole life, not just the prayer and spirituality 'bit', which remains flexible enough for me to be able to reinterpret for my context and demands (the rule keeps me, I do not keep it). I have started to find my community, the 'tribe' of which I feel part where I am refreshed, encouraged, mocked (gently and when necessary) and sent back on my way; I am exploring different ways to journal so that I can collect stories for reflection and prayer (where was God at work today, last week, last year?); and I am reclaiming old territory; charismatic and evangelical, while relishing the Anglo-Catholic tradition in which I have been a welcomed and loved tourist for over four years. I am hopeful. My prayer for pioneers is that we carry the hope of Jesus in our hearts and out to those places into which we are called; that we carry with us a dream of individual and corporate flourishing that has rocked institutions in the past and will do so again as we are called to live out a vision of reconciliation and peace.

References

Andrews, D., n.d., *The Idiot's Do-It-Yourself Guide To Turning Your Congregation Upside Down And Inside Out*, http://www.daveandrews.com. au/articles/WebSiteArticles9The%20DIYGuide.pdf.

Brown, L. M. and Gilligan, C., 1992, *Meeting at the Crossroads: Women's Psychology and Girl's Development*, London: Harvard University Press.

Bynum, C. W., 1984, *Jesus as Mother: Studies in the Spirituality of the High Middle Ages*, London: University of California Press.

Bynum, C. W., 1988, *Holy Feast and Holy Fast: The Religious Significance of Food to Medieval Women*, London: University of California Press.

Coakley, J., 1991, 'Gender and the Authority of Friars: The Significance of Holy Women for Thirteenth-century Franciscans and Dominicans', *Church History*, 60, pp. 445–60.

Foligno, A. O., 1993, *Complete Works*, New Jersey: Paulist Press.

Gallyon, M., 2000, *The Visions, Revelations and Teachings of Angela of Foligno*, Brighton: Alpha Press.

Green, L., 2009, *Let's do Theology*, 2nd edition, London: Mowbray.

Higgins, M., 2000, 'Angela of Foligno (1248–1309)', *Greyfriars Review*, 14, pp. 133–66.

McGinn, B., 1988, *The Flowering of Mysticism: Men and Women in the New Mysticism – 1200–1350*, New York: Crossroad.

Miller-Mclemore, B., 2007, *In the Midst of Chaos: Caring for Children as Spiritual Practice*, San Francisco: Jossey-Bass.

Mooney, C. M., 2007, 'Interdisciplinarity in Teaching Medieval Mysticism: the Case of Angela of Foligno', *Horizons*, 34, pp. 54–77.

Petroff, E. A., 1991, 'The Mystics', *Christian History*, 10, p. 31.

Robson, M., 1997, *St Francis of Assisi: The Legend and the Life*, London: Geoffrey Chapman.

Schaberg, J. and Johnson-Debaufre, M., 2006, *Mary Magdalene Understood*, London: Continuum.

Slee, N., 2000, 'Some Patterns and Processes of Women's Faith Development', *Journal of Beliefs and Values*, p. 21.

SSF, B. N. A., 2010, *Blessed Angela of Foligno: Mystical Theologian*, Hillfield Friary.

Underhill, E., 1949, *Mysticism*, London: Methuen.

Williams, R. C., 2003, *A Condition of Complete Simplicity: Franciscan Wisdom for Today's World*, Norwich: Canterbury Press.

6

Francis of Assisi:
New Monastic Pioneer

ANDY FREEMAN

The pardon of God

G. K. Chesterton wrote of St Francis of Assisi that he 'walked the world like the Pardon of God' (Chesterton, 1946, p. 182). Of the many things that have been written about this little man from Assisi, I found that phrase one of the most extraordinary.

We often talk of spirituality in terms of prayers, songs or traditions. Yet surely the heart of Christian spirituality is practice. Francis had a spiritual life that walked. His spirituality looked like Jesus, who was the embodied pardon of God (John 1.14).

Spirituality struggles with the question, 'What does all this mean for our lives?' So often we struggle with negative stereotypes of Christianity and of Church – that it's a matter of rules, of being made to feel judged or guilty. So many people write off faith, thinking that they will be excluded for the way they view life. Others can't quite see the reasons for a spiritual life. Why should this be important to me? Does this work?

Francis lived in a world rich in the trappings of Christendom but with an underbelly of poverty and of exclusion. It was here, among the poor, the lepers and the homeless, that Francis embodied his spirituality in practice. Here he brought grace and hope to people he met and even today he is still one of the most significant Christian lives in the history of faith.

This sort of practical spirituality is not only found in St Francis.

It embodies the desire of the early Russian classic *The Way of the Pilgrim* (1978), where the pilgrim is seeking to understand what it is to pray continually. It is found in the holistic and grounded spirituality of the Celtic saints like Columba and Aidan. It is found in the life of Mother Teresa, taking her simple prayers onto the streets of Calcutta. This same desire can also be found in movements such as 24-7 Prayer, of which I've been a part for over 15 years and where much of my learning about Francis has taken place.

Nearly two decades ago I remember going through something of a crisis in my faith. I was asking what this weekly churchgoing and daily praying was meaning for my life and the lives of those around me. I was seeking meaning for both my own spiritual life and also the church tradition and the young people to whom I was ministering.

In hindsight, this was a journey that would lead me to connect with the 24-7 Prayer movement and the time when my life would take a new direction into what we would now term 'New Monasticism'. At that stage in my life all that existed were deep questions and a desire for meaning. In the midst of this questioning I found St Francis. Despite his simple brown tunic and monkish bald patch, Francis was a different kind of monk from any others around him. Over time Francis has slowly helped me to understand my own life and in time my own calling to a world of New Monasticism.

Eight hundred years ago Francis was called by God to rebuild the Church. At first he did this literally, with his bare hands and with rock and stone at a ruined church in Assisi, Italy. Then one day he heard Bible verses that changed his life, from Matthew 10 where we hear the story of Jesus sending out the 12 disciples to preach the kingdom with no provisions nor money. Jesus called them to simple dependence on the grace of God. Living in the same way, Francis preached the gospel and cared for the poor. Others joined him. They built family and eventually formed the Franciscan orders, which still exist today. Francis prayed and his prayers sent him out into the world.

Today, God is calling us out of our meetings into the world. He is sending us among those who are wandering, hurting or alone.

God is calling us 'out' of our cloisters and churches so that we might share him who brought us home. It is this sort of practical, mission-shaped spirituality and its links with today's New Monasticism that I will explore in this chapter. I think Francis, as a twelfth-century pioneer, has much to say to us.

Renewing monasticism

In 2001 I was part of a small team based in Reading in Berkshire, which started the first '24-7 Prayer Boiler Room'. The idea was simple: a rhythm of regular prayer mixed with service to the poor and space for hospitality and the creative arts. It was not a surprise for us to find ourselves based in a disused building that we found was on the site where once the gigantic Reading Abbey had stood. We knew that monasteries were our inspiration and that our desire was to find a New Monasticism for our context and culture.

Of course, we were not alone in this. Across the world, movements like the Simple Way in Philadelphia and across the United States, the Moot Community in London, Taizé in France or the Northumbria Community at Lindisfarne had all been attempting to rediscover that same monastic spirit within contemporary culture.

For some New Monastics this desire led them to a more withdrawn spirituality that might hold more in common with the monasticism of Benedict or the Desert Fathers. Here we find the richness of contemplative prayer, of interceding for the world. Here we find a heritage of the creative arts and a renewal of monastic vows and patterns of life. Communities like these are a gift to the Church.

For others, a New Monasticism grew that was more missional in nature and deeply committed to social justice. The 2004 *Mission-Shaped Church* report recognized that New Monastic communities were one of many forms of reimagined churches growing up within the Anglican family. These new churches were named Fresh Expressions of Church and the term 'pioneers' was adopted for those who were beginning them.

For many of these New Monastic communities, a rediscovery of these traditions was a way to engage with a culture that was experiential and open to spirituality but closed to traditions and institutions. 24-7 Prayer was one of many movements that began a journey of wandering mission to places like Ibiza or St Petersburg in Russia. Continual prayer and a dependence on God in their action accompanied this wandering. In this Francis seemed like a natural companion, his mobile mission being lived out as Chesterton's embodied pardon of God.

This way of life has been challenging many. These 'New Friars' might, as 24-7's Vision Poem suggests, be 'mobile like the wind, they belong to the nations. They need no passport. People write their addresses in pencil and wonder at their strange existence. They are free yet they are slaves of the hurting and dirty and dying' (Grieg, 1999). Many friends of mine have moved to different countries and experienced circumstances that have stretched their faith to the limits. Again Francis has felt like a companion in this journey and his embrace of hardship as a joining-in with Christ has been an inspiration. New Monasticism has at times been in danger of being 'cool', but it can never be so. 'Authentic new monasticism cannot be about building comfortable, white, middle class spaces, it's a calling that will cost yet transform our own humanity and discipleship' (Cray et al., 2010, p. 17).

As I reflect back on these times I realize that St Francis has become a mentor in New Monasticism for me. He is very much a pioneer, establishing a new form of church from nothing. I find in his values of mobility, mission and engagement with the world everything that I would be at home with. Francis of Assisi might well be the first New Monastic pioneer, and I am drawn to be a pioneer living something in the way he did.

The relevance of St Francis

Despite the 800 years of history between his time and ours, Francis remains an inspirational figure to many who are seeking out a spiritual life. Each year over three million pilgrims visit Francis' tomb in Assisi, Italy. Even today the three Franciscan Orders have over one million members. Impressive though those statistics are, there is more that makes Francis significant in 2015.

Leonardo Boff argues: 'our present day culture finds in Francis a great deal of that for which we hunger and thirst' (Boff, 2006, p. 41). Writer and historian Marina Warner suggests: 'the Franciscan spirit continues to be considered by agnostics and atheists as well as believers as the most genuine expression of Christ's teaching ever approved by the Vatican' (House, 2001, p. 9). Francis seems to be able to stand in a unique position in a post-church world as someone deeply respected for his beliefs and actions. 'Through his deep humanity Francis of Assisi has become an archetype of the human ideal: open to God, universal brother, and caretaker of nature and of mother Earth. He belongs not only to Christianity but to all mankind' (Boff, 2006, p. x).

Francis is heralded as a picture of interfaith relations for his incredible journey to visit Sultan Malik al-Kamil during the Crusades and the way he respected his Muslim brothers. When Pope Francis was named in February 2013, Indonesia's *Jakarta Post* was one of many newspapers to note the significance of the new pope's name and to remember that Francis is held in high esteem in Islamic countries.

Francis has continued to be something of a figurehead for the connection of faith and environmental issues not just for the stories of his encounters with animals but with the respect he gave 'Brother Earth'. Pope John Paul II called him the patron saint of ecologists in 1979 and in 1986 the World Wildlife Fund held a joint conference with the Vatican in Assisi for just such a reason.

Francis' commitment to faith is often linked to his care for the poor and for social justice. This commitment to the least in society is particularly resonant for a generation growing with an increased sense of commitment to justice. As we remember the millennium project to 'Make Poverty History' we can appreciate that this was a commitment of Francis in his day.

Francis also brings a challenge to a consumerist world. Leaders such as Bishop Graham Cray, among others, note the significance of consumerism in today's culture: 'the culture in which we now live makes disciples more effectively than the Church does' (Cray et al., 2010, p. 3). When it comes to possessions, Francis comes like an explosive force against this immovable object. Francis quite literally rejected owning anything. He lived simply, asking for only what he needed and taking that approach as a way to empathize and relate with those on the margins.

Francis was the archetypal church pioneer. His order was different in the way it lived, simple and authentic in its lifestyle yet radically different in its culture from many other orders and monasteries. Francis' embrace of women's empowerment through the story of Clare and the creation of a women's order was groundbreaking for the time.

Francis was clear in his belief that his mission was to rebuild the Church. He was an expert at what Eddie Gibbs and Ian Coffey refer to as the Church's task of finding its place in the cultural mosaic (Gibbs and Coffey, 2000, p. 220). Francis did not over-power the world around him with his Church. Instead he listened to artists, astronomers and philosophers of his age and they shaped him as well as him shaping them. People like Leonardo da Vinci and Dante were rumoured to be Franciscans, as this move-ment influenced an entire age culturally as well as spiritually.

Many missiologists make note of his work as a key moment in the missional history of the Church. Steve Bevans saw that Francis sought to be 'more servant than institution, more communal than hierarchical, more humble than arrogant' (Bevans and Schroeder, 2004, p. 220). This was a different sort of Church from the power-ful and influential institution that existed in the time of Francis.

Francis and pioneering spirituality

So if Francis is a type of New Monastic pioneer who has a con-nection with contemporary culture, it is worth asking just what sort of reimagining of church it was that Francis envisaged. What are the dynamics of his spirituality and practice that we can apply today? At first glance it might be hard to suggest that Franciscan Orders are like these new and embryonic forms of church, yet it seems that Leonardo Boff made this same connection in his biography of Francis. 'Francis created a popular expression of the Church; the mystery of the Church becomes concrete in the small fraternity of brothers in contact with the people and with the poorest of the people of God' (Boff, 2006, p. 2).

I would like to suggest four areas of a Francis-shaped spirituality, which would not seem out of place in the field of pioneer ministry today.

1 A spirituality that crosses boundaries

I have already mentioned Francis and his meeting with Sultan Malik al-Kamil during the Crusades. This was a serious journey, and took place in 1219 during the campaign of the Fifth Crusade. Their destination was Damieta in Egypt and to get there they needed to cross enemy lines to visit the Sultan. They had no idea how they would be received or whether they would even reach their destination alive.

Francis and Brother Illuminato were travelling to see the Sultan in an attempt to stop the war. They had no tools but love and respect, and although they were probably intent on trying to convert the Sultan, they went with a tolerance and appreciation of fellow human beings that was ultimately to be their greatest weapon. Although the war did not end until 1221, both men went away from their two-day discussions with deep respect and having engaged in a dialogue that still has ripples today. In a time of considerable uncertainty in relationships between these two faiths, Francis remains a figure of respect in Islam, almost 800 years after this meeting took place.

One of the key tasks of those seeking to reimagine the Church is the willingness to cross boundaries. Pioneering itself is a task of boundary-breaking: to reach those whose feelings, experience or worldview has excluded them from the possibility of taking part in a community of faith.

In our pioneering we will each be aware of boundaries that present themselves. Whether it is a boundary of culture, belief or reason, or a wall built up from bad experiences, these boundaries need to be overcome in the act of pioneering something new. The simplest of these boundaries is something we share with Francis' journey – crossing the lines that exist around us and going to others rather than expecting them to come to us. Francis did this through hospitality, not in the offering of it but in receiving the hospitality of the Sultan.

> Hospitality means primarily the creation of free space where the stranger can enter and become a friend instead of an enemy. Hospitality is not to change people, but to offer them space where change can take place. It is not to bring men and women over to our side, but to offer freedom not disturbed by dividing lines. (Nouwen, 1975, pp. 71–2)

Nouwen's idea of hospitality as space without dividing lines is one we can emulate in order to cross boundaries. The meal table is a unique leveller as we sit together and share the same meal. Francis went out to the Sultan but then was humble and respectful enough to be his guest, to honour his religion and to have a willingness to learn from him. The space was mutual. How can we create those sorts of hospitable spaces?

As we cross boundaries it is vital too that we do not take either our rules or our defences with us. Francis managed to go as himself, yet was adept at listening to the culture and practices of those he met. He learnt from the people he had gone to share with. It has been suggested that Francis took his inspiration for praying five times a day in his Order from witnessing the Muslim call to prayer (Bevans and Schroeder, 2004, pp. 35–6).

If he were pioneering today, Francis might cross the boundaries of religion, race or culture, and try to give and receive hospitality to and from those people we might consider to be his enemies.

2 *A spirituality that sees us as co-habitors of the earth*

In his biography of St Francis, Adrian House declares: 'I propose Francis as a patron Saint for ecologists' (House, 2001, p. 10).

Franciscan spirituality is expressed in brotherhood with creation. In 'The Canticle of the Creatures', Chesterton observes that Francis 'wanted to see each tree as a separate and almost sacred thing, being a child of God and therefore a brother or sister of man' (Chesterton, 1946, p. 24).

A modern-day analysis might find it easy to criticize the romantic views of Francis' approach to the created world. Here was someone who spoke to wolves and preached to fishes. However, Francis also viewed creation practically, exhorting cornfields and vineyards to serve God willingly by producing a crop. He saw creation as something with which to live in harmony. The story of his calming a wolf expressed the idea that both might live in harmony, and although strange, spoke of relationship. His language of Sun and Moon as Brother and Sister show a dependence and mutuality of living in this created earth.

Contemporary Franciscan friaries have taken up this cause, praying for forgiveness for 'ways in which we imperil our planet earth' and instead asking that we may 'nurture in love' (*The Franciscan*, May 2011). This commitment has led US Franciscan Keith Douglass Warner to take a position of leading American Catholics in tackling environmental issues. Franciscan John Mizzoni has influenced academic thinking in biocentrism, where all creatures have unique value.

Boff identifies Francis' message in that we are 'living members of creation community' (Boff, 2006, p. 65). He saw the world as a friend with animals and the countryside as co-conspirators in the renewal of creation. The world and all that is in it was alive to Francis. His journeys were an interaction with nature. He was able to notice the birds because he was not ignoring them and because they were not superfluous to his greater aim of reaching journey's end. He could stop at a roadside and consider a lily.

Then there is this awareness of the place where we stand as our piece of the earth. In the second creation narrative in Genesis 2 it always strikes me that the first man is called Adam, or Adamah, the Hebrew for 'dirt'. We have a deep connection with the ground we walk on. Francis understood this and therefore did not seek to exert power as a human being but instead spoke of dependence. Franciscan spirituality depends on God's provision in creation but also depends on all other living creatures, plants and all created things.

Reimagining the Church in any way must involve a reorientation of our priorities and one that seems clear within our current time and setting as creation-carers. If we were to stop treating climate change as a project to be tackled, or an obstacle to be overcome, but instead began a process of 'fraternity' with the earth – that we will for evermore need to live in balance with the world we live in – then maybe we will find lessons for church and society that can help us bring about change.

3 A spirituality committed to the poorest in our world

One of the epiphany moments in the life of Francis was his encounter with a leper on the road to Assisi. Standing opposite Francis at that moment was a man who looked broken on the inside as well as damaged physically. Somewhere deep within him, suppressing all the horror he felt, Francis found grace, courage and most of all compassion. He stepped down from his horse, gave the man a coin and then gently kissed his head. Deeply moved, the leper kissed him in return. It appears that as Francis remounted his horse he looked around and could no longer see the man. Biographers suggest that at that moment Francis realized that he had kissed the face of Christ in the guise of a leper (Wintz, 2013).

Whether this was a metaphorical or actual meeting, it is clear that Jesus did indeed meet Francis at that moment and changed his heart. Days later, Francis returned to the leper colony, Lazar House, with a large amount of money and distributed it among the inhabitants, kissing each in turn. As he continued to care, he and the fellow friars who were to join him spent considerable time in the leper communities that were around them, nursing wherever they could. In his Testament, Francis writes, 'what had previously nauseated me became the source of spiritual and physical consolation for me' (House, 2001, p. 69).

It seems that each time Francis met a leper from that time on, he met Christ in their pain and suffering, he met Christ in their humanity. In this respect, the spirituality of Francis towards the poor creates certain priorities that may affect the way we pioneer.

First, he was a genuine friend to the poorest. He often chose to remove himself from the limelight and seemed happiest when he could care outside of the watch of others. He gave himself to all who were poor, in need or excluded. It was not just the leper he cared for but the impoverished family, the wounded soldier, the orphaned child or the lost and lonely. All of these and more were loved by this incredible man and his followers.

Francis believed that 'God made himself our brother in poverty and humility' (Boff, 2006, p. 23). In his naturally poetic style he would speak of the Holy Lady Poverty and esteem the lowest in the society in which he lived: those who 'mourn', the 'meek' or those who were 'poor in spirit'. To Francis people were highly valued, and in them he found Jesus. It is hard to imagine anyone who lived out the values of the Beatitudes so dramatically but also so secretly, such that many of those stories are hidden from us as we look back from the future. What would a church look like that practised this inclusive love today?

Second, there was the sense that poverty and simplicity became a way of identifying practically with the needs of those who were poorest. For Franciscans, poverty was part of their rule and part of their identity. A phrase common to many Franciscan texts is '*sequi vestigial et paupertatem eius*', which literally means 'to follow in his footsteps and poverty'. As the community developed around him, Francis' rule of life put this principle at the core of their identity – 'for those who wish to embrace this life ... they should go and sell all that belongs to them and strive to give it to the poor' (from 'The Rule of St Francis', House, 2001, p. 300).

Francis discovered that Jesus cared for the poor as a poor man. He cared for the poorest from among the poorest. Francis saw the Incarnation as the way that Jesus came to save as one of us, as a human being, the creator God cast into his own story. The humanity and divinity of Jesus seemed compelling to Francis and challenging 'a mystery of divine sympathy and empathy' (Boff, 2006, p. 23).

I wonder what our approach to money and resources might be if we pioneered a Franciscan spirituality? Where would our projects and donors be if we lived a type of simple lifestyle that relied on dependence on God and a willingness to accept the kindness of others? Can we truly find an empathy and kindness for the poor while we continue to be comparatively rich in resources? In the western world these challenges may seem particularly hard but it is worth considering how much we believe that we need money and resources and what we would be willing to sacrifice to get it. Francis took the polar opposite approach.

4 A spirituality centred on the sacrifice of Jesus

Francis began his journey with an encounter with Jesus at the ruined church in San Damiano. Kneeling before an icon of Christ, he heard God's voice and his life was changed for ever.

This call led him to rebuild the church and care for the poor but at its heart was a desire to reproduce and imitate the life of Jesus. Hundreds of years before its current popularity, here was a man genuinely asking the question, 'What would Jesus do?'

Francis tried to act in an incarnational way, as he understood Jesus did. He prayed the prayer of Jesus regularly. He meditated and understood the Scriptures in the light of Jesus. He preached Jesus. He developed his rule of life around Jesus. He told stories of Jesus. He sang songs of Jesus. He found Jesus in the lives of the poor. For him every waking moment was about living in a way that presented Jesus.

Chesterton noted, 'Christ was the pattern on which St Francis sought to fashion himself' (Chesterton, 1946, p. 48). What would it mean to focus a simple spirituality around the person of Jesus? Could we genuinely free ourselves from our denominations and traditions and instead focus on the man who revealed everything to us?

Of particular interest to Francis was the self-sacrificial nature of Christ, something found in Paul's challenge for us to imitate Christ in the letter to the Philippians.

> In your relationships with one another, have the same mindset
>   as Christ Jesus:
> Who, being in very nature God,
> did not consider equality with God something to be used to
>   his own advantage;
> rather, he made himself nothing
> by taking the very nature of a servant,
> being made in human likeness.
> And being found in appearance as a man,
> he humbled himself
> by becoming obedient to death –
> even death on a cross! (Phil. 2.5–7)

Francis clearly believed in a gospel that exemplified a self-emptying Jesus and so inferred that we believe in a humble, self-giving God. Francis would have been familiar with the Nicene Creed, setting out the core belief of Jesus Christ as Lord: a fully human and fully divine Jesus. The kenotic idea of self-emptying embraces the dynamic nature of this union. Jesus reveals much about what it means to be human but also creates a revolution in what we understand about God. This is God as the humble servant who reveals power and glory in a whole new light.

When Francis sought to reimagine the Church in his context he went first to the poor and excluded, and began by living out the core Christ-centred principle of self-emptying. Pioneering at its heart is about following the call of Christ to those on the margins of the Church and to bring them home. Jesus Christ fulfilled this task by giving himself away, and as Francis placed Jesus at the centre of his movement he felt compelled to do the same. 'We are, the great spiritual writers insist, most fully ourselves when we give ourselves away' (Armstrong, 2004, p. 37).

New Monastic pioneer

For pioneers seeking to develop new possibilities and new beginnings for the Church, I believe that Francis could be a figure of considerable inspiration and perspective. In my journey I have found this pioneer of New Monasticism to be someone who has a unique place in the history of the Church.

Francis' new beginning in his own soul took him to an understanding of the rebuilding of the Church, first through bricks and mortar then in its very institutions and structure. He created a popular and mobile New Monasticism that embraced the poor at the greatest point of need and found Jesus among them. He empowered the excluded and the broken. He created space for women to express their vocation and calling as much as men and set many women into new paths of freedom. He reimagined popular culture into songs, poems and a troubadour-style faith that captured many hearts in Italy. He challenged and inspired popes and cardinals. He created a rule of life that has brought strength to millions since. He reimagined church, set in the context of a created world with which all of us have a fraternity and bond.

We have the opportunity to bring about change and I have found that in my tiny part of this world St Francis has been a guide and mentor. I hope that some of you reading this chapter might also find this inspiration for a new future.

References

Armstrong, K., 2004, *The Spiral Staircase: My Climb out of Darkness*, New York: Knopf Doubleday.

Bevans, S. and Schroeder, R., 2004, *Constants in Context: A Theology of Mission for Today*, Maryknoll, NY: Orbis.

Boff, L., 2006, *Francis*, Maryknoll, NY: Orbis.

Chesterton, G. K., 1946, *St Francis of Assisi*, 25th edition, London: Hodder & Stoughton.

Cray, G., Mobsby, I. and Kennedy, A., 2010, *New Monasticism as a Fresh Expression of Church*, Norwich: Canterbury Press.

Gibbs, E. and Coffey, I., 2000, *Church Next: Quantum Changes in Christian Ministry*, Leicester: IVP.

Grieg, P., 1999, 'The Vision Poem', www.24-7prayer.com.

House, A., 2001, *Francis of Assisi*, Random House: London.

Nouwen, H., 1975, *Reaching Out*, New York: Doubleday.

The Franciscan, 2011, http://www.franciscans.org.uk/franciscan/franciscan-may-2011.

The Way of a Pilgrim, 1978, trans. H. Bacovcin, New York: Doubleday.

Wintz, J., 2013, 'St Francis and the Leper', www.americancatholic.org, 17 July.

7

Unearthing Spirituality: Through the Arts

GAVIN MART

I first met Martin Daws, the Young Person's Laureate for Wales, when I was introduced to him in a late-night jazz club in North Wales. I was impressed by his poetry set: 'I think you might be a prophet!?' I hinted to him; he raised an eyebrow ...

Martin and I have since shared many beautiful times on car journeys, performing on many stages, and delivering transformative creative workshops. Our talks, as wide-ranging as the long roads we drive, cover our understandings of faith and ideas about who or what God is or might be. They explore how our conceptions of a Supreme Being might relate to pagan and Christian understandings and misunderstandings, whether postmodernism fits with theology, and how pioneers successfully explore the discontinuous edges of traditional church understanding. We share new schemes and plans of how together we may try to help people unearth and gain dominion over something lost in our modern lives through the medium of our projects and performance interventions.

Martin often calls this something: simply, 'other'. I once asked him what God meant to him; 'something bigger than myself', he replied. That statement was new to me and set me journeying further out onto a fresh and crisp field of faith exploration. What might constitute this *otherness*, this *bigger-ness*? What idea of *other*, in our individualistic, consumer-driven, postmodern society might come before 'me'? What is this idea of otherness that could inspire a post-secular generation not only to reimagine the concept of a loving creator God but also to inspire social change? What is this notion of *other* that can potentially transcend contemporary scientific concepts and compete with ideas that cleave theories of space and time? How does this idea of 'something other' survive contemporary culture and break through the seemingly numbing oppression of an increasingly isolated experience of society?

Arts and artists might help us to draw out some of the underlying treasures that are hidden just beneath the surface skin of contemporary culture. Though sometimes hard to see, there still remains an underlying richness of spiritual feeling that resides deep within our communities. Spirituality often lies dormant. It waits to be mined and excavated, to be reborn and potentially to be given a new lease of life. Spirituality may even be waiting to be recommissioned by our existing models of church.

Poets as prophets

Perhaps we do not need to reinvent the wheel regarding models of church; perhaps we do not need to reorganize too much of our institutional practice. We already have the resources within our fading structures to breathe new life back into our local communities. Perhaps, and I will come to this in a moment, there is a very simple approach we can adopt that might help us to hack into a life-giving kernel offering newness and transformation into our broken societies. This approach might help to offer people a route home towards faith, and help to positively transform society in the meantime.

Martin's poem 'Here to Hold You' is a beautiful insight into the powerful medium of spoken-word poetry which is becoming increasingly popular in contemporary culture. Spoken-word poets need little introduction, props or preparation. They stand vulnerable, often invited directly into the hearts of our communities in pubs, bars, shopping centres, theatres, street corners, festivals, schools and youth clubs. These carriers of the prophetic are accepted with surprising ease across a wide range of cultures and contexts and they are deeply respected for their craft. They mix traditional reading, hip-hop culture and rap. They are judged on the content and delivery of their message. They speak boldly, like preachers of a bygone age, passionate with signs and symbols of the time, bravely unafraid and defiant beneath the ever-present eyes of power.

They are an amalgamation of the folk singer turned protester, harnessing the energies of the strikers' union leaders, while delivering the punches of politicians without the need for the election campaign. They often speak truths cutting sharply through rhetorical webs of lies. They hold up a mirror to our lives and offer insight to our prophetic imagination. Poets and prophets come down from their mountainside vistas into the midst of society and tell us how it really is, or may be; they paint colourful depictions of the state of our condition and warn about the judgement of our actions.

The words of these prophets are fair. They are poetic and soulful, carrying within them their own credence. They foster licence and permission that cut through the mundane chitter-chatter, muzak-monotone of everyday language. They challenge the royal consciousness of the status quo, appealing to our senses in an encouragement to imagine alternative possibilities (Brueggemann, 2001). They carry a conceptual currency, affording purchase power across the values of rich and poor. They delicately hang words like gospel truths on fine threads just out of reach yet visible and worth striving for. Such words are life to us when we catch them, soul food if we would only eat.

The actions and rituals of artistic expression help to unearth fossils that mirror the characteristics of a loving creator God; they point to a pattern of God's DNA throughout all creation. God becomes as recognizable in nature as in the cultural outworking of all individuals who humbly gather together to seek out something of their creator. God is found within the flow that happens during, and also in the spaces that occur after, a sacramental act. God: as in the minds of those who ponder on some exposure to a 'thin space'. God: as in the doubt of those who have carried something of faith for many years and in the freshness of a new idea or interpretation of the gospel narrative. Artistic expression helps us to reimagine God.

In the poem 'Here to Hold You' Martin Daws gifts us with his understanding of the gospel. He invites us into his non-churched framing of this otherness, and a vision of a Jesus – God/Man, made up of light and love, yearning for humanity to come home. It's a metaphor of the Father longing for the embrace of the Prodigal; it's gospel, it's family, it's joy and hope and it's desperately needed on just about every street corner of the western world.

Here to Hold You[1]

Fear not – your father will find you
a fate of cloud will break
reveal you as the truth

He's walked this path before you
left his mark upon the earth
for you to map the dark of days
and find your way home throughout the night

Listen – listen for his voice
you might find him in the light you see
his touch upon the air

He's the first and last of breath you feel
here from far beyond you – he's beside you
your father's close at hand

He's here to hold you in his arms again

Redemption calling to you
in the tears of those you love
their song lifting your name
illuminated against the sky

Beautiful bright
sun rays dissolving from your face
an epic scale of life you are
all you've ever been all you'll become

Connecting light
the space between each heart beat
still emptying endlessly
opening time into timeless love

You're light in hand
arms open like home
it's easy now to let the life weight grow

He's here to hold you in his arms again

As pioneers we are always reflecting on what it means to pass on the gospel, which can at times seem extremely challenging. Is it possible that our artists might be waiting patiently on the sidelines to help us in that very purpose? Perhaps they have been waiting for far too long?

Art and spirituality

Art has a deep purpose in our spiritual outworking and under-standing. It has a profound function that could actually help us as 'the Church' to get back on track in terms of achieving social transformation. Have we, the Church, been missing a simple trick in the commissioning of the arts? For centuries the religious institution excelled at the role of commissioning the arts to help reimagine the gospel narrative. Our cathedrals are still perform-ing well in this 'precentor' or curating role and contemporary works of art that cut to the heart of a metropolitan cultural iden-tity hang acerbically in many of our city's major landmarks. But our local churches and congregations seem to have lost their gift for retelling the stories that we hold in our local communities and indeed in wider society. I wonder how many curates feel they get to curate?

For many centuries the Church invested much of its resourcing into commissioning the arts to reimagine the cultural myths of the times. The churches were often the breeding ground for master-pieces in the arts: great works that recounted our stories and belief systems back to us so we could all understand on some level. Such stories retold our belief systems, cultural understandings and faith interpretations in a way that we could comprehend and that we could revere. Worship was centred around sacramental signs and symbols that we could honour and cherish in such a way that they would lead us into a deeper sense of relationship, conception and adoration of a loving creator-God.

Religious establishments invested in deep municipal relation-ships with the towns they inhabited. They formed relationships with local guilds, helping to identify and fund artists who were skilfully able to interpret the mood and feeling of the people. Churches would commission and instruct artisans and trades-people to retell gospel narratives employing through a wide range of multimedia disciplines, such as sculpture, stained glass, paint-ing, ceramics, employing silversmiths, blacksmiths, seamstresses, tailors, draftsmen, architects, stonemasons, poets, singers and writers.

The work that was created often became the centrepieces for the local community; such artefacts were adopted by the people as the relics that helped them to imagine their faith. They helped people to understand their own communities and their own cul-tures, as they unravelled local mythology and story. Our artisans helped people focus on a communal understanding of faith.

Perhaps in centuries past there was a deep subcultural healing function taking place through the commissioning and experienc-ing of these shared cultural collections of faith and artistic practice. Perhaps we ought to consider whether there is something deeper at play in our societies that needs to be healed in a similar way? The healing process might actually be quite simple in its praxis, so it is curious that it has been overlooked.

Putting it into practice: clumsy solutions and dangerous memories

Throughout the ten years that immediately followed the millennium I worked closely with my friend Si Smith, an illustrator by day and an extremely creative mixed-media artist by night. Together we learned how to curate art exhibitions in quirky spaces, mainly through trial and error and with varying degrees of success. Si is brilliant at reframing gospel narratives (such as 'Raised in Leeds' or '40' – see Smith, 2013), and we realized that by asking others to contribute their interpretations of how they understand biblical texts, we could open up an interesting dialogue within the context of a local community.

The exhibitions that resulted from those experimental times resulted in what I now consider to be my staple mission praxis: commissioning artists to retell the gospel story. As a pioneer for the Methodist Church in North Wales, I set out to develop these ideas alongside the idea of developing a community based around the arts and spirituality. Having been a part of a creative team responsible for the development of 'Leftbank' (a transformation of a deconsecrated gothic church building into an inner-city art centre in Leeds), I knew an exhibition project would benefit from being held in an iconic building or dramatic space.

I found the Imperial Hotel, a giant abandoned building on the market high street of Colwyn Bay, a once glorious yet fading Welsh seaside resort struggling to reinvent itself against the backdrop of a tough economic climate. The venue held out a lot of hope for local people and with the help of local photographic artist and poet Alan Whitfield we threw open the front doors and invited everyone in to help renovate and redecorate the space to host an alternative arts exhibition.

The exhibition itself would be called 'The Engedi Easter Story'. Engedi was the name of many old Welsh congregation communities and I loved the mystery surrounding the caves of Engedi in the Old Testament where David hides from Saul. It conveys the idea of an oasis in the desert and its evocation has stuck with us. Alan and I invited many local professional and amateur artists to contribute, receiving a surprisingly positive response to our call for work. We commissioned 40 pieces of art, each with a biblical passage relating to the Passion and over the months that followed we transformed the dilapidated hotel and put together the exhibition. Our opening boasted support from some 500 people, gaining national press coverage, and throughout the exhibition itself we were visited by several thousand people … we were blown away!

In the following months we tried to gather up all the contacts, connections and stories that had emerged from our efforts. We had developed quite a community of volunteers and interested people and it was a lot to try and take on board. Feeling the wave of excitement, we launched straight into our next exhibition, 'ADVENTurous'. Over 70 artists were commissioned around the theme of Advent, and the exhibition linked art centres together around the UK in a national tour which incorporated Union Chapel in London and Leftbank in Leeds as well as the Imperial Hotel in Colwyn Bay. It was an exhausting process, but the hard work paid off; we developed an expression of spirituality through the arts, a contemporary reimagining of gospel narratives and a community of folk interested in exploring faith together.

People who had become involved in 'Engedi' found themselves unearthing the meaning of togetherness through a sense of community. By no means did we all have exactly the same ideas of faith, but we shared a common ground where people felt enabled to talk about what spirituality is, and how a gospel narrative might apply in today's world. It was in the activities that were generated while working together towards the project that we found much of the community conversation taking place. We are now nearly four years into this journey together and still in the same hotel space. Although that might change, we'd be left with a strong core body of local people meeting regularly, and our stories and activities are shared by over 1,000 people on our social networks. We find ourselves as stewards that hold open a safe and non-judgemental space that partners with other agencies such as local councils, grant-giving agencies, local businesses and charitable organizations. We are patrons of the arts and ambassadors of an inclusive faith story, we are recognized and funded by established health and welfare institutions, and we help to fill a service gap in our local society. We try to maintain focus on the question, 'What are the good things that we are doing?' and constantly realign to this.

On reflection I realize that I've become a 'hacker'. Hackers use pieces of existing ideas to create better solutions for community problems. Hacking out these new and fresh spaces through curation of the arts allows for an assemblance of theologies, ideas and metaphor in combination with tradition, sacrament and liturgy. It's a kind of rebooting or reprogramming of old systems. Curators are able to use these new operating systems more effectively and creatively to enrich our religious understanding. Curators can unravel the prophets hidden within our communities, shining a light on the artists who have something new and helpful to say to our society. 'A work of art is at best an articulation of something as much as it is a representation of someone: it is a proposal for how things could be seen, an offering but not a hand-out' (Obrist in Baker, 2010, p. 184).

This artistic 'clumsy solution space' (Grint, 2010, p. 25) approach affords each participant their own voice in the mix. Conversation and discussion are prompted through the commissioning of the arts, exhibitions, workshops and shared mealtimes. People generally wander into our arts space finding that they can get involved in one way or another and begin to explore the space as a community of practice. In turn, this practice of inclusion and expression through the arts leads to people beginning to feel empowered (see Figure 1).

Figure 1: Engedi Arts: Story of impact and theory of change (Sampson, 2013, p. 3)

Artists who have contributed to Engedi's exhibitions have also become those who lead the projects on a day-to-day basis. Feeling included through the expression and commissioning, they have experienced a strong sense of empowerment. This empowerment has led them to experience social change not only in their own community through the restoration of a high street commercial space, but also through their own fresh sense of mobility in the transformation that takes place through social inclusion.

Artists have a role in bringing back to life 'dangerous memories' or ideas of a different time (Morisy, 2009). They raise hope that things do not always have to be like this. This resurrection of dangerous memories can be a key role for the pioneer, for here we begin to experience the beginnings of transformation, the beginnings of social change. They become like treasure seekers, able to reframe the stories of a people in the hope of resurrecting memories of the past, a kind of 'place maker', able to give people back the gift of their own homeland. Such memories might contain religious or spiritual pearls, stories and forgotten local myths or traditions that might help to unlock the numbness and silencing impact of the all-encompassing consumerist society. Here, in the mystery of local traditions, the gold riches of new hope lie patiently beneath the surface of our collective memory, whispering gently to be etched back into view.

It's imperative to remember that most people's outlook on religion from a wider consumer culture is that 'religion is dodgy and dangerous' (Morisy, 2009). Engel's scale (Engel, 2012) helps us to imagine where the pioneer might start in communicating the gospel narrative (see Figure 2).

Many people in today's society don't even get represented on Engel's scale; they drop off the bottom somewhere towards the '−12's, or perhaps further. They may be second or third generation non-Christians with no religious language. They may be of multifaith background with a diverse and complex religious heritage that even they don't understand. They may be completely unaware of their own cultural story.

The pioneer minister cannot rely on prior knowledge, assumed context or shared intrinsic beliefs. Therefore the challenge of ask-

+5 Stewardship
+4 Communion with God
+3 Conceptual and behavioural growth
+2 Incorporation into Body
+1 Post-decision evaluation
New birth
−1 Repentance and faith in Christ
−2 Decision to act
−3 Personal problem recognition
−4 Positive attitude towards Gospel
−5 Grasp implications of Gospel
−6 Awareness of fundamentals of Gospel
−7 Initial awareness of Gospel
−8 Awareness of supreme being, no
knowledge of Gospel
−9
−10
−11
−12 ...

Figure 2. The Engel scale of spiritual decision

ing people to unlock their histories might be just the first throw of a spade into a protracted and time-consuming archaeological dig. Communities with the ability to reflect are communities that can begin to analyse and criticize the impact of the oppression under which they find themselves (Arbuckle, 1993). Finding a voice is a step towards empowering communities to liberate themselves.

Putting it into practice: my own blank canvas

I have experienced this process myself by being commissioned. You may not consider yourself an artist, but imagine that you receive a call to express your state of mind. This commission promises you the opportunity to tell of the colour you once knew or the feelings you once shared with others; about a dream you once had or a truth you once believed in. This call is a gift of a blank canvas on which to express something deep. Your expression would be held of value within the safe walls of a community that cares and delights in your song. I wonder how such a call to respond might impact upon your life.

As a Methodist VentureFX pioneer minister, I have been given that very sense of call and commission. I know and understand how potentially daunting that feeling of being given a blank canvas can be, but also how liberating.

By way of an example, I wrote the song 'Persons Reported' as a metaphor for the condition of the contemporary Church through the eyes of a de-churched 25- to 40-year-old. The song speaks of someone who finds himself right in the middle of the so-called 'missing generation' of the Church: young adults who have switched off from organized religion and voted with their feet. There was a time when I found myself no longer able to sit through a church service, regardless of the denomination, unable to reconstruct any sense of meaning in relationship to the outside world through the ordered 'Sunday led–attractional' approach to conventional faith.

Persons Reported

We don't have a lifeboat
Is this call recorded?
There's no time for questions
Can't you tell we're desperate?

Persons reported
Don't spare the horses
We're taking on water
Send all resources

For me

We were all trying to lead
We were blind, blind as could be
There were signs but how could we read?
Now we're down, down on our knees

Persons reported
Don't spare the horses
We're taking on water
Send all resources

For me

Can't give you our number
We've all been deported
What were you expecting?
Our souls have been rejected ...
(Mart, online)

At this time I felt like I was drowning. I felt cultureless. This song resonates with the story of the yachtsman Donald Crowhurst who, on a sea of lies, reported false positions back home in the hope of creating an illusion of a successful maritime passage. During his enigmatic round-the-world race in 1968 Crowhurst radioed messages of his claimed position in various parts of the world, while keeping fabricated logbooks of his whereabouts based on weather systems which he had managed to predict. In truth, Crowhurst never left the Atlantic Ocean, having run into difficulties early on in the race and aware that his boat was never going to be able to match up to the demands of the high seas. He cut his radio communications and spiralled into his own isolated and personal world; eventually he probably took his own life, as his boat was later found abandoned.

The artist Tacita Dean reframes this tale as a sombre reflection of our own fallen, human state in her works 'Disappearance at Sea' and 'Disappearance at Sea II'. Dean's work mirrors our inner journey with its deep darkness and revelations of who we are and who we can become in times of adversity and peril. Our journey, turbulent and ungovernable, throws into light both the terrors and enlightenment of the realities we face as we set sail into indifferent waters. For we are all 'at sea'; finding ourselves at the mercy of nature's winds and tide. We set our human sanity against the sea, against nature itself, in the attempt to fathom the depths of our own souls, to chart our own emotions and to figure out who we are and might turn out to be. We hope beyond hope for rescue when things go wrong and often face despair as we age into the realization that nothing can prevent the inevitable coming, coming, coming of time ...

I felt something of what Donald Crowhurst must have experienced while he was losing his sense of reason: adrift at sea and searching for some unobtainable higher calling to give meaning to his life. Perhaps I had lost my way; moreover I had lost my part in the race, lost my sense of call and sense of focus for my beliefs. I met others in my generation who felt the same feelings of disillusion – people in their twenties and thirties were calling out for help with their spiritual lives. There were, however, no resources being dispatched.

This generation, like Donald Crowhurst, is perhaps never coming back. Cast away, they drift deeper into silent layers of grey, floating aimlessly upon a sea of relativism and no longer respecting traditional religious institutions (Sivalon, 2012, p. 57). They have left their shallow dream of faith, a kind of siren call to a euphoric worship space that had little relevance or meaning to the wider society when the music fades. They remain *out there*: detached, weary and disillusioned. They still seek something of spirituality, something of a mixed economy of faith. They may even still have some hope of a broken radio message of rescue.

Staring into this horizon, I realized that the gift of expression that I experienced might also be the resource that reaches out to others. I have now seen first-hand how allowing people to express themselves leads directly to their increased sense of empowerment. This achieves wonderful change in how people relate to their own communities. It is transformational, and that transformation is reflected in wider social change.

Refounding

A similar principle of refounding the cultural kernels of the gospel was merited as evangelization by Vincent Donovan 20 years ago, when he argued that not all evangelism is about leading individuals to the gospel. Donovan talked about bringing the 'chips' of the gospel to the culture and letting them fall where they may; evangelization in this sense is essentially unpredictable. It is not about numbers or even about an evangelist carrying a specific message. It is about the missionary carrying a sense of a story and unravelling the threads of that story within the culture they find themselves. 'The conversion, or metanoia, involved is a conversion of both the evangelist and the evangelized' (Donovan, 1989, p. 125). In this mission-praxis pioneer missionaries travel with a willingness to be changed in themselves and the lenses through which they see the gospel. They carry easily the disposition to be in the wrong and they don't proclaim to have the copyright on the religious narrative. Pioneers come as guests, they carry a gift of the gospel, and they are prepared to listen to context and culture.

It could be argued that it is impossible to be faithful to tradition in a contemporary postmodern landscape. It could also be argued that nobody even wants to be faithful to tradition anymore anyway; that history teaches us nothing and that advances in technology only serve to help us escape the crawling pace of our static past. Is it possible to reclaim premodern practices for a postmodern culture? Derrida famously states: 'I don't know ... I must believe ...' (Derrida, 1993, p. 155).

James K. A. Smith helps us out with a theory that it is possible to carry some of our postmodern 'unknowing' into this kind of mission field. Smith draws the distinction between 'knowing' and 'believing'. He understands that the postmodern theologian says, 'We can't *know* that God was in Christ reconciling the world to Himself; the best we can do is *believe*' (Smith, 2006, p. 119).

Is it still possible as a Christian to purport to *know* the truth in a postmodern culture? Claiming copyright over truth in such an expanding horizon can seem to be a challenging disposition to adopt these days. However, carrying something of a belief, faith or spiritual understanding into a new culture or community as gift often helps to spark dialogue and relationship in a society that says, 'This is my truth, tell me yours.'

This alternative, dreamlike quality of framing the gospel narrative within postmodern culture comes out of the practice of techniques whereby the individual is seduced away through the use of storytelling from the day-to-day business of consuming. Reframing history is a powerful postmodern 'sleight-of-hand' that results in producing unforeseen socio-political statements on contemporary culture. The results are often powerful, perhaps even disturbing, but they are compelling enough to break the illusion of the status quo and are entirely incarnational (Snyder, 2004).

In a ministry that practises the unearthing of spirituality, the pioneer missionary will be continually attempting to bring down boundaries. The process of 'unknowing' might help us to do this. The by-product of 'bringing down the walls' (Mart, online) is developing relationships with individuals in the community. Relationships within this context are vital and the missionary can expect to require skills in developing and maintaining ongoing friendships with individuals who emerge out of the missional practice. Relationships develop over time and are key to helping people up the Engel scale; however, it is vital that the missionary holds true to the sense of 'unknowing' in order for the spiritual seeker to develop their own faith.

This model of mission is firmly situated within the playgrounds of the 'emerging church' whose existence has been forged within the fault lines of a widespread cultural shift (Taylor, 2006). All pioneer mission initiatives are in the business of attempting to create communities of faith within cultures of change. This process takes time and requires a certain amount of developing theory 'on-the-hoof'. The pioneer must be able to hold open safe, clumsy, solution spaces within which discussion and exploration can take place. Such places might have no assets, hierarchy, ordained ministers, seminaries or bulletin boards. Indeed, these might be places where people are seen to be making it up as they go along (Caputo, 2007, p. 129).

The pioneer must be able to exist unsupported at times and maintain their own faith within this environment: the job description comes with the health warning that once they have engaged in this kind of missional activity, there is unlikely to be any real return to convention. God is in all things, deep within every molecule of creation. So there is nothing to fear!

References

Arbuckle, G. A., 1993, *Refounding the Church: Dissent for Leadership*, London: Geoffrey Chapman.

Baker, J., 2010, *Curating Worship*, London: SPCK.

Bevans, S. B. and Schroeder, R. P., 2011, *Prophetic Dialogue: Reflections on Christian Mission Today*, Maryknoll, NY: Orbis.

Brueggemann, W., 2001, *The Prophetic Imagination*, Minneapolis: Fortress Press.

Caputo, J., 2007, *What Would Jesus Deconstruct? The Good News of Post-Modernism for the Church*, Grand Rapids, NY: Baker.

Dark, D., 2002, *Everyday Apocalypse*, Grand Rapids, MI: Brazos Press.

Daws, M. and Mart, G., 2015, 'Here to Hold You' (Courtesy of the Artist, 2015), Martin Daws, Young Person's Poet Laureate for Wales (2015), https://soundcloud.com/gavinmart/here-to-hold?in=gavinmart/sets/gavin-mart-and-martin-daws-live (accessed 22 July 2015).

Derrida, J., 1993, *Memoires for the Blind*, trans. P.-A. Brault and M. Naas, Chicago: University of Chicago Press.

Donovan, V. J., 1989, *The Church in the Midst of Creation*, Maryknoll, NY: Orbis.

Engel, J., 2012, *The Engel Scale of Spiritual Decision*, http://www.internetevangelismday.com/gray-matrix.php (accessed 25 March 2015).

Grint, K., 2010, *Leadership: A Very Short Introduction*, Oxford: Oxford University Press.

Mart, G., 'Bring it Down' – mp3 (2015), https://gavinmart.bandcamp.com/album/bring-it-down (accessed 26 March 2015).

Mart, G., 'Persons Reported' – mp3 (2015), https://gavinmart.com/track/persons-reported-2 (accessed 26 March 2015).

Morisy, A., 2009, *Bothered and Bewildered: Enacting Hope in Troubled Times*, London: Bloomsbury.

Sampson, M., 2013, *Engedi Arts: Demonstrating our Impact*, A Transformational Index Analysis.

Sivalon, J. C., 2012, *God's Mission and Postmodern Culture: The Gift of Uncertainty*, New York: Orbis.

Smith, J. K. A., 2006, *Who's Afraid of Postmodernism? Taking Derrida, Lyotard, and Foucault to Church*, Grand Rapids, MI: Baker.

Smith, S., 2013, 'Raised in Leeds', http://www.proost.co.uk/raised-leeds-pdf (accessed 15 April 2015).

Snyder, S., 2004, *An Exchange: In Conversation with Sutapa Biswas*, UK: Institute of International Visual Arts.

Taylor, S., 2006, *The Out of Bounds Church: Learning to Create a Community of Faith in a Culture of Change*, Grand Rapids, MI: Zondervan.

Notes

1 Martin Daws and Gavin Mart, 'Here to Hold You'.

8

A Spirituality of Getting Dirty

JOHNNY SERTIN

Remembering and getting lost

This chapter flows from my own story, and the journey I have taken in arriving at a place I now call home in terms of reconciling the pursuit and sustainability of my Christian pilgrimage, a deep love and passion for creation and the mission of God.

I am an ordained pioneer minister in the Church of England in a local parish and my brief is to explore how to pioneer mission within this location. We arrived in London several years ago having left coastal Dorset and a movement we had been part of there since the mid 1990s, which had been at the forefront of exploring mission in youth culture and subsequently, by default, pioneering the emerging church culture that began to have a voice in the late 1990s and early in the new millennium. Though I wouldn't have said it like this at the time, the foundational aspect of our mission was that it was contextual. We didn't know it then but we were sitting on the precipice of a cultural landslide that was beginning to rumble. I took up my post at a local parish church in Dorset as the newly appointed youth worker, fresh from three years working overseas with an organization that carried a strong imprimatur of mission especially to young people. I had trained and worked with this group and was now keen to explore how missiology and cross-cultural principles could be rooted in a local environment within British society.

As is often the case as a culture begins to shift and turn towards new ideas, this was being vibrantly expressed in the arts and music at that time. So I dived into this context to see how I could embody and share the radicalizing message of Jesus. It was a fruit-ful period and I unearthed a rich seam of God's presence and grace in that place that led to a wonderful season of development.

As our tribe began to grow and change we found an increasing number migrating to the nearby urban landscape. Our vicar, who was a fine man, realized we needed help so he came up with an ingenious idea of sending us out as missionaries.

At the height of all this drama I felt increasingly uncomfortable with my own spirituality and ecclesiology as it related to mission. While seeing wonderful signs of awakening in the lives of many people, we were trapped in a cookie-cutter model of formation. Transplanting disciples didn't work. The church struggled to see the long game in all of this; it failed to recognize we were becom-ing guilty of the Sauline gaffe of trying to dress up young people in suits that did not fit them to face the Goliaths of their day. But a door had been opened to inculcate cross-cultural mission into western theology and practice through the massive sea change taking place in culture and it could not be closed up again!

I realized this road was also personal. The spiritual practices I had kicked against as a boy and reaffirmed as a young adult when my own life was reawakened by the Spirit were now cascading downhill at a pace. I could not, nor would I, be put back in the box I had so wonderfully burst out of in discovering traces of God beyond the walls of historical ecclesial culture.

Hard lessons

So cutting a long story short, I went back to exploring locally what I called at that time 'seeing if God was still God in the outposts of everyday life and culture'. To do this I launched myself into a new start-up enterprise. Along with a friend I began running a late-night venue. My rationale was to ask the question, 'Could God be found in the Saturday night worship of clubland, seem-ingly the polar opposite to the environment of Sunday worship and church land?' The quick answer was yes, God can be found on Saturday, and yes, there is light and life in said environment, as well as murky waters and blurred edges. However, what I hadn't anticipated was not so much God being found but my own life being found out. With all the travelling and platforms I had been on, with all the 'success' of what we'd been up to, I had lost my own compass and my roots were starting to fray; they were certainly not deep enough to anchor me and sustain my journey. I went into a wilderness, but while I can see now that the Spirit led me there, I went kicking and screaming! My business was not the wildly successful cutting-edge enterprise I had imagined. I learnt some hard lessons about myself, about friendship, and about faith. Some dear friends continued to walk with me through all of this and guided me towards the future and deeper waters. I realized that I needed something altogether different in the practice and ritual of my pilgrimage.

If I was going to make my home in the context of the world, I needed to know which way north was in the midst of all this. So with the help of a wise friend who had made his own path towards a deeper life, I began to look back on the monastic traditions and see what could be found. I began to explore the contemplative road of silence and solitude, to explore sacramental ministry, and to look for a stronger cord of community practice and ritual. This pilgrimage saved my life. It was frustrating, lonely and disempowering, but in the end it was a fertile space in which I eventually blossomed.

A critical question arose for me in all this around how to reconcile the being and the doing of faith. While I enjoyed the story and traditions of the monastic orders I found that the practices associated with them did not translate into my context, nor did I see much mission taking place. Many peers from this era were retreating into the contemplative and monastic traditions, or becoming atheists! I had burnt too many bridges to have faith in unfaith, but neither did I feel at home practising rituals that felt part of history. This would simply be an alternative or parallel universe as opposed to my continuing quest to coexist with God in Christ in the everyday. I did not like this binary life of retreat on Sunday and engage on Monday, to caricature the process. I was keen to find what one friend termed 'an ancient future' faith.

Reimagining and mission spirituality

So we arrive at the more recent chapter of my life, living in London. My wife and I travelled here to explore afresh what mission and spiritual formation could be like hand in hand and not as polar opposites. After nearly ten years of living here we have been through various valleys and sat on the top of a few summits as well. We have had to let go of the Christ we knew to discover the Christ we didn't, and in so doing have found a path that has led us to a place we now call home, and the sign on the door says 'welcome'.

The underlying problem we all face is how to bring together action as in mission and contemplation as formation, 'doing' and 'being'. We have tended to frame mission as engaging the world and spirituality as retreat from the world. The problem with this is that it reinforces the separation between 'doing' and 'being'. This can lead to deep fractures within our lives. My story has been one that brings together the personal and the social, one that reconciles 'being' and 'doing' – in our current cultural context. I now call this mission spirituality.

There have been two reconciliations that have been instrumental to my formation and living a missonal life: reconciliation in becoming fully human in body, mind and spirit, and reconciliation between the secular and profane.

When ordination finally found me, further down the road through the pioneer pathway, I jumped into the learning with relish. One book I was fascinated to read was by Rebecca Nye on children's spirituality (Nye, 2009). What, you might ask, has this got to do with anything regarding mission spirituality? Well, she speaks of the essential gifts we inherit in childhood. My abbreviated version frames them around the acronym WEPIC, a homemade word that stands for wonder, explore, play, imagine and create. I was reminded that for the first 11 years of my life we could walk out of our front gate and wander straight onto the grassy expanses of common ground that stretched for miles with untamed terrain and forest enclosures. For me this was an oasis of fun and I played endless games and make-believe activities. On

reading her book I realized that much of these essential characteristics had somehow dissolved from my adult life, especially in my
spirituality. Everything still felt very regimented, much like the
boarding school I had subsequently moved to, with a strong cere-
bral approach to faith through reading Scripture and Bible notes,
and, well, reading anything actually. Our capacity to know God
came from this rather modern concept of knowing by understanding and controlling not knowing through encounter and ritual. I
sensed a kind of refounding taking place in me. I believe in reason
and knowledge, and teaching literacy, problem-solving, numer-
acy and other essential elements that sit at the top of education's
hierarchy. It's just that I'm not sure we were supposed to throw
away our gifts of childhood and the pedagogy of place, learning
through creativity, making and the outdoors. I had been formed
to believe my body was a vehicle to transport my mind around.
It would never have crossed my mind to say, I am a body. What
began for me was a reconciling of a perceived image of myself to
my real or true self, and a journey to become fully human and fully
present in the world around me. I realize now that God could not
find me because I was lost to myself, sterilized by a commodified
experience of my beliefs that couldn't unfurl. I was not at home
in my own skin, so how on earth could God make her home there
and how on earth could heaven come on earth through my life?

In saying all this it is important also to speak of the other
reconciling factor that was taking place: place being the operative
word. I grew up in a binary world of opposites, so when it came
to spirituality there was secular space and sacred space, as well as
spiritual and material. It was only the discovery of a sacramental
theology that reconciled this for me. A sacrament is an outward
and visible sign of an inward, invisible grace. All of creation can
thus be a sign of grace. Sadly, within the Catholic tradition this
wonderful theology is reduced to seven main sacraments within
the life of the Church. Vincent Donovan, when describing the
sacraments to the Masai, was bemused to see in their faces confusion and dissatisfaction in his teachings, until one elder spoke
up (Donovan, 2001). They were confused because they had imagined there would be 7,000, not seven!

So what am I saying? Well, first of all, the world really is your oyster; in other words, there are pearls of God's wonder and presence to be shucked from inside creation's shell. We can find or unearth God hidden in the material and secular world. Whenever the material and the spiritual coincide, there is the Christ. Jesus accepted that full identity and walked it into history. He was fully human and fully divine at the same time. So now we can begin to imagine how they could coexist. The material and the spiritual are one, the human and the divine are for ever, the physical plumbed to its depth finds transcendence. The hiding place of God is also the place of revelation – here and now and everywhere. The gift we are given to unearth God's immanence lies in our childhood legacy that gifts us with eyes to see in full dimension.

This idea of God hidden yet revealed loops us back to the question of reconciling being and doing. We no longer need to simply walk backwards to retreat into prayer and march forwards to engage in mission. God is to be found in all creation. As we consider Jesus' own words that we need to become like little children to enter or receive the kingdom of heaven, we can refound our lives on the foundations of this childhood treasure, exploring with an adventurous heart, finding God in the mystery of the woods or the wonder of a museum, up a tree or at the top of a skyscraper, or diving into muddy waters. We can play out our life with God in full motion and with a full multisensory way of knowing that our mind is only part of what it means to be human and a playful heart is medicine to our well-being. We can imagine and create with our hands and hearts to be formed in doing, and in doing we are being.

So we are reconciled, at home in ourselves as we discover Christ in us, and at home in the world as we discover Christ in all creation – a sort of symbiotic life that ecologically works together for creation's healing as we begin to unfurl and step into the space around us with eyes to see.

Reclaiming and getting dirty

On 25 August 2006 my family and a friend moved into a house in Earlsfield, south London. We began to explore mission through sharing a common life together. Guided by a dear Roman Catholic friend with strong ties to Francis, we created four mutual pillars to life in the city: mutual mission, mutual Christ, mutual rhythm and mutual support. We were strangers in the neighbourhood and quickly felt a lack of welcome in the compulsive, hurried nature of a city whose inhabitants are either disinterested in their neighbours or too busy to care. We had made the decision at the time not simply to embed into an existing lively church, as we didn't want to become subsumed by a church culture particularly if it wasn't thinking about its own context. What started as an extended household evolved over the next three years into a group of families, and eventually after five years became the Earlsfield Friary, consisting of a cluster of working households living intentionally within a square mile of one another.

From the beginning we wanted to ensure that we moved from being guests to being fellows to being hosts in our neighbourhood. We knew that this would take time, and being committed to our local place was important. A trend we saw was how the city utilized resources without giving or investing in return. Even belief was commodified, having little interest in the locality and a very transient consumer approach to living. This created a lack of heart to the neighbourhood, or what sometimes is called a dormitory town culture: sleeping at home but living the rest of your life elsewhere. So we attempted to support local economies, communities, churches, amenities and facilities.

To do this we looked at John's Gospel in *The Message* translation. 'The Word became flesh and moved into the neighborhood' (John 1.14). We came to see how important the issue of place is in discovering God and bringing a vibrant spirituality to our lives. Place really does matter.

Walter Brueggemann said that human identity in society has been lost through the erosion of place and the up tide of meaningfulness as the definition of what matters. He suggests that we lose community, identity and meaning when we cease to value the importance of roots.

> That promise concerned human persons who could lead detached, uprooted lives of endless choice and no commitment. It was glamorized around the virtues of mobility and anonymity that seemed so full of promise for freedom and self-actualization. But it has failed ... It is now clear that a sense of place is a human hunger that urban promise has not met ... It is rootlessness and not meaninglessness that characterizes the current crisis. There are no meanings apart from roots. (Brueggemann, 2002, pp. 3–4)

This particularly links with the idea of local. Place is storied space, or the context in which we live out our lives. It is understandable that people may at a certain stage of life worship somewhere they don't live, but in the most part I believe that we lose so much of what we could see of God in the present because we hold no relationship or care to the place in which we live. This creates an erosion of identity and community in a locality.

We began to explore what the context of our place was all about and in so doing allowed this to shape how we walked faithfully with God, and equally, turning to face out, how we collaborated in what God was doing locally and translocally. To us place is made up of three interweaving stories: God's story, the story of the land, and finally the story of the people.

As we explored the history of the land we discovered a strong farming narrative in Earlsfield that existed before the mainline extended out of central London. The name Earslfield derives from the maiden name of the last lord of the manor's wife before the sale of his estate to Wandsworth council, and is also apt in that the place was made up of fields as recently as the 1950s. In particular we learnt that pig farming was a strong local economy, as well as orchards of native British fruit such as the Merton apple.

Within the story of the indigenous people and subsequent migratory groups, we also discovered that there had been a strong crafts and bazaar culture that stimulated the economy in the past.

Artistically there was a long-established local arts theatre that continues to flourish in the heart of the neighbourhood. In terms of food there used to be a vibrant marketplace, with multiple grocers, butchers and fishmongers 50 years ago, now no longer in existence. A number of great restaurants and food outlets have come and gone over the years too. It also has a reputation as a pioneer of firsts – for example, the first ever cinema was situated in Earlsfield.

The Church has been a major force in the neighbourhood over the years as well, reflecting what God has been doing. There was a strong emphasis on contextual evangelism, from early mission roots in the 1900s to the Pentecostal traditions of the newly arrived Afro-Caribbeans in the 1950s. In the 1960s the Church of England Diocese of Southwark was flourishing, capturing a trend known as 'Southbank religion'. From liberal Catholic roots the Southbank protagonists were exploring radical theology, the arts and inclusivity. More widely and further back in time, this area had a strong connection to monasticism, being a place of learning and hospitality since the establishment of Merton Priory in 1134.

So with all this recent and ancient history we were encouraged to refound the story of this place, reimagining her future life and reclaiming God's story of faith, hope and charity in this context. There have been key steps in the journey towards understanding this.

The practice of digging

We became increasingly conscious of how urban life disconnects itself from the land it is living on and as such the land becomes dismembered from a communal identity and loses her memory. So we began by finding waste spaces and farming them. This was a tactic that had been used in regenerating waste space and community identity in Detroit and we thought it was a great idea to mirror. It had become known as guerrilla farming. One primary space we became involved with was owned by the local parish. We cleared, rotivated and planted this space and over time it became a little oasis right on our High Street. From this we collaborated with a friend with hosting a beehive; this led to replanting a fruit orchard in four public spaces in the area. Finally, when we found the space to keep livestock, pigs were reintroduced to the neighbourhood!

Digging is an important principle of formation. As we unearth a fuller picture of being human we do not distinguish explicitly between where mission and prayer begin and end, or what is being and what is doing. We see both in a more joined-up way.

The biography of Peter is a great example of this. As we scroll through the Gospels we see that he had a very practical way of journeying with Jesus. Many times he was invited to feed the hungry and collect baskets, eat with strangers, navigate the boat across Galilee, fish to pay his way, or source a donkey! Peter had to learn to be from his doing. For most of us this is probably true too, but we divorce our being and our doing from each other. We lean more towards getting busy digging without listening. Peter was a digger who learnt to listen. It took him a while! Remember his lack of listening right after he reveals Jesus as the Christ and then immediately objects to Jesus explaining what this means? How often do we think we know something about God when what God is saying is not what we are hearing or not hearing! When Peter did listen, the world entirely opened up to him. Try listening and digging, you'll find another dimension to yourself and to the world. It is the synergy of digging and listening that allows us to journey and express Christ more faithfully.

The practice of listening

Brian McLaren writes in his book *Naked Spirituality*:

Could it be that the joy we pursue in life – whether the joy of playing an instrument or playing a sport, of chipping a sculpture from stone or building a business from the ground up – is the joy of knowing that there is silence, a void, a space that waits for us to fill it? And could it be that God the creator of both that void and us is the Witness, the audience, the Listener for whom we are always performing? ... In the stillness, you know there is a listener, a Witness, holding you in loving attention. You know that what you are doing has value even if there are no visible results because the Witness has witnessed it. (McLaren, 2011, pp. 277–8)

What McLaren is pointing towards is the concept that there is something more to both mission and the contemplative that occurs in humanity's relationship to the Divine and vice versa, in mutual listening. The 'magic' of God's Spirit unfolds in the creativity that arises from the void, between and betwixt this mutual listening. As 'we listen to the Listening and witness to the Witness' we curate space from the void of what we hear or glimpse in our listening. God listens too, and as First Witness responds in these acts much like an audience might at the theatre. All creation, including us, becomes present to the First Witness or Listener, and we 'see' more clearly even as we are now 'seen'. It's a reciprocal, mutual, beholding and becoming, a drama of sorts performed with space for a creative resonance born out of the void of silence and solitude, a co-creation.

The practice of co-creating

From digging and listening the opportunity emerges to imagine space differently, to reclaim the story of a place and to participate in this through what we do creatively and enterprisingly: co-creating. Here are some of the key creations to emerge in our story.

Paradise Cooperative – urban farming

Eventually the farming work grew too big for the friary to manage alone so we funded a charity interest organization called the Paradise Cooperative, made up of local people committed to their local place and focused on farming, food and community regeneration. This is a growing voice in our neighbourhood that discusses consumption, economics, environmentalism, community ethics, and spirituality.

Home – a boutique café for a local economy

We are in the process of establishing a small business enterprise that takes the form of a boutique café, using some church space on the High Street and repurposing it to offer a space for further touch points to grow community spirit and nurturing and evoking people's spirituality.

Curating liturgy in public spaces

Out of the silence and listening we discovered a way to reflect our journey personally and also to share this in public spaces with others. Four times in the year we host a week-long art installation in a part of Earlsfield, sometimes indoors, sometimes outdoors. We curate a late-night gathering on the final evening through which we invite space for reflection, encounter and change. It acts as a means both to rediscover home ourselves and to share an open home with others.

We have found liturgy to be a helpful courier of the gospel story, which acts as a womb for co-creating. At the end of this chapter is a written piece on Advent for the street from one such event. Rod Pattenden has the lovely idea that liturgy is a 'cartography of grace' that places our lives within the dimension of God's presence in the world (Pattenden, 2012, pp. 85–6). So we have explored and expressed liturgy 'in the land' as opposed to solely 'in the Church'. If mission's richest life is in mutual listening, and worship is our pouring out of this listening from the void, why confine this to Sunday practices? Why not simply continue to explore this and the creative reverberations that emerge without the need to rewire it back to a congregational paradigm?

Hospitality and care for the margins

We have spent much time growing food for our local foodbank, making meals for homeless people we meet sleeping in the community gardens and hosting street feasts and pop-up markets for locals. Possibly the most uplifting experiences we have shared through food have been cookery classes for teenage asylum-seekers who live locally, and supporting a Romany gypsy family whom we met selling the *Big Issue*. Meaningful relationships have been formed; we have welcomed them into our homes and joined together in our high seasons to share life and break bread.

Pop-up installations

We are fascinated by how space can be created in which and through which we can hint towards a better way of living, advocate for injustice, offer reconciliation, or be hope to a place. Examples include the setting up of barter stalls and swap shops, food and craft markets, a shed put up to be a quiet zone in the city, and a feast called 'wonder in a field'.

All these represent a maturing of community life, and reflect our distinct spirituality, which has emerged from living in this place and exploring faith and life from this vantage point, unfurling together.

A community rhythm

This rediscovery of place has been a major catalyst in shaping our spirituality. Several key aspects of our community practice emerged from this exploration of adopting a way of life in the city. We have adopted three high seasons in the year, while in ordinary times we have a basic rhythm that we call low time.

During low time we meet weekly for a session of devotion, reflection and conversation. This is the cornerstone of our pattern together. It's by no means the only time we see one another in the week. We made the decision to live in proximity to one another, so we find each other organically in the ritual of family life, school drop and pick up, clubs, local amenities, cafés, and so on. It is rare indeed to go through the day and not connect with someone somewhere! Wednesday nights simply act as a touch point intentionally.

Every month we host a feast in celebration of a particular occasion. This happens in and out of high season. For example, just before Lent we have 'The Feast of Dreams' celebrating Epiphany. We use this time in the new year to reflect and ask questions such as 'How is your dreaming? What are you doing to make your dreams come true? How can we celebrate and how can we help?' Then, soon after Lent and Easter we have the 'Feast of the Soul', celebrated over a weekend away. We might ask, 'How is your soul? What is going on in you? How can we help and celebrate?' So there is a particular pattern and focus that takes place around the feast, and the feast is a point in this to reflect and pause and celebrate. They are lavish, generous, thoughtful and tasty!

Once a month we share a Sabbath day together. We host a family gathering for our local Anglican church, then spend the rest of the day eating, walking, playing and resting in each other's company.

Every year we try and leave the city three or four times. We go away and retreat, share, eat, laugh, sing and reflect. These times are good for the soul and for one another. It has been our experience that having a rhythm that also includes not being in your local place gives life and perspective, and helps to recharge.

Our three high seasons of the year are grown around the church calendar – Advent, Lent and Pentecost. The first two are standard, but we felt we needed a third for the extended period of ordinary time in the summer. So we have adopted the 40 days just after Pentecost as a focus for the third cycle of our year. These high seasons keep the backbone of low season in meeting each week, sharing a Sabbath day, feasting and journeying out of the city. The difference is that this is now more focused around the season we are in. So in Advent we focus on waiting and solidarity with the poor in a season of consumption; in Lent we focus on letting go and hospitality to the stranger; and in Pentecost we focus on reaching out and being part of a global Christ.

In each high season we have a daily devotional reading. Some read this on the train to work, others after the school drop, and others later still when the mania of children has died down in the evening.

During these three seasons we host an art installation for a week and curate a gathering at the end, inviting the local community to come and join with us on reflecting and encountering together.

We have adventure days: epic, organized times where we all take off together and do something a bit more feral and off the grid. We are in the process of planning a wild camping trip over Pentecost, including going sea fishing and foraging for food from the land and sea for the weekend!

We have specific learning and sharing space for the children. We have ten children between us, and while we don't believe in sub-contracting their development to someone else we do value times in the year where they get to engage with others and explore their faith creatively, using symbols and metaphors to aid their imagination. On Good Friday, for example, all the children helped to make Easter gardens and to read and reflect together on a story mat what Good Friday is all about.

We go to seasonal activities together. Most of these are local and in going we are saying that we are part of something bigger than ourselves.

As part of a holistic approach to our formation we make and do stuff together. Sometimes it's making wreaths from materials we have foraged, or decorating Christmas trees we have sourced and harvested; or it might be working with the pigs we rear and then butcher together, or cooking food for a feast like the Easter rising. We are passionate about engaging the physical and material elements of our life in God.

Creation healed

The critical underpinning on which all this hangs is God reconciling all things to himself in Christ and through Christ, creation being healed. When Presence transfigures a space that is formed (or curated), a magic occurs that has a 'living' actuality to it. This 'living' quality has three constituents to it:

- An awakening to the wonder and magic of the Divine in and about us.
- A prophetic charism to care for ourselves, others and the world around.
- A common vocation to continually renew and transform all creation.

Each of these plays a role in our understanding of reconciliation and the transformative power of such a missional Presence to deeply render change within space and time. As such this theatre should be played out not in the confines of one domain, but in the fullness of the land in which, and through which, the story of the place and the people is held. This story, wrapped in the gospel story, is what we wish to participate in, rediscover and redeem.

So we listen, and from our listening we dig for treasure found in the history and story of a place. As we unearth these pearls we start to curate space from the darkness of the void, offering these places to the Listener or witnessing to the Witness, in the land, in a place and in the people. Through an invocation of the gospel story in the context of the narrative of our place we seek renewal through personal awakening, gifts of prophetic witness and healing. Such listening, and the reverberations, begin to reclaim the story of a missional God who is forever wooing us home and making home among us.

An Advent Poem for the Street

We remember

In this space of gentle darkness under starry night, where fused lights glimmer in the shadows of our gathering, revealing faces glimpsing shared recognition and memories of home …

We remember the stable that unstabled the world.

In this space of uncertainty and apprehension where society too glimpses for who she is in the eternity of waiting some 2,000 added years …

We remember a virgin girl who risked shame to deliver redemption's song.

In this space of deep longing to be found and to be known where fairy lights and tinsel veneer flatter to deceive our anxiety for belonging and the refugee aches in her displacement …

We remember a saviour born in another land from his own and the filth of social squalor.

In this time where we gauge relationship by the status of haves and have nots, where the highest place is measured by a ladder ascending to keep up with the Joneses we do not even know …

We remember the holy other, who did not measure equality by income, affluence, race, power or birth, but by the common bond of humanity called together to care for one another and for this land.

In this space of consumption where stocks are not shared, where capital has more followers than magic and heart is failing …

We remember wise men who risked Herod's fury, who came with gifts, kneeling in the obscurity of a stable, and hedged their bets on a baby boy who showed us that sacred is found in the mundane of dirt and grime, in the joy of love's embrace and woven knot of life together, not in ivory tower.

In this space of comings and goings, where upwardly mobile is a rite of passage and lost people hurry like busy worker ants on the treadmill of insanity …

We remember a way embedded in myth and story, which whispers to the weary, 'Come, this space is for you and the sign on the door will forever say welcome.'

We remember. We wait and remember.

References

Brueggemann, W., 2002, *The Land: Place as Gift, Promise and Challenge in Biblical Faith*, London: SPCK.

Donovan, V., 2001, *Christianity Rediscovered*, London: SCM Press.

McLaren, B., 2011, *Naked Spirituality: A Life with God in Twelve Simple Words*, New York: HarperCollins.

Nye, R., 2009, *Children's Spirituality: What It is and Why It Matters*, London: Church House Publishing.

Pattenden, R., 2012, 'Eyes Wide Open: Seeing God in an Age of Visuality', in S. Burns (ed.), *The Art of Tent Making: Making Space for Worship*, Norwich: Canterbury Press.

9

Ritual as a Tool for Hands-on Spirituality: Experiments in Discipleship with Young People

JOHN WHEATLEY AND JAMES HENLEY

Young people have generally disengaged with the Church. The book *The Faith of Generation Y* outlines the evidence of the Church's diminishing influence in the lives of young people (Collins-Mayo et al., 2010), and the resulting expression of faith:

> the everyday faith of the majority of young people tends not to be of a religious nature at all … For the most part, family, friends and self are the central axes of meaning, hope and purpose which enables young people to get on with the business of daily living. (Collins-Mayo et al., 2010, p. 84)

Indeed, young people favour the immediate experience, and the spirituality inherent in this space. This context has meant that the means and methods of the Church are out of touch with the ways and cultures of young people in the UK today.

Through our work with young people living on housing estates in areas of poverty we have learned that many of them are culturally unable to relate to the offerings of the Church. At a practical level, many of the young people we know have a limited attention span, their literacy skills can be low, and formal education is generally a negative experience. Traditional forms of discipleship and Bible study do not lend themselves to this context, often because they mirror the school environment and demand prolonged reflective exercises.

Take, for example, Adam (not his real name). We met Adam at the age of 14, just as he started his GCSEs. Now 16, he is friendly, kind, generous and warm, but he is also very chaotic, angry and disenchanted with the world. His aspirations are low, and his attendance in education is sporadic. He has a part-time job in a pub, for which he is always late. Home life is a challenge, and many of his close relationships are fractured. Adam finds reading difficult, which excludes him from lots of everyday activities. On occasion, when things aren't going well, Adam has been involved in fights, and has been in trouble for vandalizing local property. Discipleship for Adam, and many other young people, needs to be active, accessible, and grounded in the reality of the day-to-day for it to have any sense of meaning.

Inherited church has traditionally offered young people a model of vernacular reflection through study groups: drawing on a text or metaphor to initiate deeper learning through discussion. This is intended to lead to deeper self-reflection and a subsequent change of behaviour. Discipleship is taught in the form of doctrine, which in turn is expressed in practice. This model may have its merits for the educated, churched minority, but it is not reflective of the learning styles or inherent spirituality of young people on the street.

Drawing on our shared experience, we have sought to respond to the new landscape in practical ways. In this chapter you will find a brief introduction to rituals as a culture- and spirituality-shaping activity; and a collection of case studies of our work so far exploring hands-on spirituality through everyday rituals.

Resistance through rituals

Resistance Through Rituals is an anthology on youth culture in post-war Britain (Hall and Jefferson, 2006). Its title is an intriguing summary of its main thesis: that the everyday rituals and habits of living define and perpetuate cultures that resist and separate young people from the mainstream. In chapter 1, Clarke et al. write:

We understand the word 'culture' to refer to that level at which social groups develop distinct patterns of life, and give expressive form to their social and material life-experience. Culture is the way ... in which groups 'handle' the raw material of their social and material existence. (Clarke et al., 2006, p. 4)

In working with young people we must first understand the deep significance of cultures in shaping and revealing their inner and outer lives. A culture, according to Clarke et al. (2006, p. 4), 'includes the maps of meaning which make things intelligible to its members'. As youth workers and pioneers we must first navigate these 'maps' before we can even begin to comprehend how the gospel may relate. The challenge is not to resist or replace the culture that young people are living, but to participate and incarnate within the rituals that embody it.

Douglas J. Davies (2012, p. 203) describes ritual as 'a pattern of shared behaviour, repeated at appropriate times and places, that expresses some core convictions of a group'. Davies asserts that these rituals can often be subconscious, with highly individualized and emotive meanings attached to them. He writes: 'Sometimes, then, we are aware of taking part in "a ritual" even though we may not be able to spell out all its potential significance, at other times we do things without even thinking of them as ritual performances' (2012, p. 203). It is this ethereal quality that leaves scholars hugely divided on the definition of what rituals actually are, given that it is very difficult to quantify scientifically what actually makes up a ritual. Ritual Studies professor Ronald L. Grimes (2013, pp. 185–9) agrees with Davies' assessment, but goes on to suggest that, even if they overlap and interweave, it is possible to at least identify some elements that make up the nature of most rituals: (1) actions, (2) actors, (3) places, (4) times, (5) objects, (6) languages, and (7) groups (2013, p. 235).

Gerald Arbuckle (2010, pp. 81–98) goes further, suggesting that we can understand culture itself as a process of 'ritualizing life', where shared rituals are developed as a way of ordering life, creating shared meaning and identity. He observes: 'Ordering rituals are "defences against anxieties" through which we seek, establish and preserve or celebrate order and unity for ourselves and society' (2010, p. 84). However, Arbuckle also asserts that rituals can be transformational in their nature, writing that 'Ritual does at times express and reinforce the existing order, but its primary purpose is ultimately to foster transformative individual and cultural change' (2010, p. 83). These rituals are transformative where they challenge the status quo, and create or propagate a new reality within the culture itself. Perhaps this transformative, or prophetic, function holds the most potential for understanding the possible role of ritual in exploring and shaping spirituality.

Experimenting with hands-on spirituality

The landscape has changed, and the toolbox of resources for working with young people in a faith context needs updating for modern times. Building on our understanding of culture and rituals, we set out to develop a tool that would enable young people to engage with an active, lived-out spirituality, and that would build on the raw material of a social and material existence.

Our aim was to create a process that reversed the traditional model, better reflecting the ways in which young people learn; contributing and participating within the 'map of meaning' of their lives. We wanted to flip the inherited model of discipleship, which starts with an idea and then through discussion leads to action. We wanted young people to have real experiences, which would lead to conclusions and reflections, providing potential for meaning-making. Young people understand the world through the experiences that they have, and opening up spirituality needs to take the same approach.

We drew on the general wisdom of learning cycles (Nash and Nash, 2009, p. 8) to build on these four stages of learning: (1) having an experience, (2) reviewing the experience, (3) concluding the experience, and (4) planning the next step. This form of experiential learning is a model of education developed by theorists like

Kolb, Lewin, Dewey and Piaget, and is nothing new. However, its application to developing spirituality is rarely explored. Contrary to this learning cycle, many Christian discipleship resources start the learner with a reflective exercise, not based in concrete experience. We set out to create a process that would ritualize the biblical text – a resource that would invite young people into mini-rituals that would contribute to their developing map of meaning. *The Experiments* (Frontier Youth Trust, 2013) is our attempt at bridging this gap.

The Experiments is a resource to engage young people in contextual and hands-on theological reflection; it is designed for young people on the edge of both Church and society. We've made it easy to access, and it requires no experience or understanding of the Christian tradition to participate. The resource offers the raw biblical text in an accessible format, exploring and embedding it through a practical spirituality. Based on the action-learning cycle above, it starts with a set of experiments that can be tried out by the group in their own time. The stories and experiences of trying these experiments are used as the raw data for learning and discipleship. As a hands-on resource, *The Experiments* requires little reading or writing for participants. Instead each participant is given a set of cards each showing the trigger text and relevant experiments. Sessions begin with sharing stories from the previous week's *experiments* (see Figure 3). The *share* questions encourage discussion about the experiments. The following *reflect* activities are designed to unpack the text and build on the experiences from the week. The whole process is designed to be completed in 15 minutes, ideal for groups with short attention spans, and is very hands-on. We have created a *collect* process to identify learning, and help build towards a wider set of rituals that embed spiritual practices into the immediacy of everyday living.

We built the resource around Matthew 5.1–10, translating the text into contemporary language with a working group of theologically literate youth workers and young people. Concepts and biblical language were crafted into simple phrases using everyday language that would accurately capture the original essence for the prevailing youth culture. For example, Matthew 5.5, 'Blessed are the meek', became 'God is with those who choose to control their strength'. For this text, we invited young people to participate in one of the following five experiments:

- Spend the whole week without getting angry or raising your voice.
- Compliment someone you are jealous of, either in person or on Facebook.
- Let someone else have their way in an argument.
- Spend ten minutes each day standing in silence.
- Do something kind for someone else that you wouldn't normally do.

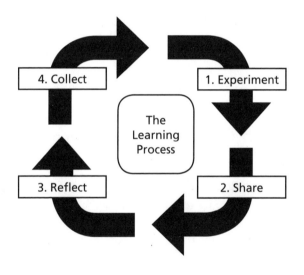

Figure 3

The intention is that these experiments tap into the spirituality and learning hidden within the text. As groups discuss, reflect and engage with their experiences, new learning will be uncovered and spirituality embedded. The experiment acts as a mini-ritual to bring concrete experience into the culture- and spirituality-shaping exercise.

One youth worker gave the following feedback:

It is going really well, and all of the young people have been heavily engaging in the activities. The make-up of my group is mostly boys and a few girls, mostly agnostic, a few church-goers, and a few atheists. What I'm finding is that the guys that are heavily engaging are encouraging the others to get more involved and are often doing 2 or 3, and sometimes 4 of the activities during the week. Something really cool happened last week. It asked the experimenter to let somebody win in an argument. An atheist who didn't really get the point of that asked, 'What if they're wrong?' and we started to get to the root of some of her feelings. She was adamant that people needed to be corrected if they were wrong, but we talked about winning the argument, but losing a friend. The following meeting we talked a bit more, and her views had completely softened.

The aim of our resource was not to produce a new programme for youth workers to run, but to begin to change the spirituality conversation. For too long, spirituality, personal faith and prayer have been portrayed as quiet, still and internally reflective disciplines. It is a classic critique of young people by the Church to say that the young do not spend enough time in contemplation, in silence, or being still. That is not to say that at one level this is not the case, but to recognize that the Christian faith can be expressed in many ways across the diverse spectrum of human activity. We have inherited a way of thinking about spirituality that is dualistic. Spiritual activity has become limited to lighting a candle, sitting in silence, walking in nature, reading a prayer, writing a poem, contemplating an idea, and so on. Why do we invest meaning in these activities, but not in the hustle and bustle of everyday living? The time has come for spirituality to be liberated.

Ian Adams (2010, p. 36) reflects:

It's interesting how often in the Gospels the better-world-now for which we all yearn (the one that Jesus spoke of as 'the kingdom of God come near') often takes place in the uncontrollable environment that is the open space, the street or the market place. The road is full of surprise and a place, if we are open to it, of learning.

If we desire to gift young people with the richness of the Christian tradition, we must find ways of connecting with the God of the everyday. Spirituality needs to become more active and engaged, and more immersed in the immediate activity of day-to-day living. It is no longer possible to divert young people into the old ways of spirituality; indeed, they have already found their own out there on the street.

Our hope with *The Experiments* is not just that young people engage with the resource, but that we enable those working with young people to navigate ways into the everyday rituals and cultures of young people on the margins. The rituals of resistance, which symbolize the things young people hold most dear, might unlock a deeper layer of spirituality.

Rituals that shape spirituality

In his *Cultural Liturgies* series of books, the theologian/philosopher James K. A. Smith (2009, p. 39) attempts to 'rethink the relationship between worship and worldview by thinking about the connection between liturgy, learning and formation'. In doing this, he begins to draw his own conclusions about the role of ritual in shaping spirituality and discipleship. His central thesis is that humans are 'liturgical animals' (2009, p. 40), whose behaviour is not actually primarily shaped and formed by thinking, but by the repetitive acting out of habitual activity. These 'habits are inscribed in our heart through bodily practices and rituals that train the heart, as it were, to desire certain ends. This is a non-cognitive sort of training, a kind of education that is shaping us often without our realization' (2009, p. 58).

Smith goes on to suggest that these habits operate on different levels, some being mundane and routine, others more exceptional, based on the level of meaning that they invoke. He writes that, 'Some habits are very *thin*, or mundane', and therefore 'aren't the sort of things that tend to touch on our identity' (2009, p. 82).

For instance, Smith suggests that most people hopefully brush their teeth every day, but it would be highly unusual for someone to think of themselves 'first and foremost as a tooth brusher'. However, other habits are 'thick, or meaning-full' and 'play a significant role in shaping our identity'. For Smith, 'Engaging in these habit-forming practices not only says something about us, but also keeps shaping us into that kind of person.' Smith goes on to assert that these thick habits could be described as liturgies, even going so far as to suggest that 'some so-called secular rituals actually constitute liturgies' (2009, p. 86), in the sense that they can express, form and re-form identity.

This conceptual framework, which Smith has formed, enables us to begin to think about the role of worship or liturgy in mission in new ways. From our discussion so far there seems to be an accepted unspoken assumption that the arena for worship is primarily, if not exclusively, the internal life of the Church. However, Smith begins to suggest that worship and liturgy regularly take place not just in religious but also in secular spheres of culture, and that there is significant overlap between the two.

Bevans and Schroeder (2004, pp. 362–6) also appear to affirm the established, dualistic understanding of the relationship between liturgy and mission, affirming that 'Christian liturgy on the "inside" empowers and equips the Christian for mission on the "outside"' (2004, p. 363). However, they begin to hint at the missionary potential that liturgy may have, writing that 'liturgy needs always to be done with a missionary intent, recognizing that the word proclaimed, the meal shared, the vocation being celebrated, the reconciliation being offered are moments of evangelization – for the evangelized and unevangelized in the congregation alike' (2004, p. 362).

Perhaps, then, rituals, in the form of cultural liturgies, could be utilized and explored as a tool for mission and evangelization among young people, by enabling the formation of identity and therefore spirituality in ways which both connect with and challenge the wider culture, as well as potentially transforming the unjust relationships and situations within it by creating a microcosm of a new ritual reality.

Rituals to transform the everyday

There are several ways in which one might approach trying to develop rituals and liturgy as a tool for mission among young people. One could begin by attempting to adapt already existing Christian liturgical practice, like that around the Eucharist, to incorporate and connect with elements of youth culture, as many have aimed to do in recent years. There are plenty of resources around the Church calendar and lectionary that might present opportunities for this.

However, another approach, which we've been exploring, begins by looking at the already existing ritual elements within the culture itself – perhaps elements that are 'thin' (Smith, 2009, p. 82) and/or are often engaged with subconsciously. By adding new layers of meaning to these elements, drawing on the Christian narrative and tradition, they may then become liturgies, which are 'thick' with meaning. These liturgies then become transformative in the sense that the original habit or ritual itself becomes transformed, holding a whole new meaning for those taking part which, over time, may form and shape a new sense of identity.

What might be some of the everyday habits and rituals that form part of young people's culture, which we could unlock new meaning within, in order to create transformative rituals or liturgies? Grimes' (2013, p. 235) earlier categories (actions, actors, places, times, objects, languages, groups) provide a good framework to identify some of these ritual elements. Turning our attention to the three that seem most significant – actions, places and objects – we can attempt to sketch out some suggestions and examples.

1 Ritual actions

Ritual actions include the 'constituent actions that make up the ritual, their phasing, rhythm and style, the connections of disconnections among them' and 'habitual vectors of bodily movement' (Grimes, 2014, p. 237). Among young people who show a preference for verbal and non-literate forms of communication, symbolic actions could be highly expressive and profound, especially ones that are unusual and counter-cultural.

Cooking

One case study comes from the work of The Lab with young people on the Alway estate in Newport, where we have used the cooking of simple meals together as a ritual means of exploring spirituality with young people who have little or no previous experience of Church. Many of the young people are used to throwing together simple meals or snacks for themselves, but the idea of a shared, communal meal is quite unusual for them, especially where everyone is involved in the making of it. During these activities we've then been able to explore with the young people issues around their own attitudes towards food and what the Christian tradition and story has to say about themes like healthy eating, body image, world hunger and fair trade. The young people then take away a new recipe with them, as a result of cooking something new, and during the week they may well remember and recall the conversations about different issues. They might even be challenged to cook and eat with family or friends more often as a result.

Make-up

Another possibility exists around the theme of vulnerability and self-image among teenage girls, or even young women. Imagine how powerful it might be at the beginning of a group meeting or a time of sharing for each girl to take the make-up they carry with them out of their bag, and place it in the middle of the circle as a sign of 'taking off their mask' and allowing themselves to be vulnerable with others in the group. This might then enable a discussion about how God has unmasked herself to the world in the person of Jesus, and the significance of this in terms of self-image and self-esteem. If the experience of sharing and being vulnerable with others is particularly striking, group members might well be reminded of the emotions they felt and shared every time in future that they put on or take off their make-up.

2 Ritual places

Particularly among the young people we are journeying with, on housing estates that are still locally focused and value local community, place can be hugely significant. Many communities have places within them, that hold both positive and negative experiences and emotions, and over which local people feel a high level of ownership. Often church buildings are hugely significant because of this – they are where funerals of relatives have taken place or where a friend was married. In my experience, this is also true for young people, perhaps those who have lost loved ones. In particular one young person attended church services regularly then struggled for many months to return after their nan's funeral had taken place in the church building because of the strong negative connection it had created for them. Some new or different rituals involving places of significance in the community could be incredibly transformative for individuals and for whole communities.

Skate park communion

In their book *Here Be Dragons*, Richard and Lorimer Passmore (2013, pp. 156–7) talk about sharing communion with a group of young people in their local skate park, which the young people themselves had campaigned for and raised the money to build:

> We took some muffins, blackcurrant squash and some candles down to the skate park ... The young people, having taken part in a discussion on communion and using the resources we had brought with us, decided to make a scooter the 'altar' (we had not used that term but they identified it) on which to put the muffins and blackcurrant squash. Later they lit the candles and jumped over them on their bikes, skateboards or scooters. Allowing space in this way meant the young people could engage with the process however they chose to, creating their own rituals rooted in their culture.

Memorials

Particular significance is often given to places where either inspiring and tragic events have occurred. Drawing on the experience of a youth work team in Weston-super-Mare, we note in particular the site of a violent crime where someone was killed by a young person in a fight. The street name on the corner where the incident happened has become a memorial or shrine in memory of the people involved. The sign is well tended, and flowers are replaced often. Following the event, local residents came together to organize a vigil.

3 Ritual objects

Among young people, culturally significant objects like clothing, jewellery and technology are often used in highly extravagant ways to express identity. Could these objects or cultural artefacts form the basis of a ritual approach to mission?

Selfies

Again with a group of young people in Alway, The Lab has experimented with using 'selfies' – self-portrait photos usually taken on a camera phone – as a starting point for theological reflection with young people. The young people were given the task of taking a selfie expressing a particular emotion or theme, such as celebration, loneliness or friendship, and then invited to unpack the significance of these together by asking two questions: what do they see when they look at the photo, and what do they think God sees? This exploration unlocks cultural issues like self-esteem, confidence and relationships, as well as theological themes like God's love, creator and creation, and Christian community. There are two lasting, habitual connections which then give the young people the opportunity to remember and repeat this process as they go back to their everyday lives: first, any time they take a selfie from now on the ritual might have a new thickness of meaning to it for them; and second, they may look over the photo on their phone again at other points and be reminded.

Christmas decorations

A second example was passed on to us by a church families' worker who each year puts on a large-scale 'stable trail' production of the nativity in her church. Local families come together and travel between different bounded-off sections of the church, with a different part of the nativity story being told in each. The worker told me how she then gives away a Christmas decoration to each family as they leave, expressing her hope that each subsequent year when they put their decorations up the family might be reminded and relive their experience, in the process revisiting the Christian story.

Breaking through the glass ceiling

In this chapter we've looked at some of the challenges of exploring spirituality in ways that connect with young people, particularly those in areas of poverty. This has led us on a journey of experimentation, utilizing rituals and practices as tools for exploring hands-on spirituality together. Finally, we have presented some examples, which might hopefully act as suggestions or starting points for thinking creatively about spirituality in your own context.

If culture provides a 'map of meaning' for the experience of life, then rituals are the way by which that culture is created and propagated. To truly respond to the call of the pioneer in our current landscape, we must take ritual seriously as a tool for spirituality-shaping and transforming the everyday. For too long we have confined spirituality to a narrow and limiting selection of activities – often the things young people find boring. We must embrace the challenge to get our hands dirty, and start experimenting with an everyday hands-on spirituality that reflects the diverse reality of the world around us.

References

Adams, I., 2010, *Cave Refectory Road*, Norwich: Canterbury Press.

Arbuckle, G. A., 2010, *Culture, Inculturation, and Theologians: A Postmodern Critique*, Collegeville, MN: Liturgical Press.

Bevans, S. B. and Schroeder, R. P., 2004, *Constants in Context: A Theology of Mission for Today*, Maryknoll, NY: Orbis Books.

Brueggemann, W., 2001, *The Prophetic Imagination*, Minneapolis: Fortress Press.

Clarke, J., Hall, S., Jefferson, T. and Roberts, B., 2006, 'Subcultures, Cultures and Class', in S. Hall and T. Jefferson (eds), *Resistance Through Rituals: Youth Subcultures in Post-War Britain*, 2nd edition, Abingdon: Routledge.

Collins-Mayo, S., Mayo, B. and Nash, S. with Cocksworth, C., 2010, *The Faith of Generation Y*, London: Church House Publishing.

Davies, D. J., 2012, 'Changing British Ritualization', in Woodhead and Catto (eds), *Religion and Change in Modern Britain*, Abingdon: Routledge.

Frontier Youth Trust, 2013, *The Experiments*, Birmingham: Frontier Youth Trust, www.fyt.org.uk.

Grimes, R. L., 2013, *The Craft of Ritual Studies*, New York: Oxford University Press.

Hall, S. and Jefferson, T. (eds), 2006, *Resistance Through Rituals: Youth Subcultures in Post-War Britain*, 2nd edition, Abingdon: Routledge.

Nash, P. and Nash, S., 2009, *Tools for Reflective Ministry* (reissue), London: SPCK.

Passmore, R. and Passmore, L., 2013, *Here Be Dragons: Youth Work and Mission off the Map*, Chard: Frontier Youth Trust.

Smith, J. K. A., 2009, *Desiring the Kingdom: Worship, Worldview, and Cultural Formation*, Grand Rapids, MI: Baker Academic.

Smith, J. K. A., 2013, *Imagining the Kingdom: How Worship Works*, Grand Rapids, MI: Baker Academic.

10

African Spirituality in Western Contexts

HARVEY KWIYANI

Introduction

A group of Malawian pastors living and leading churches in Nottingham meets for one afternoon every month to discuss the challenges that they face in their ministries. Often, their conversations lead to the question, 'What uniquely Malawian – or African – tools do we have that we can use to unlock Nottingham for mission?' This chapter tries to answer one aspect of that question by focusing on African spirituality in Britain. To do this, the chapter discusses the overarching understanding of the spirituality of personhood that informs Malawian Christianity and its implications for mission, especially in the West where any form of African spirituality is foreign and often suspicious, and highlights some practices that these Malawian pastors in Nottingham believe make missional connections with the city easier.

African spirituality and pneumatology

African pneumatology, just like many other areas of African theology, suffers the effects of the oral nature of African culture. Africans talk about the Spirit, but have yet to write about it. Apart from a few dated works published by western scholars,[1] there is very little published that shows the African perspective on the theology of the Spirit. This surprises me because Africans are particularly attentive to the spirit-world and that attention ought to find ways into their written work, no matter how meagre it is. Any African theology must reflect Africa's love affair with the Spirit. It is partly because of this interest in the spiritual realm that Christianity has spread on the continent like wildfire, especially after 1970.[2] In his *Guidelines for Christian Theology*, Osadolor Imasogie expresses concern that the role of the Holy Spirit has been neglected in Christian theologizing in Africa (Imasogie, 1986, p. 81). Of course, he makes this observation after looking carefully at the effects of western theology that fails to properly contextualize Christianity in Africa (1986, pp. 46–66). He places the blame partly on the modern western theologian who is 'not thoroughly convinced of the reality and hence relevance of the Holy Spirit' (1986, p. 81).

The African awareness of the spirits and spirit-world is based on African cosmology. This awareness greatly informs African theology, and therefore indigenous African theology often has a different starting point, in many respects, from western theology. Authentic African theology rises from a premodernist worldview, having been shaped with minimal influence by the Enlightenment.[3] Thus, the African spirit-centred worldview is similar in many ways to that of the Bible. Of course, the Bible assumes a spirit-world that has evil spirits, good spirits, the Holy Spirit, and a God who is Spirit. Both the good spirits and the evil spirits seem to be involved in human life. The biblical spirit-world, especially that of the New Testament, is a larger and more powerful reality that fills everything.

Theologically speaking, then, Africans will generally have little problem understanding the role of the spirit in religion. The reality of the spirit-world in the African worldview helps Africans make sense of God's activity in the world in a way that would not be possible without such a framework. Because of this outlook, African Christians will generally be Trinitarian in their theology.[4] Once they understand God to be Spirit, they have no need for the *filioque*. When they use various vernacular names for God, e.g.

Mulungu, Nyame, Modimo or *Nyasaye*, it is usually the God of Christianity whom they encounter as Father, Son and the Holy Spirit, and whom they understand well as Spirit. There is neither need nor room to think of the Spirit as inferior to the Father or the Son. The Triune God is spirit, and the Holy Spirit is God-at-work in their lives and in the world. God's working in the lives of Africans through God's Spirit is very important for African Christians since that is how they know to relate with the deity. Allan Anderson has rightly argued that the Spirit of God is not an impersonal, manipulable life-force, as some westerners have understood it to be (Anderson, 1991, p. 10). It is the Spirit of God acting in God's power in the world.

The Jesus of Africa is a Spirit-Jesus or, rather, the Spirit-anointed Jesus who was born by the Spirit, moved by the Spirit, and raised from the dead by the Spirit. Many African Christians proclaim that the same Spirit that worked in Christ is working in them today. Luke's summation of the ministry of Jesus in Acts 10.38 connects with the African understanding of the Trinitarian God: 'How God anointed Jesus of Nazareth with the Holy Spirit and with power, who went about doing good and healing all who were oppressed by the devil, for God was with him' (Acts 10.38). As such, even the Christologies of Africa are pneumatic Christologies. Kwame Bediako suggests: 'It is hardly surprising that the Christologies that have emerged in Africa so far are predominantly "pneumatic," presenting a Christ who is a living power in the realm of the spirit' (Bediako, 1995, p. 176).

African spirituality: cosmological underpinnings

One thing that has been said about Africans repeatedly over the past century is that they are very religious people. John Mbiti's statement that Africans are notoriously religious may seem an understatement now in the light of the explosion of Christianity in the continent since the publication of *African Religions and Philosophy* (Mbiti, 1970, p. 1). Mbiti was right; Africans are and have always been a very religious people. Even before the advent of the missionaries on the continent, Africans had very elaborate cultural religious systems. The Africans' religions fill the whole of their world – their lives. William Willoughby understood this when he wrote in 1928:

> Bantu life is essentially religious. The relation of the individual to the family, the clan, and the tribe – politics, ethics, law, war, status, social amenities, festivals – all that is good and much that is bad in Bantu life is grounded in Bantu religion. Religion so pervades the life of the people that it regulates their doings and governs their leisure ... Materialistic influences from Europe are playing upon Africa at a thousand points and may break up Bantu life; but the Bantu are hardly likely to be secularized, for they will never be content without a religion that is able to touch every phase of life and to interpret the divine in terms of humanity. (Willoughby, 1928, p. 1)[5]

Thus the human being, in Africa, is a deeply religious being living in a deeply religious world. For the Lhomwe people of Malawi (a people group indigenous to this writer), their entire existence is a religious phenomenon. Indeed, for the Lhomwe, just like many other Africans, to live is to be caught up in an overarching religious drama (see Mbiti, 1970, p. 19). Human life in its entirety is a spiritual existence, and therefore it cannot be destroyed. Persons, who are essentially spirit beings, are immortal. In agreement with Mbiti, they are 'upgraded' into the community of the 'living-dead' soon after death and moving on further into the community of the ancestors after that once they have passed out of memory.[6] For the Lhomwe, therefore, death is not the end of life but the passing on from the finitude of earthly life to immortality. It is because of the eternality of the human being – in the form of the spirit – that the Lhomwe believe that the dead continue to be part of the community even after they have died and crossed over into the invisible world. Mbiti observed that 'the acts of pouring out libation (of beer, milk, or water) or giving portions of food for the living-dead, are symbols of communion, fellowship, and remembrance' (Mbiti, 1970, p. 33).

For Africans, the spiritual universe is a unit with the physical, intermingling and dovetailing into each other so that it is not easy, or even necessary, to separate them (Mbiti, 1970, p. 97). Even among the Lhomwe, it is believed that the visible material world is enveloped in an invisible spiritual world, but the two worlds are one. With such a cosmology, the idea of a God is inherent in African culture. It is hard to find an African culture that is atheist. God is both immanent and transcendent at the same time. This being near and far at the same time is possible because God's Spirit dwells among human beings (Mbiti, 1970, p. 41).

This strong belief in the spiritual world shapes both the African culture and religious landscape significantly. Harvey Sindima has taken time to study the religious systems of the Chewa of Malawi. He observed that the livelihood of the people depended on the spirits (Sindima, 1991).[7] For the Chewas, food security, harvests, rainfall, protection against locusts and other predators, coupled with healing and defence from enemies, were always dependent on religious rituals and practices of the communities, based on a firm belief of getting help from the spiritual realm. In his ground-breaking anthropological study of the Chewas, *Kukula ndi Mwambo*, John Gwengwe highlights the role of the spirits in the lives of the Chewa throughout the life of a human being – from birth to death (Gwengwe, 1965). Thus, among the Chewa, every major event in one's life has a spiritual dynamic, and is therefore sacred.

Umunthu: towards an African spirituality

In Malawi, just like most of Africa, the spirituality of the culture is grounded in the ways in which people define personhood – *umunthu*.[8] Following the wisdom of the ancestors, Malawians say that *munthu ndi mzimu* (a human being is a spirit). Among the Chewa, *umunthu* is the word for personhood and it is also used to mean 'spirit' (Sindima, 1991). Among the Lhomwe, in addition to 'spirit', *umunthu* can also be translated *nthunzi* (vapour, breath). Lhomwe hermeneutics, therefore, believe that the spirit that God breathed into Adam at creation is that which makes the human being to be a spirit being (Gen. 2.7). Sindima adds that, '*Mzimu* [human spirit] is the principle of life, the divine element in people, which is able to transcend death' (Sindima, 1995, p. 146). Indeed, the Lhomwe believe that the spirit is the essence of the human being, the centre of a person's gravity.

In South Africa, *umunthu* describes the much popularized African philosophy of *ubuntu* which has been used in the reconciliation process in post-apartheid South Africa. It embodies the Nguni proverb, '*ubuntu ngubuntu ngabantu*', which translates as 'a person is a person through other persons'. *Ubuntu* exemplifies the great communal values of solidarity, compassion, respect, human dignity, conformity to basic norms, and collective unity. At the root, it means, 'I am because I belong, I am because we all are; you are because I am, and I am because you are.' Desmond Tutu's attempt at a definition of *ubuntu* says:

> A person with *ubuntu* is open and available to others, affirming of others, does not feel threatened that others are able and good, for he or she has a proper self-assurance that comes from knowing that he or she belongs in a greater whole and is diminished when others are humiliated or diminished, when others are tortured or oppressed, or treated as if they were less than who they are. (Tutu, 1999, p. 31)

To have *umunthu*, or to be a *munthu*, is to be at one with one's spirit-self and the spiritual realm. It is because of this that to have *umunthu* is a moral issue, since African spirituality is a communal endeavour. Among the Malawian Chewa, to have *umunthu* is to be a person who helps others. Anyone who does not help others is not a *munthu*. Anyone who is individualistic does not have *umunthu*, and therefore is a beast, for he or she does not know the meaning of living together as a people (Sindima, 1995, p. 203; also see Chigona, 2002). Personhood is a communal spiritual journey that one cannot embark on alone. Individuality is encouraged as a building block for the community. Individualism, however, is scorned, rejected, and ostracized as poison that corrupts community. Musopole observed that among the people of northern Malawi, *umunthu* is established on two pillars: moral integrity and economic productivity, and these two make generosity possible (Musopole, 1996). To have *umunthu* is to have *mtima wabwino* (a good/generous heart). It is to be humane, hospitable, dependable, sociable, and many other aspects that would make a person live favourably and in harmony with the society.

In this sense, *umunthu* makes possible a discussion of spirituality that could enrich western missiology. First, in establishing the spiritual nature of the human being – in saying that a person is a spirit being – *umunthu* highlights the fact that there is something transcendent about the human being. This transcendent aspect of the person allows the human being communion not only with the spiritual realm but also with the Spirit of God. Africans live well aware of the presence of spirits in the world around them. Indeed, once the human being is understood to be essentially a spirit being, living in a spiritual world, significant parts of the Bible begin to make sense in ways otherwise difficult to understand. For instance, the Spirit is understood to be the *ruach* (breath) of God that was breathed into Adam. The divine interactions between the Spirit of God and the prophets like Isaiah, Jeremiah and Ezekiel are also seen in a different light. However, it is the pneumatology of the New Testament that becomes even more relevant. The spiritual realities that inform much of the New Testament are similar in many ways to that of Africa. As such, the spirituality of *umunthu* is a helpful lens for the preaching of the kingdom of God, and the eschatological presence of the future that has broken into the present. The powerful Spirit of God is active in the world in which many other spirits are active.

Second, *umunthu* recognizes and pays serious attention to the existence of a spirit-world. There is no doubt about the presence of invisible spiritual forces in the Africans' world, and that these invisible spirits have great influence on human life. Some of them are evil, others are good. In *umunthu* spirituality, then, demonic powers and principalities are understood to be real spiritual forces that resist the *humanizing* impact of the kingdom of God. It is with this in mind that Jesus is understood to have said,

'If I cast out demons with the finger of God, surely the kingdom of God has come upon you' (Luke 11.20). Just like the ancestral spirits are thought to protect the community from calamities and harm, the Holy Spirit, in its power, is understood as the provider and the defender of the community. For *umunthu* spirituality, it is possible, then, to talk about spiritual warfare. Among the Lhomwe of Malawi, it is commonplace to perform rituals for *kuchotsa mphepo/mizimu yoyipa* (removing bad wind/spirits) from a village after there has been a funeral, or other misfortunes. The rituals involved in cleaning up the spiritual atmosphere (usually led by the *sing'anga*) amount to waging war in the spiritual realm (2 Cor. 10.3–5). Even in day-to-day life, the effort taken by people to stay protected from evil spirits is enormous.

Third, *umunthu* spirituality is always a communal spirituality. Community forms the foundation on which life is built and the platform on which it is shared. This community includes all that are living now, those that are dead, nature, spirits, and deity. The Lhomwe, for instance, are always conscious of the fact that they live in communion with the spirits of the living-dead and the ancestors who are involved in the everyday lives of human beings. One does not have to know or like a person in order to be helpful and hospitable to them. Helping to meet the needs of others is a spiritual act done as if it is done to the spirits of the ancestors. In *umunthu*, life is about humanizing others, and therefore person-hood is always a shared commodity. The whole of life is, thus, a communal endeavour. To be individualistic is to lack *umunthu* – a very unwelcome label in society.

African spirituality in Britain: missional implications

With these three cultural pillars of *umunthu* spirituality discussed above, we now consider what a missional spirituality based on *umunthu* will look like. Here, we explore two of what I consider to be the main characteristics of missional spirituality. After this, we look at how these characteristics would show themselves in a western context.

Holistic spirituality

A missiology conceived in the context of African spirituality will be holistic in its approach to theology and human life. This holistic spirituality will inform theology on several planes. First and foremost, African spirituality will not only be interested in the spiritual work of the salvation of the human being. While, indeed, salvation is an important work of the Spirit, for Africans, salvation is not just about the saving of the human spirit. Indeed, within the African context, salvation is not only spiritual. It is holistic. As such, salvation must include healing and deliverance, which are also central to Christianity. Salvation is about humanizing the entire person and helping the person become more whole in every sense of the word. This includes spiritual wholeness, but must also include emotional, physical and even economic wholeness, among many things. To be whole is to have life. To be sick or needy is to have less life. As a matter of fact, any life-saving act in Africa could be easily attributed to the Spirit of God. Prayers and sacrifices are made for the harvests in the fields, and for jobs and bank accounts. Fasting in order to receive a spouse is a common thing among Africans, for here, too, to lack is to experience a failure in salvation. In many cases, to be free from need is to be well cared for by God. That is also understood to be salvation.

Furthermore, this holistic spirituality is not only an abstraction that is a matter of the mind and the heart. African spirituality involves the whole of the person's being, including whatever that person owns. It involves the person's whole body and their entire estate, which is usually understood as the extension of the person's being. Be it in celebration or in worship, or any other religious activity, the participant's entire body engages in the process. In most cases, when people come for a major religious service, like annual sacrifices, they will bring an offering with them. This offering may be in the form of a goat, chicken, a piece of cloth, or money. When performing sacrifices to ancestors, or invoking the god of the harvests, or when the rainmaker leads the community in intercession for the rains, people will participate by singing and dancing. The drum that is often used to invoke certain spirits is also an invitation for the community to dance. Certain ritualistic dances are spiritual, symbolically inviting the spirits to come and impregnate the earth. When the spirits come, there are usually many bodily manifestations, like people falling in trances, prophetic utterances and healings, glossolalia and, in rare cases, levitations.

Communal spirituality

The African understanding of the spirit-world demands a communal understanding of spirituality. A popular Malawian proverb, 'chala chimodzi sichiswa nsabwe', reminds us that 'a single thumb does not kill a louse'. This reflects the general understanding that spirituality is a communal event; it is best done in company. Be it in ancestral veneration, or a simple pouring of libation, there is a way in which the community is represented. In most cases, the community will be present and actively involved. Just as umunthu says that one's personhood is constituted through other persons, in this communal spirituality one's spirituality is constituted through the spirituality of others. Any person with umunthu will pay attention to the spirituality of others as well as that of the community. Individual spirituality is never consummated if it does not end in communal spirituality. Together with the community, one worships the God of the community. In addition, the entire spiritual experience is a public phenomenon. For instance, when a soothsayer enters a village, life stops for the whole village in order that the community is able to hear what the spirits have to say. In those cultures where trances are a means of spiritual communication, when someone falls into a trance, the elders of the village are brought together to listen and mediate with the entire community. Individual spirituality has its telos – purpose and goal – in communal spirituality. Religion and the matters of faith still reign greatly in the public arena.

Looking at this the other way round, it is also quite true that the communality of African culture is a spiritual endeavour. The spirits of the ancestors desire this to be. For example, it is common belief that the spirits of the ancestors direct people to care for the needy and strangers, or to prepare meals for communities as a way to restore harmony. This orientation towards the community, both in the elders and the ancestors, is what makes the community itself a spiritual endeavour. To engage effectively in a religious activity, one needs company. The arrival of a new-born into the community or the beginning of a new family by way of marriage are junctures in the community's life when, through rituals, the spirit-world of the ancestors and God is invoked. In some cultures, a strict set of ritualistic religious activities will shape the initiation rites by which children are accepted into the society. A community broken, for instance, by death, has to go through rigorous ritual cleansing in order to restore itself. The existence of community itself is a spiritual process. The community is a spiritual phenomenon. Unity and connectedness, peace and harmony are the marks of a community that is in tune with its ancestors. These ancestors will not hesitate to intervene through dreams or divination, for example, when such a harmony is destroyed. Jesus may have had something similar in mind when he said, 'For where two or three are gathered together in my name, I am there in the midst of them' (Matt. 18.20).

Christian community, be it in a congregation or a *fellowship*, is important for African Christians. These are places where they embody the belief that they need the community just as the community needs them. As such, Christian communities give them space to engage the Spirit communally. There, they listen and learn from other Christians. They also share and teach other Christians. They recharge their spiritualities in readiness for the mission, but also they help recharge other Christians for the same. Based on *umunthu*, these communities (more at the fellowship level) emphasize an openness encouraging every member to give their best in order for the whole community to thrive. If one has a song, or another has a psalm, this is the place to contribute. If one has a need, this is the place to receive help. In addition, *umunthu* tells African Christians that they need one another. More so, congregations need one another for their own good. Indeed, even at the congregational level, individuality is discouraged. Congregations live in a mutually edifying community, and are thus more likely to help one another in their efforts since they believe that existence in isolation is never an option, spiritually speaking.

Furthermore, this communal spirituality is not afraid to welcome the stranger. From its foundations, both in *umunthu* and in African cosmology, the African Christian spirituality is particularly optimistic about engaging with the stranger. In fact, it is the possibility that the stranger is being guided to this community by the ancestors or the Spirit of God, or that the Spirit's hidden charisma in the stranger is the Spirit's gift to the community, that excites this kind of spirituality. It is thus inviting others into the experience of its deity.

Malawian spirituality in Nottingham: hospitality

The Malawian pastors in Nottingham are very aware of the two characteristics of African spirituality discussed above. Their conversations seek to embody these aspects of their spirituality and worldview in a British city. When they engage people in Nottingham, they want to be holistic in their approach. They focus not just on the whole person but also on the person's family and community. This is generally possible through communal effort. It takes a team of people working together to minister to another person holistically. The pastor's work is just a small portion in a wide network of Christians who offer integration to the people they evangelize. Hospitality has become their major missional practice for the city of Nottingham. But this has not come easily. They have struggled to begin to see fruit.

On the one hand, they realize that most of what they do needs proper interpretation for their non-Malawian neighbours in order to understand and to appreciate them. As such, they are convinced that the practice of hospitality is one way to engage their neighbours. Hospitality among Malawians is a very important spiritual practice. It is a way to share one's personhood, humanizing oneself by humanizing others, especially those in need. It is what makes *umunthu* the bedrock of Malawian culture, and thus religion and spirituality. Malawians are welcoming in nature, and their culture is celebrated for offering hospitality to strangers.

Malawian churches in Nottingham are trying to practise hospitality as a means of reaching out to their neighbours. However, they are realizing that hospitality in Nottingham means something different from what they knew in Malawi. On the one hand, in Malawi, hospitality is expected and easily accepted. In Nottingham, often people do not expect others to be hospitable. It is generally those at the margins of society that will accept hospitality from a stranger – the needy, homeless and others. These communities are where Malawian churches are making connections. Malawians, I suspect, are equipped with the patience and the listening skills needed to minister at the margins. One church is running a foodbank that is not patronized by Malawians at all. Another church has intentionally opened their building to the youth in their host community for unstructured use of their premises.

On the other hand, these Malawian churches are noticing that their non-Malawian Christian neighbours find the demands to be hospitable difficult to manage. Of course, hospitality is a risky business. To some, it does not make sense to be so hospitable to strangers. Hospitality takes time. Usually, it disturbs their schedules and forces them to talk to people they would not otherwise engage with. More often than not, Malawian churches in Nottingham find themselves entangled in messy situations because they have been hospitable to risky people. For the Malawians, this is not at all unfamiliar, because even in Malawi, hospitality can be easily abused.

Conclusion

This chapter has discussed some elements of African spirituality at work in the West. Using the example of Malawian pastors in Nottingham who meet regularly to discuss their missional engagement with their city, it has suggested that African spirituality could actually work in western cities. The Malawian philosophy of *umunthu* enables us to talk about people in ways that respect and humanize others, even strangers or those in need. In conclusion, it seems to me that African spiritualities in the West enable us to engage critically with western culture, where individualism and capitalism usually shape human relations. These African spiritualities, if intentionally engaged, could also find ways to strengthen and reinvigorate other spiritualities and churches in Britain.

References

Anderson, A., 1991, *Moya: The Holy Spirit in an African Context*, Manualia Didactica 13, Pretoria: University of South Africa.

Bediako, K., 1995, *Christianity in Africa: The Renewal of a Non-Western Religion*, Maryknoll, NY: Orbis.

Chigona, G., 2002, *Umunthu Theology: Path of Integral Human Liberation Rooted in Jesus of Nazareth*, Balaka: Montfort.

Gwengwe, J. W., 1965, *Kukula Ndi Mwambo*, Limbe: Malawi Publications and Literature Bureau.

Imasogie, O., 1986, *Guidelines for Christian Theology in Africa*, Ibadan: University Press.

Kim, K., 2007, *The Holy Spirit in the World: A Global Conversation*, Maryknoll, NY: Orbis.

Mbiti, J. S., 1970, *African Religions and Philosophy*, Garden City, NY: Anchor.

Musopole, A. C., 1996, 'Religion, Spirituality, and Umunthu: A Perspective from Malawi', in *Agitated Mind of God*, D. T. Irvin and A. E. Akinade (eds), Maryknoll, NY: Orbis.

Sindima, H. J., 1991, 'Bondedness, Moyo and Umunthu as the Elements of Achewa Spirituality: Organizing Logic and Principle of Life', *Ultimate Reality and Meaning, Interdisciplinary Studies in the Philosophy of Understanding*, 14(1), pp. 5–20.

Sindima, H. J., 1995, *Africa's Agenda: The Legacy of Liberalism and Colonialism in the Crisis of African Values*, Contributions in Afro-American and African Studies no. 176. Westport, CT: Greenwood Press.

Tutu, D., 1999, *No Future without Forgiveness*, New York: Doubleday.

Willoughby, W. C., 1928, *The Soul of the Bantu: A Sympathetic Study of the Magico-Religious Practices and Beliefs of the Bantu Tribes of Africa*, Garden City, NY: Doubleday.

Notes

1 For instance, the works of Bengt Sundkler, published mid twentieth century, still inform much of African theology as far as the African independent churches are concerned. Allan Anderson's *Moya* was published in 1991. Both these works need to be updated and the geographical region of their studies need to be broadened, as African Christianity is developing at a very fast pace.

2 The years between 1960 and 1970 mark a very important season in African Christianity and theology. The colonial agents and most of the missionaries and western traders returned to the West, leaving African Christianity under the leadership and theological ownership of indigenous Christians. As a result, both African Christianity and theology would be decolonized, and an explosive growth of Christianity would follow, adding on average a hundred million new Christians every decade between 1970 and 2010.

3 Indeed, modernity has found its way to Africa, especially urban Africa. However, its influence on African religiosity, be it African traditional religions, Christianity, or Islam, is limited. Many Africans will go to church, but also visit a *sing'anga* (spiritual consultant/soothsayer/diviner) when they fall sick. This is seen especially on such spiritually potent occasions like a funeral. Church members will be around the house of the deceased the whole time the body is there, singing, preaching, etc. But oftentimes, a *sing'anga* will be around, taking care of the people's spiritual needs.

4 Kirsteen Kim observes the same kind of theological convictions among Indian Christians (Kim, 2007, p. 67).

5 Bantu is a collective name for some 600 people groups that use Bantu languages and covering most of sub-Saharan Africa. The root '-ntu' in its many variations (-nto, -nthu, -ndu, -ndo, -mtu, etc.) is translated 'person' in many of the Bantu languages. The word 'bantu' itself means 'people'.

6 This is Mbiti's terminology used to describe the state of the recently deceased people who are (through their spirits) still very active in the community. They are still remembered in active memories of the people. In some cultures, food is left for them to come and eat at night, etc. Libations are made to them. They are invoked when the community needs spiritual help, etc. These people are dead, and yet they live. The spirits of the recently deceased linger around, communing with the people left behind while at the same time slipping slowly beyond memory and closer to the gods. Once they have slipped beyond memory, they become ancestors. The ancestors that will be involved with the people living on earth will be the ones who lived good lives on earth. They become intermediaries between the people and the gods.

7 The Chewa people are the largest people group in Malawi, comprising between 6 and 8 million of the 16 million people in Malawi. There are also many Chewa in Zambia, Zimbabwe, Mozambique and South Africa.

8 *Umunthu* means personhood. *Munthu* is person. Among other African peoples, the concept of *umunthu* is known by other names: *ubuntu* in Xhosa and Zulu, *utu* in Swahili, *obonto* in Kiisi, *nunhu* in Shona, *bunhu* in Tsonga, *numunhu* in Shangaan, *botho* in Sotho, etc.

We Are One Body Because We all Share in One Bread: Pioneering and the Eucharist

KIM HARTSHORNE

Introduction

I write as someone leading a small, new form of church that serves a group who have no connections to Church. Many have low levels of literacy, mental health difficulties, childhood trauma or other struggles. We operate under a Bishops Mission Order from the Church of England, but began our life as a non-denominational mission project led by people who considered themselves 'low' church regarding the Eucharist. This is the story of how our eyes have been opened to its unparalleled power and beauty.

I have had quite a steep learning curve to understand the myriad rules around how the ritual of the Eucharist is celebrated in the Church of England, but this has been a positive process in the main, driving us to clarify how we understand ourselves in relation to Scripture, tradition and the wider body of the Church. We have also come to see that participating in the ritual of the Eucharist has formed and shaped us into becoming church, and over time has formed and drawn the participants into becoming baptized Christians. Communion has proved itself to be hugely valuable as a missional practice, drawing people into its orbit from those who are outside the walls of Church. Finally it is a ritual that constitutes and contains the entirety of our faith in a microcosmic dramatic performance and is therefore hugely effective as a practical, demonstrative tool for teaching and communication.

In this chapter we examine some historical and contentious issues, discuss contemporary approaches to eucharistic inculturation, and the struggle to re-appropriate and reimagine the ritual for people new to the Christian faith.

Eucharistic liturgy

The Eucharist, and its associated liturgy and practice, is a huge subject. It encompasses several thousand years of history, stretching from Jewish Temple practice through the early years of the Christian Church, via its appropriation by the state under the Roman Emperor Constantine, to the Protestant Reformation, which sought to rid it of associations of power and corruption. Today pioneers and new faith communities often wrestle with its controversies, contradictions and paradoxes as we try to identify its core meaning for new people coming to faith. For most faith communities, that will necessitate some grasp of history and how it influences our understanding of contemporary eucharistic practices.

It is important to note at the outset that there is not one 'right answer' when it comes to the theology that underpins Holy Communion, or the practices and liturgy that embody it. Each church and denomination has its own history, doctrine and practice; some are informal and occasional, while others, like the Church of England and Roman Catholic Church, have complex formal, legal and liturgical structures that determine many of the practices around it. The Salvation Army, on the other hand, celebrates Holy Communion once a year only.

All churches have some rules and behaviours around this ritual and it is important to get to know and understand something of the history and theology of the denomination or stream we may be associated with or supported by, in order to understand this. For pioneers working with no denominational or congregational ties or commitments, this issue is both easier and harder to deal with, and may require the focused commitment of the community over a period to decide where to locate the practice and what theology and meaning underpin it. For those of us with complex territory to negotiate, prayer and good collaborative working relationships will help to establish a place of integrity from which to explore the possibilities of inculturating the ritual.

Almost all churches and denominations have liturgies associated with the taking of bread and wine, even if they consider themselves to be non-conformist or non-liturgical. For example, is the bread sliced and out of a packet; does it comprise tiny wafers or one large one; is it unleavened or freshly baked? Is the wine alcoholic or a grape juice; is it served from paper cups, ancient gold vessels or tiny plastic or glass cups? Who is allowed to touch and serve the elements; is communion taken weekly, monthly or even annually; who is allowed to receive it? Is it served from behind a rail or passed around the room? All of these are liturgical practices that speak of the identity and underpinning theology of each community of faith. Does the community view its participation as an act of obedience to Christ and a memorial of the Last Supper; do they understand Christ to become literally, mystically or symbolically present in the breaking of the bread? Are the words fixed and unchanging, performed by one role only, or is it a largely improvised and informal ritual that can be led by anyone?

For new church communities that are being shaped around the needs of people unfamiliar with church culture and history, there are important decisions to be made about the place of Holy Communion and in what ways it may have meaning for the new groups that are being reached. How can we negotiate the complexity surrounding it in order to enable people to access the meaning of it in ways that are culturally appropriate and resonant? I believe that these are questions of huge importance but they may require us to wrestle like Jacob to grasp the blessing within. If we grapple with these questions seriously, we may discover this rite to be one of the most important shapers of new communities of faith.

Hands off? Understanding the Anglican approach

It may seem hard to understand why there is so much stricture regarding the exact words and actions used to celebrate the Euchar-ist in the Anglican and Roman Catholic churches, particularly for pioneers from other denominations who are working ecumenic-ally, and for others who are new to the Church of England. It's worth bearing in mind that it is considered a very wonderful and precious matter and so is taken seriously out of reverence and not just to be difficult!

One of the historical reasons is because it used to be thought that Christ had handed down the actual words that were to be spoken from the Last Supper, and these had been passed on via apostolic succession, lending some of the sacredness to the act. However, in the late nineteenth century the discovery of some scrolls known as the *Didache*,[1] which recorded many details of the worshipping life of the early Church, actually revealed a wide variety of different prayers and liturgies that were used. This shift to a greater variety of words has manifested itself within the Anglican Church, which moved from having only one eucharistic prayer in 1928 to the authorization of eight with the publication of *Common Worship* in 2000.

I learned about the 'rules' as part of my journey of leading a new church, and discovered that the Church of England has a process of authorizing the words that are going to be used in its services via the systems of consultation and governance of General Synod and the Liturgical Commission. Anglican history, stemming from the earliest Book of Common Prayer, has had a huge influence on how the Church of England regards worship and it is important to understand a little of this.

One reason why Fresh Expressions may have attracted criticism from some quarters of the Anglican Church is that the possibility of diverse congregations springing up with greater freedom in shaping worship opens up a possible weakening of commitment to common prayer, which is the idea that we all say the same things in our worship services, and this represents doctrinal and ecclesial unity.

The Book of Common Prayer (1549, 1552 and 1662) is very important to Anglican identity. The principles held within it underpin theology and doctrine expressed via the liturgy. Its author, Thomas Cranmer, was keen for the people to understand and take more responsibility for their own Christian faith, and the reading of Scripture was important for this. Cranmer developed the lectionary and a book of homilies, and these gave preaching the word a central place in the service: 'Cranmer's chief reason for implementing standard liturgies was to provide a venue [for] the Bible' (Jacobs, 2013, pp. 26–7). This may surprise some who are of the opinion that the Anglican Church has prioritized the liturgy over the reading of Scripture.

It is hard now to imagine the huge impact of the introduction of the Prayer Books, which put prayers, psalms and liturgy into the hands of parishioners, in their own language, for the first time. The notion of 'Common Prayer' has been one of the strongest identities expressed in Anglican worship ever since and is perhaps increasingly important today when 'a degree of commonality in liturgy is needed to maintain and enhance the unity of the Church' (Gray-Reeves and Perham, 2011, p. 12).

All these points of history are not reasons why new things cannot be tried or introduced, but they may explain why at times a warning klaxon seems to sound when we try to discuss changes to practices around the Eucharist. For Anglican pioneers, it helps to understand the sensitive issues from history and become familiar with the themes and rhythms found in the liturgy, drawing on them when creating prayers and services that may be simpler for new people, but maintain a 'family resemblance' to the original.

In 2005, Steven Croft (now Bishop of Sheffield) proposed that Anglican unity had begun to shift from definition 'by common worship texts, to unity defined by common worship shapes'. He proposed a definition of Anglican unity on the basis 'of the common values which lie at the core of our corporate life and ... heritage' instead (Earey, 2013, p. 87). Mark Earey suggested a core set of values or principles that relate to Anglican identity in worship, asking if we can move away from a liturgical 'policing' strategy to a commitment to our shared history and an 'eye to the needs of our particular context' (Earey, 2013, p. 68). These proposals can give us confidence as pioneers to shape worship that is appropriate for our people and makes a connection with our shared history and identity.

In my experience the single biggest factor in giving pioneers appropriate freedom and creativity in an Anglican context is the relationship to your bishop. In the Diocese of Gloucester, Bishop Michael Perham undertook a tour of Fresh Expressions in the UK and the Episcopal Church in the USA several years ago and wrote a book exploring what he had seen in new ecclesial communities. When we approached him, despite being a committed liturgist, he was very willing to listen to the reasons why we felt we needed to create new and shorter services and prayers, and he gave us written permission to explore this, within a framework of serving people missionally from outside of church culture. His letter ended: 'The most important thing is that the worship should honour Jesus Christ and be filled with the Holy Spirit!'

Sacrament and participation

The name Eucharist derives from the εὐχαριστία (*eucharistia*), meaning 'thanksgiving'. It is not a word used in the New Testament as a name for the rite, but the related verb is found in New Testament accounts of the Last Supper:

> For I received from the Lord what I also delivered to you, that the Lord Jesus on the night when he was betrayed took bread, and when he had *given thanks*, he broke it, and said, 'This is my body which is for you. Do this in remembrance of me.' (1 Cor. 11.23–24)

Some churches, Anglican, Orthodox and Catholic among them, consider the Eucharist to be a sacrament. A sacrament is something that points to a greater reality, and that also helps that reality to come into being; a small action that helps us to be drawn into Christ's life and body in a fuller and more mysterious way. It speaks of his provision for us in creation through bread and wine, his desire to gather in and offer a welcome in the body of Christ which is the community of the Church, building us together as we are reminded of his grace to us in his life and death, and allowing us to offer our own response as a sacrifice of praise and recommitment.

The Salvation Army believes 'that it is possible to live a holy life and receive the grace of God without the use of physical sacraments and that they should not be regarded as an essential part of becoming a Christian'. Salvationists see the sacraments as the outward sign of an inward experience, and it is the inward experience that is the most important thing.

However, anthropologists have noted that as physical beings, the creation of ritual is universal and helps people make meaning and develop self-understanding. So I believe the Eucharist to be an important part of the journey of faith. As a ritual it also points us to greater self-awareness, a necessary part of being human, as we engage in self-examination to recognize our life, our mistakes, repetitive habits and selfish behaviours. The Eucharist offers an opportunity for penitence as we consider the relation of our own mess and mistakes to the grace offered through the sacrifice of Christ, and draws us to reflect on our need for forgiveness. If we celebrate it often, this penitence helps us keep 'short accounts' with God, forming the habit of becoming aware of when we have caused hurt or damage to others or the planet. I believe that this regular habit of opening ourselves up to the gaze of God via the Eucharist helps us hold the paradox of our own weakness and failure together with the fact of our deep acceptance and forgiveness by the Father.

However, it has been noted that people unfamiliar with church today may have a different approach to 'sin' from regular churchgoers (see Emma Nash in Baker and Ross, 2014, p. 197), and this may impact what is understood by the relationship between communion, the sacrifice of Christ and our individual and corporate need for forgiveness. One of the shifts in scholarship over the last 50 years has been to relate the ritual of communion to the metaphors and themes found in the whole life and ministry of

Christ, rather than locating communion solely in the narrative of the Last Supper, with its backdrop of Passover and the sacrifice of the paschal lamb for the sins of the people. We will explore this shift further.

The Eucharist is a rite of participation, one that forms us on the journey of faith. It allows new believers and old to appropriate the metaphors of resurrection life again into our own lives. It is hugely important that it is a participatory rite, engaging our senses and bodies:

> By receiving the body of Christ I become a little more a member of his body, the Church. The symbol (sacrament) produces in me what it signifies ... and brings me into contact with a Reality, by acting on me, in me ... The fact of receiving the consecrated bread brings into existence the reality of communion with Christ. (Lebon, 1987, p. 9)

A mutual recognition of ourselves and our relation to others is an important part of gathering together as the Church to undertake the eucharistic celebration: 'Men and women are ritual animals [and] this symbolic action allows individuals or groups to recognize one another at the deepest level of their identity ... Rites are social practices' (Lebon, 1987, p. 15).

Rowan Williams writes in *Lost Icons* that our development as a person and a self grows over time in community with others, and our self-awareness is shaped by our shared understandings (Williams, 2003, pp. 140–1). We need to be aware that we each bring ourselves into dialogue with a faith community, along with our own understandings of tradition and culture, and are shaped by the people and practices in that place.

Shared understanding of the Christian narrative has broken down in some parts of today's culture, so new spaces need to be made for this dialogue and self-understanding to occur. Williams believes that we need a sense of ourselves being held within a narrative as part of human development, even as this narrative is constantly being re-edited over time. Every event that happens connects to others and to the gospel story and reorders who we are and will be, so that 'every telling is a retelling, and the act of telling changes what can be ...' (2003, p. 144). In this way, new identities can be explored and inhabited. Participating in the gospel narrative, via the Eucharist, helps us to develop our humanity.

Eucharist as plausibility structure

People working in ministry and mission ponder how to help people who have never heard the good news of the gospel to access it in a way they can understand and which makes sense. We also need to consider how we ourselves live, show and tell the Jesus story with integrity so that our actions and words work together to communicate clearly.

What we have learned, over the last seven years in a UK context, is that telling, proclaiming, witnessing and evangelizing is not enough; nor is inviting people into 'our church' and then expecting them to get the hang of it because it makes sense to us. This is partly to do with British postmodern society, where experience and authenticity tend to help people make sense of things, but it is also because our shared cultural framework and foundation for understanding faith is now largely lost among some groups in our culture.

When establishing a new church community, one of our tenets has been about offering a space where people who have lost their thread of connection to the gospel can come and be introduced to the Christian narrative and try it on for size; to question and explore, begin to find where they may belong in the story. We hope they can taste and see and participate in it in ways that reduce the cultural hurdles that church can present. We offer a 'plausible structure' to others, sharing the story of Jesus, who he is, what his coming, living, dying and rising is all about, and showing what belonging to the family of God feels like. This is experienced along with a community of fellow journeyers who are still exploring and asking questions, but who have been travelling for a while and can share their own experiences.

The sociological idea of 'plausibility structures' was explored by Sam Richards regarding the Eucharist (Ward, 1999, pp. 116–30). Richards develops the idea that people need spaces, relationships and experiences to enable us to process, internalize and begin to believe and live the gospel. In a surrounding culture that no longer has this explicit in its daily story, this space becomes important. People need to be able to experience it in order for the narrative to make any sense and to participate in it, chew it around, see what it feels like, try it out with others, see how others live in it and how it makes sense to them, and to do this over a period of time with others.

The need to 'have a go' is a very human characteristic and is a facet of learning and growing. We need spaces to practise, and learn from one another's questions and reactions. A community that is open to questions and diverse perspectives is helpful to people at the start of a journey towards faith, and to all of us as we continue on that road.

Richards posits reception into the ritual of communion as access to tasting and experiencing the action that surrounds the death and resurrection of Christ. In joining in, sharing the peace, tasting the bread and wine, people are drawn into the welcome of God at the heart of the faith community. This is why we ask the newest person to offer the cup of wine to others at communion (if they are comfortable, of course) and why we welcome all to take bread and wine. The invitation and participation have proved transformative to many on the journey towards faith. It seems that being given a role at the centre of the action enables people to process and explore the ritual and its meaning for themselves. Communion is a place where we retell and reshape our own stories in the light of Christ's redemptive story.

Table fellowship or Last Supper?

The theology underpinning our community life and our Eucharist draws from the coming and the life of Jesus, as well as his death, and resurrection. It does not focus solely on his death on the cross.

The notion of the Eucharist as primarily based upon a metaphor of sacrifice seems to have been introduced by Augustine around the fifth century, when he suggests that the Church is herself offered on the altar as an invisible sign shown by the symbols of bread and wine she offers (Gorringe, 1997, p. 10).

In recent years there has been a dawning awareness of the connections between the meal of the Eucharist and the radical behaviour of Jesus regarding his dinner companions. The influence of Hellenistic culture relating to meals is also important and provides the context for the Gospel accounts (Bradshaw and Johnson, 2012, p. 1). There is therefore a need to set the Last Supper in the broader context of Jesus' teaching, practices and miracles around eating, hospitality and the kingdom of God, where the metaphor was more often about abundance of life and nourishment than of sacrifice (Bradshaw and Johnson, 2012, p. 21).

In Hellenistic culture, diners reclined on couches around a room with food laid on tables in front of them. 'They would be ranked according to their social status' (Bradshaw and Johnson, 2012, p. 2). There was a sense of *quid pro quo* and patronage, whereby the host might expect support from guests in local matters at a later date. For those of lower social status, food of lesser quality might be served in a separate room; for others who could not be offered a seat, a food parcel might even be given to eat at home.

There was a definite social order around the eating arrangements and we see Jesus confront and repudiate this in the Gospels when he provides the best wine for everyone at the wedding at Cana (John 2.10); when he addresses the pecking order at the table (Luke 14.8); the expectation of the host's getting something in return from the guest (Luke 14.12); and in the invitation of the poor to the banquet (Luke 14.21).

These form part of Jesus' teaching around the kingdom of heaven, where the paradigms of culture and society are turned upside down by grace, and radical inclusion is modelled to a divided society. Religious piety expressed by ritual purity around food was a major issue of social hierarchy in Jewish culture and Jesus deliberately contravened every one of these cultural norms: 'His feeding miracles functioned as *performative* versions of his teaching ... moving the boundary markers with regard to those whom his contemporaries deemed acceptable to God, challenging the divisions in society' (Bradshaw, 2012, p. 9).

Through the actions of his life and ministry, Jesus showed his intention towards radical social inclusion and the breaking down of hierarchy and exclusion in the kingdom, modelled throughout his ministry:

> For a first century Jew, having dinner with someone was making a statement about acceptance and about religious fellowship. Supper was not just sustenance; supper was spirituality. Doing lunch was doing theology. And Jesus was a guy who would chow down with just about anybody. He accepted dinner invitations from upstanding Pharisees ... [and] he also swapped snacks with less savoury souls. (Gempf, 2005, p. 132)

This clash of covenants explains the root of the conflict between the Pharisees and Jesus; while they were still adhering strictly to the law based on Israelite worship at the Temple, Jesus has begun reinventing covenantal practice in anticipation of his death and resurrection, the birth of the new Church and the destruction of the Temple around AD 70. Jesus may have been paving the way by his example for worship and hospitality described in the book of Acts: the new Church was being built on 'radically different principles from those of honour, shame, patronage and clientage. For Jesus, healing ... calls forth hospitality ... The table hospitality practised by Jesus recreated the world' (Bradshaw and Johnson, 2012, p. 9). Perhaps we need to allow its power to recreate us as the Church.

The unity and equal sharing of a meal among a diverse group marked out the new Church from all other gatherings in Roman society, which was highly stratified, 'yet the Christians had declared that there was neither Jew nor Greek, male nor female, master or slave in Galatians 3:28' (Zizioulas, 1985, p. 151). This radical equality and hospitality are such important motifs for the Christian faith and need to be rediscovered and emphasized in our eucharistic practice.

Eschatology and eucharistic community

'Gathering together is a prophetic act which reveals God and makes his presence known' (Lebon, 1987, p. 45). Jesus did not coincidentally eat with people who were socially excluded from the Jewish community; his deliberate act of eating with people considered unacceptable caused a scandal among the Pharisees and even his own followers. That a ritual of gathering and eating is given to us by Christ as our act of remembrance is significant for us in a number of ways.

For Martelet, there is significance in the elements of bread and wine as representing the joint work of God in creation and humankind in cultivation and culture: 'bread and wine are ... part of humanized nature ... It is the [hu]man in his [her] entirety ... that is signified in our Eucharists.' He continues: 'In his Incarnation and in his Eucharist God is strictly inseparable from love and bread ... and the inestimable value of the human itself which bread and wine symbolize' (Martelet, 1976, p. 35). This resonates with the value Jesus accorded to people who suffered from sickness or mental illness and were further harmed by their enforced separation from society imposed by the purity laws.

They were restored as much by their restoration to social and relational life as by his direct healing (John, 2001, pp. 23–4), working with the grain of how humans are made physically and socially and relate to one another in community. In the Orthodox tradition the main focus of the Eucharist relates to this power of gathering and community; the very nature of a eucharistic community is found 'in its inclusiveness of all' (Zizioulas, 1985, p. 154). It is an eschatological picture of the kingdom of God, where the first shall be last and the hungry will be filled.

As we have gathered together around the communion table with people who often remain hidden due to shame and exclusion, we have found that they begin to be revealed after a time of journeying with others in a safe environment (Rom. 8.19). People begin to confess brokenness and be healed, freed to participate again in the life of the local community, their family life or taking responsibility for their health, reviving ambitions and educational journeys, and exploring their spiritual journey. These are our common human journeys.

Gathering together to break bread encompasses all our brokenness and shame within the brokenness of Christ at Calvary, and unites us equally in our need of healing and restoration. We begin to hold our heads up higher. This is foretold in the banquet in Matthew 22.9, when all are invited to the marriage feast to be wed to Christ, and in Matthew 21.31 when Jesus declares that tax-collectors and prostitutes are entering the kingdom ahead of the religious elite. The bread and wine remind us of our equal need of bread for survival; none can outlive human frailty and limitation, whatever our status.

'If Christ himself suffered "outside the camp" (Heb. 13.13) it was in order to show that the offering he made of himself was directed to the profane and commonplace life of [people] ... that were regarded as profane.' Martelet here draws our attention to the requirement of justice imposed upon us in receiving the Eucharist, challenging us to ask whether we are a 'community where the poor cannot possibly feel at home' (Martelet, 1976, p. 182). 'Can those who have more than enough happily retain what they do not need so long as a member of Christ ... is destitute, without breaking up the communion? This practical awareness of others is an exact measure of our belonging to the risen Christ.'

Participation in the Eucharist brings with it a powerful challenge to each of us and to the Church, regarding our commitment to justice. Stretching our understanding of who may access the rite, and in what way they and their life experience can be incorporated into the life of Christ, is a work of justice that calls for the practice of inculturation.

Inculturation

Finding a way to share the importance of the eucharistic message today requires inculturation: the practice of listening to the immediate context and the timeless mysteries of the faith together.

Contextual theologian Steve Bevans advocates for the inclusion of context and our present lived experience to be brought fully into the life of the Church: 'Theology that comes out of a world church, a minority church, a multicultural church, a poor church, can open our ears to new voices – some right in our own back gardens ... and others very different from our own' (Bevans and Tahaafe-Williams, 2011, p. 14). He argues that this type of new voice, derived from the development of contextual theology, 'offers the church a new look at itself'.

The idea of inculturation began to be articulated in the Church of England by the *Faith in the City* report in 1985, which identified the entrenched poverty of the white urban working class, trickling away from the Church of England, and discussed ways in which the gap could be bridged. It recognized that 'the failure of the Church today ... is ... a failure to attend to the voices, the experience and the spiritual riches of the "poor" in its midst' (*Faith in the City*, 1985, p. 62).

It goes further:

A Church which has only a single highly intellectual style of doctrinal formulation and which orders even its most contemporary forms of worship by reference to a closely printed book of over a thousand pages can never hope to bridge the gulf which separates it from ordinary people. We must recognize that ... authentic Christian faith ... can be expressed and achieved in a variety of styles and idioms, by imaginative story-telling, for example, as much as by expositions of doctrine. (*Faith in the City*, 1985, p. 66)

The report critiques the intellectual assumptions around how faith is learned and identifies that our liturgy may be written from a narrow cultural perspective which limits its adoption by those from other cultural standpoints. It is doubtful that this issue has yet been addressed fully 30 years later.

Experience and experiment

The Upper Room was formed in response to the exclusion of people from the Church by social barriers. We opened a space that provided welcome to listen to people and begin an experimental process of inculturation together: 'To engage in dialogue it is essential that one speaks the same language, uses the same code. If I want to speak with someone else, first of all I have to listen in order to learn his language or [her] code' (Lebon, 1987, p. 57).

We heard people express in their own language their sense of exclusion from church because they did not wear the right clothes, espouse the right morality or lifestyle, or were unable to read in order to follow the complex services. They expressed shame when they thought of attending church, feeling that they would be unwelcome, unacceptable, that church was not possible for people 'like me', and that they couldn't possibly 'go in there'. And yet, Lebon reminds us that our rites are meant to be 'at the service of humanity' (Lebon, 1987, p. 17). What does it mean in this scenario that Jesus said the Sabbath was made for people, and not the other way around?

The people we serve have little previous contact with the Church and little theological foundation for understanding the symbolism, allusions and scriptural references, so we decided to begin simply and strip back to the basics of Jesus' activities on earth. These seemed to be based around eating and drinking with excluded people as often as possible. We saw this led him to reciprocal opportunities for listening and sharing with people.

We began by offering tea, toast, listening and prayer at two drop-in sessions per week. Over time, people who were homeless, mentally ill, suffering chronic illness or domestic abuse came and brought their friends. They welcomed prayer, listening and sharing together. We celebrated birthdays and hosted get-togethers. Over time, we added a monthly community meal. People were drawn to being together and eating with Christ seated at the table, just like the crowds that followed Jesus.

Seen through the lens of the table fellowship of Jesus, consider a homeless man eating birthday cake, being sung to among a new church family, celebrating his birthday for the first time in many years: could this also constitute a celebration of communion, of restoration of identity and healing? I am uncertain that we can contain the longing of Christ for his people in our formal official services and I believe that he draws a chair up to the table to eat and be present among us when inclusion is mingled with love and food in his name.

After several years together we began a communion service, using bread baked by a community member and grape juice out of care for the people with addictions in our family. This was followed by a picnic lunch. People began to encounter Jesus in the breaking of the bread, as on the Emmaus road, and ask to be baptized. We began to witness something revelatory taking place.

Our most recent venture centres around growing food on an allotment and a class learning to cook nutritiously and cheaply, as well as developing relationships among isolated people in the groups. Angel Méndez-Montoya has written movingly on the connection between the love that goes into cooking food for a meal together with others and the self-giving love of Christ poured out in the Eucharist. He describes food coming from creation as a 'cosmic banquet' (Méndez-Montoya, 2012, p. ix) and the process of preparing food for others 'a form of theological rejoicing' (p. xi). Drawing on the levelling need of all humans for food and love, he believes that 'food ... can be envisioned as a means of the highest spiritual experience of God's love and of human's love responding to God', and that eating is the means of 'physical and emotional change and ... spiritual transformation; the Eucharist is the paradigmatic example' (2012, p. 2).

Conclusion

As a community we have come to understand the power of the Eucharist, seeing it as a performative rendering of Jesus' teaching on the kingdom of heaven. We have learned that it is no coincidence that he instituted a physical act of ritual to enable remembrance of his radical eating and socializing habits, and that when we participate in sharing this welcome and hospitality, people are drawn towards him and changed. This learning has emerged from the welcome and hospitality offered to us by the Church of England, and our resultant grappling with its rules and doctrines as we sought to find the blessing in them for people who were far off. Whether our stream takes this ritual seriously or lightly, I recommend that pioneers forming new church communities seek after the blessing and the life that flows from the Eucharist and its power to shape all our faith journeys.

References

Baker, J. and Ross, C. (eds), 2014, *The Pioneer Gift: Explorations in Mission*, Norwich: Canterbury Press.

Bevans, S. and Tahaafe-Williams, K., 2011, *Contextual Theology for the Twenty First Century Church*, Eugene, OR: Wipf & Stock.

Bradshaw, P. and Johnson, M., 2012, *The Eucharistic Liturgies*, London: SPCK.

Earey, M., 2013, *Beyond Common Worship*, London: SCM Press.

Faith in the City: A Call to Action by Church and Nation, 1985, London: Church House Publishing.

Gempf, C., 2005, *Mealtime Habits of the Messiah*, Grand Rapids, MI: Zondervan.

Gorringe, T., 1997, *The Sign of Love*, London: SPCK.

Gray-Reeves, M. and Perham, M., 2011, *The Hospitality of God*, London: SPCK.

Jacobs, A., 2013, *The Book of Common Prayer*, New Jersey: Princeton University Press.

John, J., 2001, *The Meaning of Miracles*, Norwich: Canterbury Press.

Lebon, J., 1987, *How to Understand the Liturgy*, London: SCM Press.

Martelet, G., 1976, *The Risen Christ and the Eucharistic World*, New York: Seabury Press.

Méndez-Montoya, A., 2012, *The Theology of Food*, Oxford: Wiley Blackwell.

Ward, P. (ed.), 1999, *Mass Culture: Eucharist and Mission in a Post-Modern World*, Oxford: BRF.

Williams, R., 2003, *Lost Icons: Reflections on Cultural Bereavement*, Edinburgh: T&T Clark.

Zizioulas, J., 1985, *Being As Communion*, London: Darton, Longman and Todd.

Note

1 The *Didache*, or apostolic teachings, are ancient writings dated around the second century, containing detailed information on the practices of the early Christian Church. These were discovered in the late nineteenth century and they showed that there were a whole variety of prayers used by the early Church when celebrating communion. Prior to this, it had been thought that there was one handed down by Christ himself.

12

Doors in the Air: Baby Spirituality

TINA HODGETT

The opening credits of the Disney Pixar movie *Monsters, Inc.* take place against a background of different doors. The doors refer to the connecting doors between the bedroom of every child in Monstropolis and the secret factory run by the eponymous monsters where the children's screams (and later laughter) are bottled as fuel for the town's energy grid.

The concept of mystical doors acting as a point of entry to a hidden alternate reality is well known. It is common in fantasy fiction, and famously employed by C. S. Lewis in the Narnia series. Apart from the well-known wardrobe door into Aslan's kingdom of Narnia, Aslan himself places doors in the air wherever he chooses to allow people to transfer from one world to another. It is easy to trace the connection between this image and the metaphor of Jesus as 'the gate for the sheep' (John 10.7), the one 'through whom' people must pass to come to the Father (John 14.6), and the 'narrow door' (Luke 13.24). Jesus is the door; but he also places doors in the world wherever he chooses, opening the way into the kingdom of the Trinitarian God.

Sometimes the task of pioneering includes discerning where these doors are. Since they are 'in the air' (code for spiritual, mystical places), they are not necessarily obvious to human sense perception. The events described in this chapter grew out of a hypothesis that biblical metaphors might give a hint to where doors are situated: like a map in a hunt for invisible treasure.

Stripping down the metaphor

The biblical writers use metaphors of pregnancy, labour, new birth and parenthood in all kinds of contexts to describe impending change, distress, joy, weakness, tenderness, sin, hope, and mystery (among other things!).

When we read about the lives of women in the Bible, we find them encountering and engaging with God as they try to conceive, give birth, or protect their children. Sarah, Rebecca, Rachel, Hannah, Elizabeth: the women who conceived against the grain of nature ... Tamar, Ruth, Bathsheba, Mary: women who gave birth in what you could only call interesting circumstances ... Moses' mother, the Hebrew midwives in the time of Pharaoh: women who fought for the lives of infants.

It ought not to surprise us that God knows the processes of pregnancy and birth from inside out (literally!). If this common but extraordinary life event is exploited by the biblical writers as a source of metaphors for the spiritual life, perhaps there is also an argument for exploring the actual concrete experience of being pregnant and giving birth as a spiritual space: a place generative of new spiritual life, flourishing and potential growth. Perhaps conception, pregnancy, labour, birth and even baby loss (Jones, 2001, p. 242) can act as a door into the kingdom of heaven.

There is a growing body of theological writing testifying how spiritual growth may take place for women in connection with their experience of conception, pregnancy, birth and parenthood. Pregnancy – or on the other end of the conception spectrum, infertility – are intense, life-changing events. The birth – or death – of a baby is so huge it is hard to put into words. By its very nature it is a spiritual occurrence, whether we acknowledge it or not.

Baby Days begins

Since May 2012 I have been sharing a spiritual space with a group of five women in Portishead who had just had their first baby. This is a very strange area of ministry in many ways for me to get involved in, as I am single, have never been married, and never been pregnant. This was definitely a case of having 'the gift of not fitting in' (Baker and Ross, 2014, p. 1). My friend and co-missioner Nicola, on the other hand, is a mother of three, sought-after ante-natal teacher, open to God, passionate about supporting mothers in pregnancy, and still amazed at every new human being that arrives on the planet.

At a post-birth reunion she asked one of her ante-natal groups if anyone was interested in exploring the spirituality of pregnancy, birth and first parenthood with us. We told them we had no idea what we were doing; they would be guinea pigs in a six-week project. Two came along to the first session, and by the third we had five mums attending. As time went on it turned out they were all 'open de-churched' according to the Richter and Francis scale of churchification (Richter and Francis, 1998, quoted in Bayes, 2004, p. 37).

We met in Nicola's house, created a spa-type ambience with candles, gentle music, sofas, homemade cake and black-and-white photos of babies. All the babies came. We talked and they were fed, jiggled, rocked, cuddled. Every week we began in Nicola's spacious kitchen with tea and cake, then transferred to the lounge. The course outline can be found at the end of the chapter.

We did very little theology as it is traditionally understood. I read bits of Scripture, and encouraged them to engage with it, but mainly we created the kind of therapeutic space I had encountered during ordination training on placement at a psychiatric unit for young people with anorexia. I had been so impressed by the open and accepting atmosphere, and struck by the contrast with most of the church groups I had been part of – it seemed more truthful, more holistic.

In the first weeks of the Baby Days group there were sudden surprising moments of deep spiritual connection. One afternoon Katherine[1] broke down in tears, suddenly realizing how moody and unappreciative she had been of her partner who was working hard to support her and the new baby … and suddenly we were witnessing an act of genuine, spontaneous confession and repentance such as I had never seen in 45 years of church attendance and membership of home groups. On another day Emma told us that before her baby arrived, she was perfectly happy; the baby had added 'something extra' to a completely contented existence, something undeserved, and I found myself thinking she was describing grace. We were 'doing theology' in a way that arose from the circumstances of the women's lives, rather than arising from the givens of church requirements, or the non-negotiables of catechism or scriptural text.

As for the Baby Days ladies,[2] they were taken by surprise as well. Emma wrote after the six weeks finished: 'Becoming a mum reignites your spirituality in a way I didn't expect and your group has really brought that out for me at a perfect time.' She said it was like 'an hour's spa treatment' and a chance 'to take time once a week to be thankful'.

Lucy said: 'It was really refreshing to discuss topics you wouldn't automatically discuss. As you know the five of us are together every week but we've never talked that deeply – just having the time to think about how you feel is priceless.'

So they received it as gift, something they said they would have asked for if they had known it was available.

Where we live is unusual. It is a rapidly growing town being settled by what Nicola calls 'aspirational families', lots of whom work in engineering and IT on the west side of Bristol in the aerospace industries and Ministry of Defence. Physically beautiful couples with higher education, family support, money, good housing, reliable income and future prospects move here to start a family or settle down with young children. The icing on the cake is their first baby, and it seems that their lives can be enriched by an opportunity to reflect more deeply on what is in many ways an ordinary life event.

They didn't want to stop meeting when the six weeks came to an end. Katherine set up a secret group on Facebook so we could share YouTube clips of miracle babies, arrange dates and share prayer requests. The online space has become a significant part of our community, allowing us to stay connected when the demands of family life make it hard to meet face to face. As the group has grown in faith, we have together wrestled in prayer for families we know who have been going through extreme challenges, and God has answered prayers in beautiful ways. Facebook has kept a record for us of the ups and downs of the stories, and of the prayers posted on line.

Baptism

For the rest of the year we discussed baptism (using parallels from the birth experience to interpret symbols in the baptism service) and all the babies were baptized. It was a privilege to have journeyed with the families for so long through the adventure of pregnancy, birth and the formation of a new family before the baptism. In many cases churches (those that baptize infants at least) meet families for the first time when they present babies for baptism, missing the opportunity to offer spiritual resources, guidance and support much earlier in this formative, stretching, blessed stage of life.

Through Advent we read Luke chapters 1 and 2 and discussed Elizabeth and Mary, their pregnancies and birth stories, which helped bring the Christmas story closer to the new mothers. The problem with babies, though, is they grow, and once they were toddlers the nature of our gatherings changed. It was impossible to have deep conversations about anything, and eventually we stopped meeting.

Nicola and I thought in many ways that was the end of the story – gloriously worth it for its own sake, but not generative of deep connection to God and a life of discipleship. However, giving birth to faith seems to be a long, complex process with a number of stages, just like giving birth to a human being.

It is clear now that God was already at work in the lives of the Baby Days ladies. The seeds of faith were already in them, just as eggs are already in a girl's ovaries when she is born. The first gatherings caused some kind of conception to take place. The awareness of God started to grow in the women, but it was slow, and you would not have seen much evidence that they were pregnant with faith. The 'bump of faith' did not show very large to begin with, and although there were the signs of God at work, as described earlier, I was not confident of continuing growth, particularly after we stopped meeting. I feared their faith had stopped growing under the pressure of toddler-care and juggling other priorities. It had miscarried, perhaps ... It had brought joy and hope and insight for a short time, but had not grown into a viable faith with a life of its own.

I do not have the space to tell the whole story in detail. But over the following year Katherine decided to be baptized. She had wrestled for many years with questions of faith, had had periods of engaging with faith traditions, and had good Christian friends. After months of agonizing, she made up her mind to go for it. We held a beautiful Baby Days baptism service in the parish church, with the group and partners and children. She sent me a card saying that she was proud to call herself a Christian; soon afterwards she began bringing her two young children to the traditional family service on Sundays.

Katherine and three of the other ladies had a second baby after Baby Days came to an end, which heralded a season for the group of different kinds of crises. Extraordinarily, three of the newborns were hospitalized with serious complications in the few weeks after birth, while Louisa hit a wall of exhaustion and anxiety. And it seems that those experiences of pain and struggle in particular initiated another trimester in their faith development. It gave birth to a hunger for a more spiritual life ... When Lucy's second baby was taken into the children's hospital with a serious condition, her instinct was to turn to the Baby Days Facebook page with a request for help, sure of the deep, prayerful acceptance and understanding she had become accustomed to finding in the group.

She was instrumental in calling a Baby Days reunion a couple of months later, and in that September – at their request – we began Baby Days Mark 2, which meets monthly in the evening, and the ladies prioritize it in their calendars.

What kind of spirituality is this?

If there are countless different doors in the air from this world into the kingdom of God, then the path leading from each door towards Christ at the centre of the kingdom will be unique. It will begin from differing starting points, travel through its own local landscape, and draw on easily accessible resources at the start; as a result of all this, it will also develop its own particular spiritual characteristics.

In the following pages I attempt to describe as objectively as possible the spirituality of the Baby Days group.

Applied spirituality

Primarily, this spirituality is *for* something. It is about lifestyle, about trying to find an answer to the questions, 'How do we live? How do we mother, how do we connect, how do we survive in a world that expects so much of us?' The question of how to surf the waves as new parents in the twenty-first century, with all the pressures that this entails, has been the underlying momentum for the group, particularly in its second manifestation, when the Baby Days ladies told me they felt a deep need to reconstitute the group, almost for their sanity. As such they fit the pattern of postmodern, corporate achieving, holistic spiritual seekers of Drane's 'spiritual spectrum' (Drane, 2008, pp. 80, 83). They seek an expression of faith and spirituality that resources and sustains them in their everyday life and does not add burdens to it, resisting any pressure to join a form of church that makes demands and adds to the diary overload and endless 'to-do' list.

This kind of spirituality does not begin with tradition, Scripture or church culture, but with life, and the joys and challenges it offers – in this case, the often disorienting joys and challenges of a first-time parent. The Baby Days ladies have privileged lives on the whole, and probably belong to that category of people who have largely been able to choose and control the circumstances of their lives. Interestingly, most of their husbands are away from home during the week because of work, and the responsibility and demands of parenting alone have thrust them into situations where they have felt overwhelmed, or where money and education cannot always determine the outcome they want.

So this spirituality is about being able to ride the rollercoaster of life as a parent of young children – with help from a deeper source of life and power than they have had before. It is also pegged into the routines of life and rites of passage, so it has a strong focus on God in the everyday, encountering him in nature, relationships, children and community.

A spirituality of deep connection

The women knew each other socially before I knew them, and they get together in between our meetings for all sorts of reasons. They are astonished at the depth of relationship and quality of conversation we are capable of. Katherine said in her evaluation of Baby Days 1 that she was amazed at how honestly Nicola and I shared our thoughts and feelings with them in those first six sessions. I sometimes wonder if what Nicola and I have pioneered here is simply a capacity on behalf of a few individuals to relate to each other deeply and compassionately.

When we reconstituted the group in September 2014, they said one of the things they valued hugely was having a place where you could say anything and not be judged. They wanted to be free of the need to perform and pretend, to escape the tyranny of the parenting textbooks and the mantras around babycare, to have a safe space where they could throw off the mask and be themselves, vulnerable and imperfect and yet accepted and loved.

Relationships are enormously important, and so is the fact that we are all travelling together. The group is definitely journeying as a group. I did not have an individual faith conversation with any of them till recently.

When we were discussing our five core group values for Baby Days 2, Lucy surprised me by offering the word 'cherish'. She said she felt we cherished each other. 'Cherish' is not a common word in today's world. It appears in the traditional marriage vows and includes the idea of love, but also of holding something precious and fragile, something you need to truly appreciate and almost hold your breath when you think about it, because of its great value.

The quality of the relationships in the group struck me again when I went to chat to Emma about the baptism of her second baby. She opened the door, threw her arms around me and burst into tears, very atypically emotional. As we talked, it turned out that she was not personally in difficulty; rather, Louisa was going through a very challenging time and Emma was deeply distressed to see her suffering. Emma's willingness to allow Louisa's pain to become her own was a voluntary act of co-suffering unique in my experience.

Rooted in prayer ...

When we met for the six-week trial in 2012 and talked about prayer, Lucy told us that she realized she had been praying all the way through her pregnancy. She wouldn't have called it praying and didn't know to whom she had been praying, but she was constantly addressing someone in her head asking for the baby to be born healthy and for everything to go well in the child's life.

Prayer seems to come naturally to some pregnant women. I think the body prepares, expands, opens in so many ways, and emotions come under the influence of hormonal changes; so if body, mind and spirit are interconnected it makes sense the spirit will awaken and prepare to co-create new life with God. All aspects of a woman's body mobilize for motherhood; of course, her spirit will be roused to call upon the divine resources to hand. She simply needs to bring that call to awareness.

Prayer seems to go well with the act of breastfeeding. Breastfeeding can be (although is not always) a deeply satisfying experience of connection with another, of giving nourishment. It is a period of enforced inactivity that can be peaceful. The mother nourishes the baby physically and at the same time draws on spiritual nourishment for herself (cf. 1 Pet. 2.2–3). The metaphor of God as mother is indicated here as in parts of the Scriptures, holding the child close, delighting, cherishing and comforting, expressing tenderness and providing security (e.g. Isa. 42.14; 49.15; 66.13). As the human mother relates to her child in this way, she can imagine God as mothering parent relating to her with the same nurturing, unconditional love. She can take her place in the cascade of love from God to herself to her child and onwards.

I have begun to think of prayer as the spiritual equivalent of 'latching on', the term used in breastfeeding circles to indicate that the baby has got its mouth in the correct position on the nipple to feed. Latching on to the life of God! Once a person has latched on through a regular rhythm of prayer that supports their everyday life, their leader can relax because then they are no longer dependent on you, but open to leading of the Holy Spirit.

Embodied ...

It is an embodied spirituality. In our gatherings we used our bodies to cradle babies and we marvelled at the miracle of creating a new human being, who at three months has primarily bodily ways of expressing his or her humanity. A baby does not rely for its life on engaging the mind in analytical discussion, but is welcoming and accepting of physical touch as a way of showing value. So we embrace physical forms of prayer (prayer walking, prayer running, and breathing prayers, for example) and welcome appropriate physical expressions of care and spiritual connection.

In her book *Women's Faith Development*, Nicola Slee (2004, p. 110) quotes research by Maria Harris into women's experience of spiritual awakening 'which will include a claiming of the self, especially an affirmation of the body' (Harris, 1989, p. 5). Slee also refers to research by Belenky and others demonstrating how a woman's intuitive and bodily ways of knowing begin to be prioritized during the time of awakening over authoritative dictates of others, as was the case with Emma (Slee, 2004, p. 116).

Emma described how she had gone against the strong advice

of her consultant gynaecologist when she had her second baby. The doctor wanted to have the baby turned, but Emma refused, telling me later that she had been certain about this because of her new openness to God's Spirit within her. She was right, too, as the baby was born with the cord wrapped twice around her neck. Being turned would have put her life at risk. She made a choice based on what 'her body and her need were telling her' (Slee, 2004, p. 116).

Using metaphors of pregnancy and birth

Once you begin to use metaphors of pregnancy and childbirth to explain concepts of faith, the possibilities are almost endless. Apart from the idea of connecting up with God through prayer as 'latching on', the role of the Holy Spirit can be explained as a kind of umbilical cord that keeps us attached to God, delivers God's goodness and sustenance into our life, and helps to take away harmful waste products. The symbols of an Anglican baptism service can all be explained in terms of physical birth, and the place of a spiritual guide and mentor equates to the role of midwife. The phrase 'born again', used by Jesus in conversation with Nicodemus, gains a fresh resonance when it is closely associated with the realities of an actual birth and the detailed illuminating metaphors for the early stages of faith that can be extrapolated from the birth experience.

This insight from Baby Days is not new. Many writers use birth imagery to describe the process of becoming aware of the life of God within:

Conception, labor and birthing ... offer a body parable of the process of awakening. The parable tells us things we need to know about the way awakening works – the slow, unfolding, sometimes hidden, always expanding nature of it, the inevitable queasiness, the need to nurture and attend to what inhabits us, the uncertainty about the outcome, the fearful knowing that once we bring the new consciousness forth, our lives will never be the same. (Monk Kidd, 1996, pp. 11–12, quoted in Slee, 2004, p. 112)

Awe, wonder and mystery

This kind of spirituality is not based in the kind of awe and wonder found in a worship gathering, but in the awe and wonder that comes from contemplating the wonder and the everyday miracle of life. The impossibility of 'you being you' – of that particular combination of egg and sperm ever having a chance of coming together – is comically described in a novel about an alien from an advanced mathematical society who comes to earth and inhabits the body of a human. He falls in love with a human woman and is driven to reflect:

> Mathematically, rounding things up, there was no chance at all that Isobel Martin could have existed ... A zero in ten-to-the-power-of-forever chance. And yet there she was ... Suddenly it made me realize why religion was such a big thing around here. Because, yes, sure, God could not exist. But then neither could humans. So, if they believed in themselves – the logic must go – why not believe in something that was only a fraction more unlikely? (Haig, 2014, p. 207).

In addition to the unlikelihood of one's own conception, awe and wonder is evoked from the thought of having a complex creation growing inside you from a few cells, the awesome responsibility of being co-creators with God, of receiving from him the gift of a new human being. Our Facebook page is used to celebrate life, its conception and richness. Increasingly the ladies express their thankfulness for the gift of their children and for the privilege of the gift of life itself. This gives a sense of perspective in the face of the day-to-day challenges of life and the juggling required by all the competing demands of homemaking, work, marriage and family life with pre-schoolers, community and wider family commitments and responsibilities.

Mystical

There have been one or two extraordinary moments in the past year when God has been powerfully present when we have met. I have described these as an 'overshadowing' in reference to Mary's being 'overshadowed by the Holy Spirit' (Luke 1.35). While not claiming a similarity with the magnitude of Mary's experience, I wonder if believing women who make themselves available to God may share in some way her experience of being overshadowed by him. These experiences are emotional and mysterious. After the last occasion Emma said it was like 'a cleansing'. When I asked what she meant, she said it was like 'the rubbish in your head ... the rubbish of the everyday to-do list ... is cleared away ... all that matters is this right here, right now. About the things that are important.'

In his sonnet 'The Nativity', Roman Catholic priest and poet John O'Donohue wrote of Mary giving birth to Jesus, 'Someone is coming ashore inside her' (O'Donohue, 2001, p. 65). In some ways at Baby Days it seems as if God is coming ashore in us as well. We are certainly happy to describe what is happening in poetic, mystical terms, and living with the uncertainty and mystery of what is happening beyond our control.

Subversive of social norms around birth and parenting

I want to suggest that this kind of spirituality is subversive of twenty-first-century culture. The culture around giving birth today is largely consumerist, rationalist and humanist. It reduces the experience of conception and birth, as well as miscarriage and infertility, to questions of biology, medicine and material goods. What Baby Days has shown is that people need permission to talk about the spiritual, emotional and relational aspects of having a baby. When we can provide that, we undermine the meta-narrative that sidelines the Creator in the process of creation, and offer a view that is potentially more rounded and respects our full humanity.

The fascinating thing about birth is that you cannot – however much you try – say, 'It's just science at work.' It is impossible to get away from the fact that the baby is profoundly imbued with value and meaning; even babies born with great physical defects are called 'perfect' by their parents. So a spirituality that puts the Creator back into the birth process is subversive.

This spirituality also subverts the myth of perfection that is dominant in middle-class circles. There is an idealized image of perfect family life, with a perfect home and perfect children, that many parents – particularly mothers – find themselves trying to live up to. The anxiety to meet this unspoken expectation leads parents to be constantly measuring their child's progress against that of other children, creating an unintended competitive environment which in turn prevents warm and supportive relationships from forming of the kind that many women seek.

Subversive of church culture

I might also claim that this kind of spirituality critiques church culture. The Baby Days ladies call their group a 'freestyle' church. It has values of honesty, celebration, deep connection, compassion and cherishing each other.

I have been concerned sometimes that they have little knowledge of current church culture. The Baby Days ladies and their families occasionally worship at an Anglican church – Christmas, weddings and baptisms – but are otherwise refreshingly free of Christian cultural baggage. I recognize the danger that Nicola and I offer a very narrow range of Christian thought and spirituality. We risk giving rise to a church in our own image and likeness (although today the internet offers a much wider range of theologies and spiritual resources than have been available before, so there is no boundary to what they may be exposed to, both good and bad). We constantly walk a line between being faithful to the Scriptures, tradition and wider contemporary church life, and looking for newness and creativity within a specific context.

Nevertheless, there are advantages in growing faith largely outside established church culture (of all traditions). The ladies use

language freshly and creatively because they have not been taught
Bible-speak or church jargon. Emma said recently that Baby Days
was like 'a voile curtain over an open door ... not one of those
heavy church doors ...'

It is refreshing to trace the work of God's Spirit in their lives not
by their conformity to church subcultures but by tracking developments in their prayer habits, attitudes to others, accounts of their
conversations, and adventures with God. It has felt important not
to impose expectations on them – though this has been hard –
in order to leave space for God to do 'a new thing' (Isa. 43.19)
should he so desire.

Why this story is worthy of attention

This story is in many ways minuscule in scale, involving numbers
too small to have broad significance. Against the background of
today's vigorous missional activity, it is as fragile and ephemeral
as gossamer. Just how fragile it is was demonstrated when Alex,
the fifth mum I have not mentioned so far, decided to withdraw
from the Baby Days group after the first meeting of Baby Days 2.

It is a minor experiment, but somehow it feels significant and
strong regardless. The growth in faith that has taken place is
organic, responsive to what is happening in their lives; it is slow,
deep and integrated, and it is still continuing.

The story shows that there are deep wells of spirituality around
pregnancy and childbirth and encourages us to consider how we
help draw that water from those wells. Nicola and I have recently
launched a Church of England ante-natal course with an intentional spiritual strand, to offer women the opportunity to become
aware of the God who is creator and sustainer of the child unfurling in their womb, and to be alongside as pastors in the highs
and lows of pregnancy, birth and first parenthood (www.birth-
and-beyond.org.uk). Potentially from this may grow ante-natal
and post-natal groups in the future that could lead people to a
life-giving faith. If that happens we may find that there are doors
in the air from the bedrooms of many newborn children leading

into the hidden kingdom of God – the experience of pregnancy, birth and first parenthood becoming 'an open door that no one can shut' (Rev. 3.8).

Baby Prayer Course Outline

Session 1: New Beginnings

Light a candle. Welcome and introduce ourselves and the babies.

Explain the purpose and outline of the session.

Sing (selection of appropriate songs with and without God content)

Baby Days Gathering Prayer

We praise you, God, Father, Son and Holy Spirit,
for the Life that overflows from you into us.
We praise you for your wisdom, kindness and generosity.
We come in joy at the gift of a child.
We come with thanks for the love and support of a family.
We come together to share our joys, our sorrows,
our hopes and our fears in community,
and to draw comfort from one another.
Help us to meet with you today.
Help us to care for our children's needs in body, mind and spirit.
Help us to be the people you want us to be.
Amen.

Big question
Discuss: *Think about the fact that birth can be a time when people ask big questions about life, themselves, creation, God, family. Ask them if it is true for them? What sort of questions have opened up for them? How do they explain this phenomenon of a new human person being formed inside them?*

Read Genesis 1.26–28 (from *The Message*). Ask for any responses ... comments ... questions ...
We would say that God is the author of all new life. He is the Creator of all things.

Sharing
Ask what has been the best and worst thing about the past week. Allow people to share.

Prayer
Nicola and I say TeaSPoon prayers (thank you/sorry/please) for each person aloud re the issues they've shared, or more generally.

Craft activity: memory-making
Take a photo of each baby and print, then insert into a keyring with a suitable quote. Allow conversation to revert to day-to-day matters.

Session 2: Who am I?

As above, except:

Big question
Discuss: *Who is the new baby? What do you already know about the baby's personality? How are they the same as you? How are they different? What do you think has contributed to the baby being as they are?*

Read Psalm 139.13–15 (from *The Message*). Ask for responses.
We would say that God has designed us to be unique and is the only one who truly knows the baby inside out.

Craft activity: handprint
Take a handprint of each baby in clay.

Session 3: Who will I become?

As above, but:

Big question
Discuss: *How did you choose the baby's name? Do you know what it means? Was it to do with the past or the future? Does the name say something about what the baby means to you? Or to your partner?*

Read Psalm 139.13–16 (from *The Message*). Ask for responses. *We would say God knows the baby's potential and purpose ... who they'll become if they hold to that purpose and allow God to shape them as they grow.*

Craft activity: handprint
Paint the clay handprint of each baby (from last week).

Session 4: Where do I fit in?

As above, except:

Big question
Discuss: *The family – the couple – has to make space for the new baby. So physically in your body; practically, in your house; and then emotionally and spiritually within your relationship or your family. How do you feel about making space for this stranger? What changes are likely to happen, have happened?*

Perhaps discuss the Nativity story or read 1 Corinthians 13.4–7. Ask for responses.

Craft activity: photoframe
Decorate and find a new family photo to put inside.

Session 5: How do I grow?

As above, except:

Big question
Discuss: *For you, what are the essentials for your baby to thrive? Do they cover the material, physical, social, emotional, spiritual? Which is most important? How will you provide these or enable the child to receive them?*

Read Mark 10.13–16. Ask for any responses.
We would emphasize the importance of the spiritual ... the spiritual nature of childhood ... the connectedness of young children to the kingdom of God. Point out the inconsistency of taking a guiding role as a parent in every area of children's development except the spiritual.

Craft activity: candle-holder

Session 6: What about Mum and Dad?
As above, except:

Big question
Discuss: *What about you? How are you doing as a couple through all of this? How do you stay sane, healthy, keep your relationship strong? How is your support system? Are you part of a community? How do you celebrate?*

Read Deuteronomy 16.9–11, 13–15. Ask for responses.
Discuss the importance of having a wide network of supportive relationships if possible. 'It takes a village to raise a child.' Point out the weaknesses of a rigid adherence to the culture of a nuclear family.

Craft activity
Write affirming words/prayers for each other.

References

Baker, J. and Ross, C. (eds), 2014, *The Pioneer Gift*, Norwich: Canterbury Press.

Bayes, P., 2004, *Mission-shaped Church*, London: Church House Publishing.

Drane, J., 2008, *After McDonaldisation*, London: Darton, Longman and Todd.

Haig, M., 2014, *The Humans*, Edinburgh: Canongate.

Harris, M., 1989, *The Dance of the Spirit: The Seven Steps of Women's Spirituality*, New York: Bantam.

Jones, S., 2001, 'Hope Deferred: Theological Reflections on Reproductive Loss (Infertility, Miscarriage, Stillbirth)', *Modern Theology*, 17(2), pp. 227–45.

Monk Kidd, S., 1996, *The Dance of the Dissident Daughter*, New York: HarperSanFrancisco.

O'Donohue, J., 2001, *Conamara Blues*, New York: Bantam.

Richter, P. and Francis, L., 1998, *Gone But Not Forgotten*, London: Darton, Longman and Todd.

Slee, N., 2004, *Women's Faith Development*, Aldershot: Ashgate.

Notes

1 Real names used with their permission.

2 The term 'ladies' is used for these women solely because of its alliterative quality. They are the 'Baby Days ladies'.

13

An Active Spirituality for Mission

ANN-MARIE WILSON

Introduction

Mission is taking part in God's plan and sharing it with the world (*missio Dei*). Yet how does one keep a real sense of passion while working in mission, and not succumb to the threats of burnout, loss of faith and giving up the calling due to the challenges of the mission?

While working in West Darfur in 2005, I met a little girl aged 11, who had experienced FGM (female genital mutilation) at the age of five and become pregnant at ten from rape by armed militia who left her orphaned in her burned village where she was the sole survivor. This experience changed the course of my life, and led me to retrain in midwifery and fistula rehabilitation skills, Islamics, gender, anthropology and development, in order to start an anti-FGM charity, 28 Too Many.[1] This journey so far has taken ten years and travel across over a dozen African countries, and diaspora countries in the Middle East, Asia, Europe and Australasia where FGM is practised. It would not be possible if the work was not a calling, tested and confirmed by the Church, by CMS, and supported by individual donors and over 20 volunteers across Africa and the UK.

This chapter explores my journey to find a meaningful spirituality from the vast range of options on offer; this has now led to a lifelong commitment to the Christian faith, and unexpectedly a calling to lifelong mission. It also explores how I have embraced an active spirituality while travelling overseas for up to four months each year in some of the most troubled places in Africa.

Journey to find a meaningful spirituality

Born to a staunch Methodist father whose childhood embraced the disciplines of alcohol abstinence and an entire Sabbath rest day, and an Anglican mother who was expected to eat only fish on Fridays and attend multiple weekly church activities, it was a surprising decision to send me to a convent school and avoid church. The Sisters of the Holy Cross embraced vows of poverty, generosity, teaching, simplicity, celibacy and diligent hard work. Being a 'non-Catholic', yet taking part in weekly donations to African mission and work activities during Friday Mass, my curiosity in spirituality was birthed. At the age of eight, the death of a teacher and abuse at the school led to my seeking my own spirituality, and I took myself to Sunday school. A Holy Spirit 'experience' and confirmation followed with church attendance until the end of university, although the practice felt somewhat ritualistic and empty of something.

During my twenties, after the death of my father and having met two Jewish partners, I embraced Judaism; after three years of study, a Mikvah (Jewish bath), a Beth Din (court) conversion and synagogue acceptance service, I became Jewish. With its similarities to Catholicism, I found it an easy adjustment, with its focus of faith as a 'way of life'. After more than 20 years of living and practising Judaism, the death of my mother led to a life crisis. All aspects were questioned: relationship, work, family, friends and faith. Although I kept the practice of Judaism over the following years, synagogue, workshop and community membership stopped.

This somewhat existential crisis led to exploring the elements of faith 'other' than Catholicism, Anglican and Judaism. First, after studying psychology, I explored the elements of New Age practice. It seemed appealing with its use of liturgy, angels, candles, meditation and healing. Travel to Hawaii and Sedona brought an exposure to chanting, yoga and rituals associated with ancient indigenous peoples and spiritual places. Although attractive, after much reading and reflection I still felt something was missing, and sought elsewhere. The spiritual journey continued and I enrolled on a transcendental meditation course, at the end of which I was offered the possibility of attending a practising community. Again meditation and candles were present and the quieting of the mind seemed appealing in my busy western culture. Then came the opportunity to join the movement, which meant mailing a photo and money to a guru living in California. As this seemed slightly strange, I visited the guru at a conference in Edinburgh that December. After listening to very discordant 'inspired' sitar music and having the chance to buy the guru's 'heavenly' art, I drew an end to this path, as this also did not seem to be the route to spirituality.

A psychology course led to my meeting two Islamic brothers. My course project was 'exploring spirituality', and they helpfully offered tutoring in Islam; the reading of many books, lessons and teaching followed. While this gave a good foundation in Islam, some of the attributes of God seemed distant and unapproachable, and once again I did not adopt this path.

The visit of a friend to the UK to hear the Dalai Lama speak on Buddhism seemed like a good opportunity. After three days of teaching he addressed the 'white converts' in their red robes. He asked, 'How many of you have explored your own faith before converting? You should never convert without fully studying the faith of your land.' This point struck a chord, and caused a reflection on the spiritual journey so far: Catholicism, Anglicanism, Judaism, New Age, Indian Sect, Islam, Buddhism. Realizing that an adult study of Christianity was missing from the list, upon a friend's recommendation I enrolled on an Alpha course.

The course seemed extraordinary timing. Not only were the ten weekly evenings free for me to attend Holy Trinity Brompton's Alpha Course,[2] but the course offered an evening on 'Can God Heal?'; on that occasion prayers were sought and miraculously worked providing my healing from seven years of chronic ill health. The course came to an end just as a three-month sabbatical, which had been booked, began; this enabled time for me to start Bible study, prayer, reflection and the beginning of the seed of calling to mission.

Nearly 20 years later, looking backward enables me to reflect on a tapestry rich in colour, diversity and wisdom. I have embraced the wisdom of the Catholic nuns in integral mission and a life of calling; the liturgy of high Anglicanism now sits comfortably with Charismatic low-church Christianity; a Jewish soul has merely added a completed Messianic expression of the belief and embracing Passover and high holidays of the Torah; the practice of transcendental meditation, the Indian sect and Buddhism began a path to silent reflection; a study of Islam has opened a way to spiritual discipline, daily rhythms and an understanding of women dressing modestly. Finally, attending the Alpha course, after much personal spiritual seeking, enabled my questioning of faith which was not always possible within a community of believers. This legacy was the perfect stepping stone for intercultural mission.

An active spirituality

Spirituality encompasses devotion to God through pursuit of holiness and cultivation of core virtues, whereby the whole of one's life is lived under that direction, influenced by the role of key texts, disciplines and practices by which spirituality is achieved. This involves a process of spiritual formation. *The Westminster Dictionary of Christian Spirituality* (Wakefield, 1983, pp. 1–6, 26) notes that 'Christian spirituality is not simply for the "interior life" or the inward person, but as much for the body as the soul, and is directed to the implementation of both the commandments to love God and show grace to neighbours in daily life'. In reality, it takes a wide diversity of forms, and differs greatly over key seasons of life, in response to changing and challenging circumstances and with natural spiritual maturity.

While volunteering at the New Wine summer camp with children aged six to ten, and in north London at 'Our Place'[3] with those with special needs, I found it moving to witness these young people's honesty of prayers: to end bullying; bring parents back together; heal the health of siblings; stop anxiety or disturbing dreams. Hands were placed on heads and prayers were said in honest, open, uncomplicated language; and, as ever, were often answered. Those with special needs communicated with a depth of faith that was as rich and full of hope as any other believer.

A very different spirituality is often found with those who are terminally ill. I nursed my dying father who had witnessed much loss in the war and while working in the defence industry, and it was reassuring to see his simple acceptance of his illness and mortality. He seemed to seek neither answers nor cures, nor more surgery or medication. In contrast, when my mother was terminally ill she sought the reassurance and pastoral care of her minister, she refreshed her faith practice on an Alpha course and sought healing and the solace of prayer. While being spiritually active in her four years of remission, she requested a 'celebration of life' funeral to mark the end of the early earthly days, and the beginning of her heavenly era.

When a close friend was diagnosed with cancer recently I had the privilege of meeting him weekly for prayer, conversation and companionship. Until three days before his death he was a joyful optimist, praying for healing and full of hope. He asked for all at his funeral to wear yellow, as the mourners celebrated his life, if a shortened one.

So what are the markers of an active spirituality? Here are six suggestions:

1 Community

Community is very important to me. I have attended my home church for over 15 years. This church suggests various levels of engagement for spiritual activists: attendance at Sunday worship; membership of a missional community and engagement in mission service; commitment to a 'two by four' prayer group with two or three others; and generous giving. Over the years I have experienced the good sense of these aspects. As a London church, the population is partly transient. Those that manage regular weekly attendance become known to others, and become friends. People notice if they are absent, and check if they are unwell. Regular attendance enables engagement in Bible study sermon series and hearing of bi-termly key speakers.

The core congregation, around 25 per cent of listed members, all hear the same message and the 'church' journeys together, under the spiritual direction of the pastors. The church becomes a community of spiritual activists, not a building filled with ad hoc attendees. This helps me feel part of a sharing communion as 'a family' with whom I can share my overseas experiences, and we can focus on key projects such as planting a church to a new area.

I am also part of a missional community at this church. This is a new model which encourages 'up, in, out, of',[4] and it has replaced small groups, which were rather too inward-looking. The new model comprises over 20 missional communities focused on geographical patch (estate, borough, postcode), a community (Asian, Spanish-speaking, Iranian, Japanese) or a ministry (justice, prisons, homeless, crossing cultures, English classes). My missional community is called Justice Matters, and they have been able to support me in my anti-FGM work. These give all church members an opportunity actively to engage in mission outreach to unchurched or de-churched. Many of these communities have the potential to become Fresh Expressions of Church, led by pioneer ordained or lay ministers. Unlike many churches, the purpose of these missional communities is to attract non-church members who might be deterred by the cultural barriers of attending more traditional communities.

2 Service

I believe in the ethos of 'every member ministry', so that we all engage in the work of the church and community, whether paid clergy, lay leaders, committed volunteers or church members. This enables new skills to be learnt, gifts to be honed and church membership to be active rather than passive, as all members 'are' the church.

For me, it worked out like this. Following a three-month sabbatical to Indo-China, it became clear that there was a world of diverse need. The first global issue that grabbed attention and broke into my comfortable career and lifestyle was the heart-wrenching plight of the Romanian orphans. As television news channels pumped images into living rooms each evening, a growing personal heartbreak was occurring, possibly out of God's hatred of injustice. But how to act? Neither driving a truck to Romania nor knitting blankets seemed very useful or possible. I made a personal pact to God to 'go' to the next crisis.

In preparing, I dedicated three months a year to voluntary work – to a housing trust, an eating disorder charity, to Alpha International, and Medair, a Christian relief charity. The latter involved volunteering in human resources (HR) at their Swiss head office. After three months with them, I went to debrief the team working in Kosovo, the 'next' crisis. The difference this time was that, unlike Romania, my skills and experience as an HR professional and psychologist, in debriefing people who had been there for four years, were directly relevant to the need. During that tour I witnessed suicide, poverty, homelessness, bombing and amputees in an active warzone. It involved debriefing those with burnout, eating disorders, trauma and loss of faith. The UK volunteering of the last few years was all directly transferable and supplemented work skills and gifting.

The next two years were spent working part-time in Africa, and were followed by two years working full-time in North Uganda, Northern Kenya, North and South Sudan and West Darfur. There I witnessed death, murder, injustice, poverty, rape, disease, disability and untold trauma. During this time, others lost their faith, burnt out, became disheartened and lost their calling. Others, of course, kept going, saw miracles, experienced all the blessings of overseas cross-cultural mission, including hospitality given and received, new life, new faith and skills learned. Service is a vital part of an active spirituality.

3 Prayer, worship and hospitality

A third mark of an active spirituality is a committed prayer life. This, for me, involves following a daily devotional: intercession for self and others, prayers against global injustice, prayers for healing and those in need, giving thanks and worship. This has grown my experience in praying publicly, gifts in prophecies, enabling me to lead at national prayer events. It also involves setting a 'rhythm' for life, built up from a daily period of prayer (morning, midday, close of day, beginning of night) as part of a weekly cycle (extended prayer at home or church) on the Sabbath. This has formed a monthly day retreat or quarterly extended retreat. The annual calendar can also give form to cycles such as fasting as part of prayer at Lent and Advent. These can provide periods of spiritual refreshment, and by altering the pace of life deeper spirituality can be accessed with an incremental greater intimacy with God. This pattern has given me structure and rhythm in my life even though I am travelling several months a year.

Retreats have been very important for me, helping me to gain a greater understanding of the monastic life and how the benefits could be applied to a difficult and complex ministry such as helping to end FGM. After attending a spiritual retreat to St Katherine's with the Diocese of London, I developed a taste for the monastic life. In the twenty-first century, it might seem strange to suggest that not only monks and nuns but also lay people could learn from the writings of St Benedict of Nursia from around AD 530. Benedictines have provided light, prayer, hospitality and refuge to the Church and the world for the last 1,400 years. The Rule, developed by Benedict, has provided spiritual inspiration to monks and nuns searching for God in the life dedicated to a monastic path (see Barry et al., 2005). It has also been used by Benedictine laity who are oblates and friends of monasteries and abbeys. The Rule was created in a period of social and economic chaos in the sixth century, and is highly relevant and accessible to a wider group today who are seeing a balanced, focused and simple common life, through television programmes and books on monastic life which offer people spiritual inspiration of their faithful service, and greater connection with God.

The monastic life, a retreat to a Benedictine abbey or a study of the Rule all offer a taste of silence, a simpler life and distance from ordinary distractions. Retreats encourage courtesy, listening, respect and attentiveness to others. The space can be filled with intimacy with God through prayer and worship, community life and refreshment.

I have enjoyed many retreats at Malling Abbey which has existed since 1090. There are seven daily offices (services) from Lauds at 6.50 a.m. to Compline at 7.25 p.m., and four meals, which are silent except for tea. These provide the frame for my day, to which I add periods of community work or study, from 9 to 1 p.m. and between 2 and 3 p.m., with recreation from 3.15 to 4.45, as is the pattern of the Sisters. This enables a rhythm to be adopted, or readopted, of prayer, worship, work, leisure and sleep, which is often lost or becomes unbalanced in a busy 24/7 work pattern. The benefits of time in the abbey are for me to reflect on the last season, and regroup for the next. I take a retreat four times a year, three times at the abbey and once to New Wine. These enable time to rest; for prayer and worship at the seven offices, to seek spiritual direction, to hear from God for next steps and to contribute to the community, such as help in the guest house and in the linked community of Pilsdon at Malling.

So what are the aspects learnt from the abbey that enhance an active spirituality? For me one of the disciplines is doing everything for God in worship, so that all activity becomes purposefully done in thanks and praise, liberating me from anxiety and worry. Another aspect has been to learn about *lectio divina*. This practice comes from Guigo the Carthusian (*c.*1188), who suggested a dynamic form of reading, meditation, prayer and contemplation with the idea that reading repetitively assists in digestion and assimilation (Colledge and Walsh, 1981). One of the nuns who coached me had spent six months on half a verse in the book of John, so I did the same until I gained from the lessons and moved to the next verse.

The practice of prayer at the monastery (seven times a day, with an eighth period of pre-dawn vigil for the Sisters), combined with *lectio divina*, has enabled a pressing into God despite the challenges of having witnessed trauma, death, poverty and injustice over the last 15 years, in over 15 countries for four months of the year. Other aspects learnt at the abbey include the value of work, including the mundane requirements of life, God's ministry and church activity. I have revaluated the value of work and recreation (creativity, craft, singing) and have better understood a need for greater balance, which has been achieved by keeping one day of rest per week and ensuring that work hours do not exceed 50 over a six-day week. I plan annual times for holiday, retreat, study and recreation to ensure that ministry does not take over, with the concern for burnout, breakdown or physical illness. I embrace the rule of discipline and find it very helpful in a pioneering context where focus is needed, while being flexible to the unknown possibility. This has made me more joyful and creative, less irritated and stressed and more accepting of my calling, and the costs that come with it.

Spending regular quiet time alone helps connect with one's inner spirit, hopes and fears, and hearing from God. With practice, mindfulness can also quiet a busy mind and bring relief from anxiety and unhelpful repetitive worries. Mindfulness also helps gain acceptance and reduces judgemental attitudes to self, feelings and others. Over time, mindfulness helps develop a greater sense of intuition and self-trust. I have learnt to use this to protect me from free-floating anxiety about things I cannot change.

Finally, one of the values embraced in mission and community living is hospitality, which is expressed in Benedictine life. This is practised by living in a shared home and working in a volunteer culture where many give of their time at no charge. I have just recently taken a vow to become a Friend of the Benedictine Order as a commitment to these practices and as an indicator of the journey already started to a life of dedication to active spirituality to the end of one's days.

4 Generosity

Another commitment to an active spirituality involves generosity – both financial and more. Christians are encouraged to be generous and to give joyfully to the Church, Christian charities, charities addressing injustice, gifts to friends, family, church members and others in need. For me this has meant living by faith for over ten years and being humbled to be dependent upon the generosity of others, while still giving myself.

Another form of generosity is offering skills and gifts to those in need which enables connection with those who are suffering, isolated, or dealing with loss or hardship. It is often the volunteer rather than the beneficiary who is most blessed and yet the volunteer gains confidence in new contexts or skills, and the experience can often lead to new directions or opportunities. I mentor others to share skills and this helps balance the gain I have from being mentored.

5 Lifelong learning and creativity

An active spirituality is achieved when sufficient time is given to lifelong learning and personal growth. I have attended courses in healing and wholeness, character development and gifting. Other sources of help have been via books on skills such as time management and mindfulness. Sermons at church or downloaded from podcasts or the internet can also be a great source of growth to assist an active spirituality. Conferences such as New Wine and Holy Trinity Brompton's leadership conferences have been great for new ideas, personal reflection and to hear global authors or speakers. Many churches offer leadership modules – I attended missional entrepreneurship and leadership modules with CMS pioneer training. These have helped me grow as a leader and pioneer a new focus for the Church in FGM.

Reading directly improves spiritual growth by gaining knowledge from experienced authors, leaders, role models and practitioners. Growth can come from reflecting on the lessons of others and applying the parallels to one's own spiritual path, selecting the useful reflections. I make action plans from reading and focus on a couple of priorities for six months until I have embraced the change.

I also believe in creativity. Creativity is present in everyone, and being open to one's creative potential broadens skills and develops giftings. This may involve singing or playing an instrument, dance, photography or art, poetry or creative writing. Journalling is also a way to explore creative talent and reflect on experiences. Journalling has helped process the challenging experiences witnessed; I wrote my life story in Nigeria where there were no books, people, light or leisure. This discipline has developed my journalling skills, which offers self-debriefing for an extrovert in an isolated context. The experiences can then be prayed through and reflected upon later. Another aspect of being creative is doing something in a novel or different way, or approaching a task or relationship differently. I use creative art and singing to relax and balance this with the edgy ministry I have been called to, and to cope with hearing traumatic stories daily.

6 Thankfulness

Despite the terrible events that I see, I try to be thankful. In countries where 28 Too Many works, there is stigmatization, deep trauma, sorrow and isolation for many FGM sufferers. Let me give you one 'good news' example, from the West African country of Mali.

FGM in Mali has not decreased in prevalence in the last 20 years. The figure for FGM in women and girls (15–49 years) in 2013 was 91.4 per cent, not significantly different from 92.0 per cent in 2006. The prevalence rate by faith shows a Muslim rate of 92.8 per cent and Christian rate of 65.2 per cent; over 60 per cent incorrectly perceive FGM as being a religious requirement. Seventy-three per cent of girls in Mali have FGM at age five or younger and the age of cutting is decreasing. There also seems to be a worrying trend that some women without FGM have had their daughters cut. There is no Malian law specifically criminalizing FGM. FGM is 'known about' by over 98 per cent of men and women, and yet patriarchy gives authority to older men and women over younger women who cannot question the 'authority of wisdom or age' and have little voice to stand against FGM. However, I retain hope, encouraged as I am by the meetings with a number of organizations in Mali who are seeing progress in tackling FGM locally. Successful interventions reflect the specific context of each community, and a good example is the use of *griots* (traditional storytellers) to take anti-FGM messages to communities where literacy rates are low. The good work of NGO Sini Sanuman shows that change is possible, as nine villages signed the following declaration:

> We, the women and men of Moussala, in Kalabancoro, circle of Kati, Mali, have taken the decision to never again excise girls in our village. We have seen that there are many drawbacks and no advantages to this practice. Our girls don't deserve this traumatizing and degrading experience and they have the right to their whole bodies. This decision has been taken for the health and well-being of our girls, the women of tomorrow. We encourage every Malian to take this same decision, individually and collectively, so that excision will disappear from Mali.

Here is a story where it was easy for me to be thankful. It is not always like that but I try to remain positive and thankful as part of an active spirituality, knowing that God is in everything, however hard that may be to know and to experience. A daily discipline has been to adopt a philosophy of thankfulness – ensuring that at least one good thing is reflected upon last thing at night, despite the challenges of the day.

Keeping an intimate spirituality while working in highly challenging mission contexts that involve violence and trauma to others and personal risk to self requires similar disciplines to those of military personnel. Personal routine, discipline, structure, determination and focus are necessary as well as sensitivity to physical, emotional and spiritual safety and protection. Mission assignments need to be balanced with times of spiritual retreat and leisure in order to keep life in perspective and maintain a joyful and thankful spirit.

Conclusion

This chapter has explored how an active spirituality can be achieved despite the challenges of a missional life of campaigning and advocacy. My journey is just one example of a 20-year life in mission, and is offered as a simple case study that can offer hope or an example to others. I recommend that you dedicate time to being in community, to prayer and worship, to practising generosity and committing to lifelong learning. Spiritual disciplines such as regular retreats and the practice of *lectio divina* can help develop and deepen an intimate spirituality.

Spirituality is often enhanced by being creative, positive and thankful as well as enjoying and offering hospitality. An active spirituality can be formed by serving, by connecting with others and by volunteering to give back. In my experience I have discovered that all of these aspects can enliven a journey to achieve a mission spirituality.

References

Barry, R. et al., *Wisdom from the Monastery: The Rule of St. Benedict for Everyday Life*, Norwich: Canterbury Press, 2005.

Colledge, E. and Walsh, J. (trans), 1981, *Guigo II: Ladder of Monks and Twelve Meditations*, Collegeville, MN: Liturgical Press.

Wakefield, G., 1983, *The Westminster Dictionary of Christian Spirituality*, Philadelphia: Westminster John Knox.

Notes

1 See http://28toomany.org/ (accessed March 2015).

2 See http://www.alpha.org/try (accessed March 2015).

3 See http://www.stbarnabas.co.uk/Groups/184020/St_Barnabas_Church/Whats_on/Our_Place/Our_Place.aspx#.VQK6no6sV48 (accessed March 2015).

4 See http://www.freshexpressions.org.uk/guide/about/proper (accessed March 2015).

14

From Missionary Incarnate to Incarnational Guest: A Critical Reflection on Incarnation as a Model for Missionary Presence[1]

BERDINE VAN DEN TOREN-LEKKERKERKER AND BENNO VAN DEN TOREN

Introduction

'Incarnational Ministry: A Critical Examination' was the title of a 1990 article in the *Evangelical Missions Quarterly* written by Harriet Hill. This article turned out to be a plea to mission educators to be more realistic in their teaching about the role of missionaries. After her studies to become a missionary, Hill was fully convinced that she needed to be incarnational – to enter fully into and become one with the host-culture, a rural village in Ivory Coast, in order to follow Jesus and his call to mission. She writes:

> But I failed miserably. Even after years of trying, vast differences remained. The model that sounded so wonderful in my missions classes wasn't working for me, but rather than question the model, I assumed the problem was myself. I was doing something wrong, I was failing God, and guilt overwhelmed me. (Hill, 1990, p. 196)[2]

We resonate with this experience. In 1997, we left the Netherlands for what became eight years of ministry in the Central African

Republic. Similar to Harriet Hill, we went with the conviction that we wanted to be one with the local community. Our living conditions made that much more feasible than for Hill: we lived on a campus of a theological school in the same kind of home as a number of our colleagues who had studied abroad and were relatively well off in their own context. And yet so often we felt guilty for being different: for having access to medical care that was far beyond the reach of our colleagues, for the protection of a European passport. And though we felt very welcome, we realized that we were always considered foreigners. And in certain relationships we would also feel resentment to us as westerners, because of our association with the world from which we had come and to which we still belonged. Today, we continue to meet people living and working across cultures, sharing their lives in mission, highly motivated to serve, yet burdened with feelings of doubt and guilt because of the distance they perceive between the high ideal of incarnational mission and the practice of their daily life.

In this chapter, we will primarily reflect on the Incarnation as a model for cross-cultural missionary presence. In the next section, we hope to bring some clarity to the understanding of the use of the notion of 'incarnational' in relation to mission. In the subsequent section, we want to analyse some of the practical and theological drawbacks of the Incarnation as a model for cross-cultural missionary presence. Finally, we propose the metaphor of the 'guest' as an alternative image to clarify the role of the missionary: a guest is someone who is invited to a reciprocal sharing of life with the host community in an attitude of humility, meeting each other deeply and authentically in the presence of Christ, God incarnate, through the Holy Spirit.

These reflections on incarnational mission and the role of the missionary have grown out of our experience in cross-cultural mission 'overseas', but those involved in pioneer ministry and mission across cultural and social boundaries in their own country are facing the same challenges and questions.

Defining incarnational mission

The complexity of the discussion of 'incarnational mission' partly comes from the fact that the meaning of the expression is not always clearly defined. The word 'incarnation' in relation to mission seems to be used with at least three different meanings in different contexts. In the documents of both the World Council of Churches (WCC) and the Lausanne Movement, the Incarnation is seen as a model for the Church as Christ's ongoing 'Incarnation' in the world. Mission in Christ's way could bring evangelism as verbal proclamation together with evangelism through social action (Guder, 1994; cf. Min, 2011).[3] In missiological literature, the notion of Incarnation is also used to refer to the need or ideal that Christian communities become 'incarnate' in their local contexts and live out the gospel in culturally appropriate and recognizable forms.

In this chapter, we focus on a third use of the notion of incarnation in mission: incarnation as a model for the behaviour of the cross-cultural missionary. Christians are encouraged to enter into the unknown host-culture, to identify with the people in this culture as followers of Christ, who entered into our humanity, emptied himself, and died on the cross. The 'incarnational missionary' is called 'to following the way of Jesus' as he or she 'moves across boundaries of geography, culture/language, social class, or other such distinctions' (Allison and Allison, 1993, p. 22). 'As Jesus entered fully into our level of living and working, we as missionaries are also to fully enter into and work at the level of others so they can relate to us' (Thomas, 2012, p. 46).[4]

The missionary incarnate

We believe that the use of the model of the incarnation of Christ for the understanding of *Christian mission* has profoundly enriched Christian mission. In this section, we want to argue, however, that a misappropriation of the metaphor for understanding *the role of the missionary* can lead to unwarranted demands on the missionary. The model is furthermore unhelpful in a globalizing and multicultural world and can easily hide a paternalistic attitude towards the community in which the missionary works.

The incarnational model is unrealistic

In her article referred to earlier, Harriet Hill asked two crucial questions concerning this model as far as the missionary is concerned. Is it realistic? And is it honest? (Hill, 1990, pp. 198f). The ideal of incarnation in the host-culture seems not to be realistic in the long run: maybe I can become a real part of a culture, a community, a family for a shorter period of six months to two years in order to get to know a culture profoundly. But it is not realistic for a ministry over a longer period. We cannot completely share the lives of the people we are working with. And we do not want to completely share their lives. It is therefore dishonest to suggest that we are completely part of their community. Let us illustrate this with two examples which have created tensions in our own ministry. First there was the question of the education of our three boys. We knew that their futures would not be in the Central African Republic, but in the Netherlands or elsewhere. That is why we sent them to the *Lycée Français* in Bangui and to a boarding school in neighbouring Cameroon. Yet, that made us different from the community and even from our closest colleagues. These schools were far beyond the reach of our African colleagues.

Even in our ministry itself, we often used resources that were much less accessible to our colleagues: as teachers, we used our furloughs to read up on recent academic publications and had an extensive study-leave that our colleagues at the school in which we worked could not have afforded. But that study year allowed us to support the development of the new doctoral program.

We also shouldn't underestimate how hard it is to relate and communicate according to local cultural expectations. Communicating is not just about mastering a local language, but it demands mastering the nuances of how needs, commitments and attitudes are expressed in both verbal and non-verbal communication. The local people may tacitly know these things without being able to express them for themselves, let alone teach them to others. After returning from Africa, we lived for over eight years in Oxford, England, culturally much closer to us than Central Africa. Yet, we are far from mastering the nuances of local English communication. We often do not get the unspoken messages, either critical or affirmative that the Oxonians so craftily hide in their formal and understated conversations. We need our non-English accents to remind people that we are not one of them. We need this, because, otherwise, people would constantly presume that we have understood what was only implicitly communicated. We need this so that they know that when we do not master the nuances of polite exchange, this is not because we are rude and offensive (cf. Loewen, 1976, pp. 240f).

The critical questions mentioned so far may of course mean that we are just not dedicated enough, not radical enough in our love and identification, not patient enough in our efforts to adapt to the local culture, and that both contemporary missionaries and contemporary mission agencies have become too willing to embrace the luxuries and the safety of the modern western world to be effective and true ministers of Jesus in a foreign place (cf. Thomas, 2012). We do not, however, think that the answer should only be to develop more fully, radically and truly incarnational missionary ministries. The fact is that the limitations of this incarnational model do not only come from the missionaries, their families and their agencies, but also from the expectations of the host-culture.

The incarnational model is inappropriate in a globalizing world

The basic idea of the 'missionary incarnate' is that the missionary becomes as much as possible part of a local culture. This ideal presupposes that the host-culture is a relatively isolated and a relatively homogeneous reality. That is why the incarnational model is most attractive in contexts such as the remote and rural parts of China where Hudson Taylor worked, or the isolated Micronesian Island of Yap in the late 1960s that formed the training ground for the Lingenfelters. In our globalizing world, these presuppositions only apply in an ever-decreasing number of isolated communities, and even there they never apply fully.

An important consequence of globalization is that many communities are going through a period of *cultural change*, most often more rapidly than ever before in their history. They are confronted with new forms of education, with western media, with the economic and political opportunities and pressures of a globalized world. Profound tensions are developed between traditional cultural views and values and new ones that are brought in from the other parts of the world. In Bangui, you can for example choose between traditional medicine, western medicine, the Muslim *marabout*, the Christian prayer healer and Chinese acupuncture, all with their own understandings of illness and health. With very few exceptions, contemporary missionaries work in such situations of rapid cultural change, of cultural conflict and often of cultural crisis, fuelled by global developments and flows of information.

These issues have consequences for the ability of missionaries to enter incarnationally into the culture of the host community. They do not enter a homogeneous culture in which they can only fit if they become part of that community. They have to choose among a number of different cultural strands; they cannot equally identify with all of them. Furthermore, they enter into a community that is probably linked to the wider world of which their own culture forms a part. The host community does not receive the missionary as if coming from a neutral foreign culture. The missionary represents a particular culture and often a culture with which the host-culture has had many experiences, sometimes good, often bad.

This was already sharply expressed in the 1950s by David McDonald Paton, an Englishman who had worked as a missionary in China. 'In a country revolutionised by the invasion of the western world [China] a Christian missionary who comes from the western world, be he [sic] as harmless as a dove, as unpolitical as Jane Austen, is by himself by his very existence a political fact' (Paton, 1953, p. 66).

And in our globalizing world of the early twenty-first century, missionary presence is itself also an expression of the globalizing forces that fuel cultural encounter, cultural exchange and cultural clashes.

Incarnational mission can be paternalistic

It is important to note that the incarnational model of missionary service is developed out of a deep respect for local cultures, a belief that the gospel can take root in every culture and a desire to serve and identify with the local community. In this respect the incarnational model of mission is a huge step forward compared to the Eurocentric shape of mission of earlier generations that saw the spread of 'Christianity, [western] civilisation and commerce' (Livingstone) as one single package. Yet, it is also important to develop a sensitivity for the inherent paternalism that can hide behind the respectable face of incarnational ministry.

In this model, the cultural encounter is, after all, controlled by the missionary. The missionary engages with a receptor culture but does not allow the receptor community a similar insight in his or her own culture. Missionaries might even consider modernity so dangerous that they want to protect the receiving culture from having to engage with it. The missionary is allowed to form both an appreciative and critical view of the local culture but does not necessarily entrust and empower the receptor community with the possibility and tools to appreciate what the modern West has to offer.

The incarnational model risks diminishing the uniqueness of the Incarnation of Jesus Christ

Is it possible for people in mission to truly incarnate into the culture and community of the other as Christ became incarnate in Jewish culture in first-century Palestine? Is not Christ's Incarnation unique? Christ entered into humanity and became one of us in order to share in our lives and to save us from sin, shame and death. He became fully human, but also remained fully God. That is why he could bring salvation. Garrard writes that the Incarnation of Christ is 'soteriological, unique and unrepeatable' (Garrard, 2006, pp. 103f).

This unique character of the Incarnation of Christ then raises the question as to whether we are diminishing the work of Christ by talking about the incarnational character of our missionary life? Are we not underestimating the sheer magnitude of Christ's saving death and resurrection when we as human and fallible beings identify with his Incarnation? How can we ever 'be Christ' to others in such a saving and redeeming way?

Yet, 'as the Father sent me, so I send you' (John 20.21) is much quoted in the literature around the incarnational role of the missionary (Whiteman, 2003, p. 409). And so is Paul's Christological hymn in Philippians (Allison and Allison, 1993, p. 24; Lingenfelter and Mayers, 1986, p. 17). The disciples/apostles (plural!) are called to follow Christ, to live as he lived, to serve as he served. Fully abandoning the incarnational model for missionary presence may not be an option. In mission history and current praxis, there are too many instances of inappropriate relationships, where inequality in power and resources and cultural barriers are taken for granted. A possible way for a continuing understanding of the missionary role as incarnational is by realizing that we use the incarnational language as a metaphor when applied in mission. A metaphor takes the model very seriously, but not literally. Therefore when we speak of the Incarnation as a metaphor for the missionary role, we are not speaking of a missionary incarnate, but of a missionary who seeks to shape his or her life by the values of the Incarnation, and is motivated by the reality and example of Christ incarnate (cf. Langmead, 2004, p. 36). The precise role of the missionary in relation to the host-culture is, however, better expressed as the role of a guest.

The missionary as guest

The incarnational model is not the only model available for cross-cultural missionary presence and engagement. In recent years anthropologists (Loewen, 1968, 1975, 1976; Loewen and Loewen, 1967) and missiologists (Bevans, 1991; George, 2002; Skreslet, 2006) have proposed a great variety of metaphors and models. These models have various functions. Some concentrate mainly on the way the Christian message is shared and how one learns from the other (prophet, teacher (Bevans, 1991), participant-observer, learner (George, 2002)), others on the roles that are available in the receptor culture that the missionary can inhabit (friendly alien, merchant, foreign aid worker (Loewen, 1976, pp. 228, 232–3), patron (Kay, 2006, pp. 131f; Loewen, 1976)). These models are therefore not all mutually exclusive and may make different, sometimes contrasting, sometimes complementary contributions to the understanding of cross-cultural mission.

In this chapter, we want to explore the model of the 'missionary as guest', which has also been mentioned by Bevans (1991, pp. 50f). We propose this model because we focus on a limited question: how do we understand the relationship between the cross-cultural missionary and the host community and culture in which s/he works? The model has the strength of strong biblical precedent and may be recognized in a great variety of cultures. The host–guest relationship will be experienced and lived out differently in diverse cultures. Two traits of the guest-metaphor are central to the following argument: mutual respect and the dependence of the guest.

Biblical precedents and theological value

Jesus himself accepted the hospitality of many of his friends and supporters, such as Peter and his mother-in-law (Mark 1.29) and Martha, Mary and Lazarus (Luke 10.38). His living conditions in Capernaum are uncertain, but on his missionary journeys he depended on the hospitality of people who would welcome him into their homes (or boats) so that he would have a base from which to work and a place to minister and preach. Interestingly, the role of a guest allowed him to engage and be part of a much wider range of communities than if he had simply been, as the Son of God, living as a carpenter's son in Nazareth. As a guest, Jesus was received across the different Jewish people groups and beyond, and often among people who would not consider him a natural part of their in-group, such as Pharisees (Luke 14.1) and tax-collectors (Luke 5.29). He also accepted the negative side of depending on local hospitality: the need to move on when he was no longer welcome, as was the case in the region of the Gerasenes (Luke 8.37).

The same pattern was repeated among the disciples and apostles. When Jesus sends out his disciples in pairs, he encourages them to accept the hospitality of the people they will encounter on their journeys but also to 'shake off the dust [of their] feet' and leave if they were not welcome (Matt. 10.14, NRSV). We see a similar pattern in Paul's ministry; he stayed with a wide range of people, such as the Cyprian Proconsul (Acts 13.7) and Lydia, a trades-woman (Acts 16.16), but moved on when he had overstayed his welcome or became a liability to the local Christian community, as in Thessalonica (Acts 17.10).[5]

The understanding of missionaries as guests in their host-cultures also makes sense theologically. It links in with the profound truth that Christians, wherever they are, are always 'aliens and exiles' (1 Pet. 2.11, NRSV) or 'strangers and foreigners' (Heb. 11.13, NRSV), 'resident aliens' belonging to a different kingdom (Hauerwas and Willimon, 1989); they are a pilgrim people (Walls, 1996, pp. 8f). We can be at home, wherever we are called to live, but will in an important sense always remain strangers. In more sociological terms, Christians always have a 'marginal identity'.

This tension between being both 'in the world' and 'not of the world' can also be understood and lived out with the help of the metaphor of the Incarnation. However, 'incarnation' strongly suggests that we are embodied in one specific cultural form. This embodiment in one particular cultural context may be characteristic of the presence of God the Son in Christ, but it is less appropriate to describe the presence of God the Spirit in his people. In our reflections on missionary presence, we should not only take our clue from the Incarnation, but also, and perhaps even more, from the nature of the work of the Holy Spirit. From the day of Pentecost onwards, the Church has characteristically been a multicultural community in which the gospel is proclaimed in multiple languages and embodied in many cultural forms. The body of Christ post-Pentecost is a multicultural body of 'Greek and Jew, circumcised and uncircumcised, barbarian, Scythian, slave and free' (Col. 3.11, NRSV). It is as a member of the Jewish people that Paul is willing to be 'all things to all people' (1 Cor. 9.22, NRSV) and considers himself called to be a blessing to the nations (Rom. 11.13).[6]

It is practical and realistic

When we speak of the guest model for missionary presence, we are not expecting the missionary to live in the home of the local host. Hospitality should be understood from a community perspective. The missionary is the guest of the local community, living among them and participating in their life as a community.

As guest of the host community, the missionary will need to make the greatest effort to understand the culture, learn the language and to adapt to the lifestyle of the community as appropriate. Yet, at the same time, both the host community and the missionary realize and accept that the guest is coming from somewhere else, where life is different, and with different values and expectations. Where this dual reality is both communicated and accepted, both the missionary as guest and the community as host will be able to meet the other in relationship, yet also accept the other as different. Authentic relationships become possible over barriers of cultural difference. This authenticity is also emotionally healthy, since the missionary does not have to pretend to be someone s/he is not. Their personal identity can even be seen as a contribution to the wider host community, because of the new perspectives and opportunities that s/he can provide.

Even though a guest can behave with a condescending attitude, most of the time a guest realizes that s/he is dependent on the host. The missionary needs the host community to learn how to live in this particular context, to learn to speak the language; s/he needs the host community for many practical matters, and much more. This relationship of need leaves little room for a superior power relationship on the part of the missionary, but rather encourages humility and teachability.[7]

Yet, such a humble and respecting attitude does not preclude curiosity and the discovery of new things. It also allows for reciprocity in the relationship between the guest and host. When the guest and host really meet, they will realize that in their relationship there is mutuality in needs as well as in gifts. The host may be in need of the specific skills and knowledge that the guests bring into the host community, precisely because they come from a foreign culture and community. The guest is in need of the hospitality of that community, and will also find wisdom and understanding in the host community that she would never have encountered, had she not entered this community as a guest.

It is anthropologically appropriate

Hospitality is an important value in many cultures, making the guest metaphor for the missionary role even more appropriate. The guest metaphor does not only help the missionary in their self-understanding, it also provides the host-culture with a recognizable role for themselves and for the missionary, giving dignity, space and responsibility to both parties in the encounter.

Being recognized as an outsider takes seriously that cultures in general do not allow for the integration of a stranger in a short period of time. In the region where we grew up in the Netherlands, people can still be seen as an outsider after more than ten years of living and participating in the community. Pretending to be a member of the host community is unrealistic and may be disingenuous.

To state this more positively, the outsider role also brings advantages. A guest is not expected to have the same alliances as members of the host community. They do not have to support everything that the host community supports, such as the local caste system or, in the UK, the class system. This gives more freedom and can provide fresh insight. And if the guest does make a wrong judgement and behaves inappropriately, she can be excused for a lack of understanding of the situation precisely because she is an outsider. And if the relationship between the guest and the host is really good, the host community might be able to speak with the guest to explain the offence and help the guest to find a good solution (Bevans, 1991, p. 52).

It is relevant in a situation of globalization and cultural interaction

Half a century ago, Loewen drew attention to the opportunities presented by outsider roles, such as the guest. These considerations have become even more relevant in our globalizing world today in which cultural exchange and interaction is part of the fabric of life. In this world, missionaries are automatically seen as representatives of the culture to which they belong either for good or for bad. This identification with another culture may in fact provide a positive point of contact, where they can be seen as 'cultural brokers' (Loewen, 1976, p. 233). They may be able to help negotiate the relationship with other cultural streams that profoundly influence the communities with which they work. They can help local communities to develop critical insights into the blessings and curses of global modernity and postmodernity, blessings and curses that are multifaceted and that often elude us if we focus on the most obvious, visible, material aspects of this influence.

Yet, cross-cultural guests can only effectively work as cultural brokers if they develop a real empathy, possibly even an 'incarnational empathy' (Hill, 1993, p. 266), with their host community. The guest needs empathy to learn to see through the eyes of the host-culture, to learn to hear through the ears of the host-culture, and learn to interpret through the values of the host-culture, without necessarily fully agreeing with or adhering to these values and interpretations. This will allow the development of a mutual trust, which is a precious gift in the midst of cultural clashes which keep producing mistrust and misunderstanding. It also allows the missionaries themselves to gain a deeper insight into their own culture, to share these insights with their host community and to grow in a joint learning process of what it means to serve Christ on the cultural crossroads of our world.

Conclusion: the incarnational guest

The Christian community is itself a global and multicultural community which embodies the message of the gospel in a variety of local contexts and cultural forms. As a result, it can flourish in a variety of cultural and social contexts and also engage in a critical intercultural dialogue between different parts of the body of Christ about how to faithfully relate to this multicultural environment. One of the crucial ways it can model Christ's making one body out of many peoples and languages is in modelling in an attitude of humility, learning and mutual respect what a multicultural community and cross-cultural engagement can look like. This means that the cross-cultural missionary will follow Christ in his 'kenotic' ministry in an attitude of costly service (Phil. 2.5–11), with an 'incarnational ethos' (Kok and Niemandt, 2009). We have argued that such service is most authentic, and that the gospel can therefore be faithfully shared and served, if cross-cultural missionaries understand themselves as guests, accepting in humility that they depend on the hospitality of the host community, adapting as far as possible to local customs and expectations as a guest would do, while staying authentically themselves, and contributing the gifts that a guest can bring from elsewhere.

Our reflections have not led us to abandon the value of the example of the incarnate Christ for Christian mission. Guder writes: 'An incarnational (adjective!) understanding of mission is precisely not a continuation of the once-and-for-all incarnation (noun!), but the continuation of the incarnate Lord's mission as he shaped and formed it' (Guder, 1999, p. 23). And this continuation is realized through the work of the Holy Spirit. It is the Spirit who makes Christ incarnate in our lives and beyond, in and through the Christian community (Billings, 2012; Langmead, 2004, pp. 53–5). This dependence on the work of Christ for us and the work of the Spirit in us helps us avoid an unbearable burden that only spiritual heroes can shoulder and that for most of us – and possibly for all – would lead to dishonesty (Langmead, 2004, pp. 231f). As Ross Langmead aptly wrote, with a reference to Bonhoeffer's notion of 'costly grace': 'Mission in Christ's way emphasizes the cost; mission in Christ's presence emphasizes the grace' (Langmead, 2004, p. 52).

References

Allison, D. C. and Allison, N. E., 1993, 'The Doctrine of Salvation: Mediated through the Incarnational Missionary', *Southwestern Journal of Theology*, 35.2.

Baker, K., 2002, 'The Incarnational Model: Perception of Deception?' *Evangelical Missions Quarterly*, 38.1.

Bevans, S. B., 1991, 'Seeing Mission through Images', *Missiology*, 19.1.

Billings, J. T., 2012, 'The Problem with "Incarnational Ministry": What if our Mission is not to "be Jesus" to other Cultures, but to Join with the Holy Spirit?' *Christianity Today*, 56.7.

Flamming, P. J., 1995, 'Incarnational Leadership for Ministry', *Theological Educator*, 52.

Garrard, D. J., 2006, 'Questionable Assumptions in the Theory and Practice of Mission', *Journal of the European Pentecostal Theological Association*, 26.2.

George, S. K., 2002, 'The Quest for Images of Missionaries in a "Post-missionary" Era', *Missiology*, 30.1.

Guder, D. L., 1994, 'Incarnation and the Church's Evangelistic Mission', *International Review of Mission*, 83.330.

Guder, D. L., 1999, *The Incarnation and the Church's Witness*, Harrisburg, PA: Trinity Press International.

Hauerwas, S. and Willimon, W. H., 1989, *Resident Aliens: Life in the Christian Colony*, Nashville, TN: Abingdon Press.

Hill, B. N., 2000, 'Toward a Theology of Evacuation', *Evangelical Missions Quarterly*, 36.3.

Hill, H., 1990, 'Incarnational Ministry: A Critical Examination', *Evangelical Missions Quarterly*, 26.2.

Hill, H., 1993, 'Lifting the Fog on Incarnational Ministry: Friendship is Key to Developing Needed Empathy', *Evangelical Missions Quarterly*, 29.3.

Kay, P. K., 2006, 'Personal Reflections on Incarnation as the Model for Mission', *Journal of the European Pentecostal Theological Association*, 26.2

Kok, J., and Niemandt, C. J. P., 2009, '(Re)discovering a Missional-incarnational Ethos', *HTS, Teologiese Studies/ Theological Studies* 65.1. Available at: http://www.hts.org.za/index.php/HTS/article/viewFile/274/705 (accessed June 2013).

Langmead, R., 2004, *The Word Made Flesh: Towards an Incarnational Missiology*, Lanham, MD: University Press of America.

Lausanne Movement, 2011, *The Capetown Commitment*. Available at: http://www.lausanne.org/en/documents/ctcommitment.html (accessed May 2014).

Lingenfelter, S. G. and Mayers, M. K., 1986, *Ministering Cross-Culturally: An Incarnational Model for Personal Relationships*, Grand Rapids, MI: Baker.

Loewen, J. A., 1968, 'Relevant Roles for Overseas Workers', *International Review of Mission*, 57.226.

Loewen, J. A., 1975, *Culture and Human Values: Christian Intervention in Anthropological Perspective: Selections from the Writings of Jacob A. Loewen*, South Pasadena, CA: William Carey Library.

Loewen, J. A., 1976, 'Roles: Relating to an Alien Social Structure', *Missiology*, 4.2.

Loewen, J. A., and Loewen, A., 1967, 'Role, Self-image and Missionary Communication', *Practical Anthropology*, 14.5.

McElhanon, K., 1991, 'Don't Give up on the Incarnational Model', *Evangelical Missions Quarterly*, 27.4.

Min, A. K., 2011, 'The Church as the Flesh of Christ Crucified: Toward an Incarnational Theology of the Church in the Age of Globalization', in L. M. Cassidy and M. H. O'Connell (eds), *Religion, Economics, and Culture in Conflict and Conversation*, Maryknoll: Orbis.

Paton, D. M., 1953, *Christian Missions and the Judgement of God*, London: SCM.

Skreslet, S. H., 2006, *Picturing Christian Witness: New Testament Images of Disciples in Mission*, Grand Rapids: Eerdmans.

Thomas, A., 2012, 'Money and Missionary Lifestyle in the Buddhist World', in P. H. De Neui (ed.), *Complexity of Money and Missions in Asia*, Seanet Series, Volume 9. South Pasadena: William Carey Library.

Walls, A. F., 1996, *The Missionary Movement in Christian History: Studies in the Transmission of Faith*, Maryknoll: Orbis; Edinburgh: T&T Clark.

Whiteman, D. L., 2003, 'Anthropology and Mission: The Incarnational Connection', *Missiology*, 31.4.

Notes

1 An earlier and longer version of this chapter has been published in *Transformation: An International Journal of Holistic Mission Studies*, 32 (2015), pp. 81–9. We are grateful to the publisher for permission to use this material in this volume.

2 The issues raised in this article are clearly important to the *Evangelical Missions Quarterly* readers, given the number of passionate contributions to the debate. See further, McElhanon (1991), Hill (1993), Baker (2002).

3 *The Cape Town Commitment* (Lausanne Movement, 2011), written at the Third Lausanne Congress in Cape Town, does not speak of incarnational mission as such, but uses the term 'integral mission', which is based on the ethical implications of the life and love of Christ.

4 These three uses of the notion of 'incarnational mission' or 'incarnational ministry' are the most important ones, but the list is not exhaustive. P. J. Flamming, for example, understands 'incarnational leadership for ministry', as following Jesus' strategy and methods (Flamming, 1995).

5 B. N. Hill (2000) uses this Thessalonica episode as a starting point for developing a 'theology of evacuation'; this theme is relevant for our question, for evacuation may sometimes be proposed by the host community and is therefore a prime instance when the desire to complete identification proves undesirable *from the perspective of the host-community.*

6 On the affirmation by the Holy Spirit of cultural plurality in the body of Christ, see Billings (2012).

7 Both Lingenfelter and Mayers, and Allison and Allison, rightly stress the dependence of the cross-cultural missionary using the image of the socialization of a child: 'They must enter a culture as if they are children – ignorant of everything from the customs of eating and talking to the patterns of work, play and worship' (Lingenfelter and Mayers, 1986, p. 23; cf. Allison and Allison, 1993, p. 23, on the example of Jesus in this respect). This is a valuable insight, but it seems that the image of a guest is equally able to express this dependence while giving the guest a greater responsibility than a child would have.

Index

Music 15, 59, 110, 114, 184, 204

Mystic 1, 39–41, 43 (ref), 65–7, 71, 73, 81 (ref), 165, 182, 194

Narrative viii, 2, 4, 28 (ref), 90, 100–4, 106, 111, 121, 129, 141, 170–2, 194

Nature xiii, 23, 35, 49–50, 73, 76, 84, 86, 90, 94, 99, 109, 120, 132, 134–5, 138, 147, 153–4, 159, 175, 183, 186, 189, 192, 200, 226

Nazareth 34, 149, 160 (ref), 225

Neighbour 8, 78–80, 158–9, 205, 219

Neighbourhood 6, 120, 122–4

New Monastic v, vii, 82–5, 87, 95

Nourish 20, 173, 190–1

Nouwen, Henri 23

Oral vii, 23, 26, 47, 53, 79, 148, 152–3, 178, 206, 219

Order 2, 9, 12, 16–17, 29, 49, 53, 63 (ref), 68–9, 71, 73–4, 78, 83, 86–7, 89, 108, 112, 116, 134–5, 141, 154–8, 163–5, 172–3, 176–8, 196, 202, 211, 214, 216, 219, 223

Orthodox 34, 168, 175

Outsider 10, 13, 227–8

Palmer, Parker 8

Pardon 82, 85

Parish 78–80, 114, 122, 167, 187

Participation xii, 4, 17, 20, 22, 24, 168–70, 172, 176

Pastor 23, 26, 53

Patience 25, 39, 159

Paul viii, xi, 19, 28 (ref), 57, 81, 86, 94, 223, 225–6

Peace 3, 34, 36, 42–3, 58, 81, 157, 172, 190

Penitence 68, 71, 169

Pentecost 122, 127–8, 226, 230–1 (ref)

Performance 97, 134, 163

Person 3, 4, 8, 16–17, 27, 35, 37, 66, 69, 93, 137, 142–4, 152–6, 158, 170, 172, 191, 197–8

Peter 19, 29–31, 38, 123, 224–5

Pilgrimage 5, 8, 13, 44–52, 54, 116

Pneumatology 147, 149, 153

Poetry 4, 13, 46–7, 53, 64 (ref), 97–8, 113

Politics 2–3, 150

Poor 17, 26, 34, 68, 84, 86, 91–5, 127, 173, 176–7

Postmodern 46, 97, 111–12, 113 (ref), 171, 188, 228

Posture 1, 10–12

Poverty 24, 68–9, 71, 82, 86, 92, 132, 145, 177, 208, 210

Power 2–5, 7, 11–12, 15 (ref), 16, 20, 22, 26, 33–4, 35, 49, 53, 65, 58, 68, 76–7, 79, 87, 91, 94–5, 98–9, 105–7, 110, 112, 126, 129–30, 140, 142, 148–9, 153–4, 163–4, 174–6, 179–80, 189, 193–4, 222–3, 227

Practices 3–6, 10, 12–13, 16, 18, 21, 25–7, 28 (ref), 46, 80, 89, 111, 115–16, 125, 136, 139–40, 145, 147, 151, 160 (ref), 164–5, 167, 170, 173, 181 (ref), 205, 211

Praxis 102–3, 113, 223

Preach v, 29–34, 36, 38, 42, 76, 83, 90, 93, 99, 153, 161 (ref), 167, 225

Pregnancy 183–4, 186, 190, 192, 196–7, 202

Presence 6, 29, 31, 33, 37, 46, 49–51, 61, 63 (ref), 75, 115, 125, 128–9, 153, 175, 217, 222–4, 226, 230